UNDERSTANDING
SCREENWRITING

ALSO AVAILABLE FROM CONTINUUM

How to Write: A Screenplay
Revised and Expanded edition
Mark Evan Schwartz

Me and You and Memento and Fargo:
How Independent Screenplays Work
J. J. Murphy

Screenwriting:
The Sequence Approach
Paul Gulino

How to Be Your Own Script Doctor
Jennifer Kenning

The Historical Epic and Contemporary Hollywood:
From *Dances with Wolves* to *Gladiator*
James Russell

UNDERSTANDING
SCREENWRITING

Learning from Good, Not-Quite-So-Good, and Bad Screenplays

TOM STEMPEL

continuum

NEW YORK • LONDON

2008

The Continuum International Publishing Group Inc
80 Maiden Lane, New York, NY 10038

The Continuum International Publishing Group Ltd
The Tower Building, 11 York Road, London SE1 7NX

www.continuumbooks.com

Continuum is a member of Green Press Initiative, a nonprofit program dedicated to supporting publishers in their efforts to reduce their use of fiber obtained from endangered forests. We have elected to print this title on 50% postconsumer waste recycled paper. For more information, go to www.greenpressinitiative.org.

Printed in the United States of America

Library of Congress Cataloging-in-Publication Data

Stempel, Tom, 1941-
    Understanding screenwriting : learning from good, not-quite-so-good, and bad screenplays/Tom Stempel.
        p. cm.
    Includes bibliographical references and index.
    ISBN-13: 978-0-8264-2939-1 (pbk. : alk. paper)
    ISBN-10: 0-8264-2939-4 (pbk. : alk. paper)
    1. Motion picture authorship.   I. Title.

PN1996.S79 2008
808.2'3--dc22

2007044304

For Ilana.

CONTENTS

ACKNOWLEDGMENTS

This current book evolved out of my 1982 textbook *Screenwriting*. To fill out that volume, I put at the end of it an Annotated Study List, a list of scripts I felt writers could learn from, with short notes on what they should look at in the scripts. I did not just limit myself to great scripts, but also had two other categories, Flawed Gems (the equivalent of the Not-Quite-So-Good section in this book) and Disasters to Learn From (the Bad). So my first thanks go to the readers of that book who suggested I could make it into a book of its own.

I had other writing projects I wanted to do, but a few years ago Erik Bauer, the publisher of *Creative Screenwriting*, and I had a conversation about books on screenwriting, and it occurred to me to go back to it. So Erik deserves a round of thanks, and another round for starting up *Creative Screenwriting*, where a few sections of this book appeared in more extended articles. (The notes on sources will tell you which ones.) *Creative Screenwriting* is also one of the major sources of information for the background of several of the scripts discussed here. Its current editor, Den Shewman, and writer director Bill Condon's assistant Jack Morrissey, enabled me to get the scripts for *Kinsey*.

As always, thanks must go to Linda Mehr, the head librarian of the Margaret Herrick Library of the Motion Picture Academy of Arts and Sciences, and her staff, who can find anything a person writing about film needs.

Jerry Hendrix, who taught television writing at Los Angeles City College for over twenty-five years; Jim Desmarais, a television movie writer who also teaches screenwriting at LACC; and Elaine Lennon, who worked in development for director John Boorman for years, all read the first draft of the manuscript for this book and gave copious and detailed notes that have greatly improved it.

The second draft was read by Patrick McGilligan, the editor of the esteemed *Backstory* books; Claus Teiber, a film historian at the University of Vienna; and an anonymous reader at the University of Kentucky Press. Their notes, comments, and disagreements improved the book even more.

And of course thanks to Evander Lomke, Gabriella Page-Fort, and all the people at Continuum.

INTRODUCTION

This book isn't about me; it's about you.

I am a teacher, not a guru. As a wise teacher once said, with a guru it's all about the guru—his vision and his students' loyalty to him—whereas with a teacher it's all about the students learning. I have, I hope, over the years avoided gurudom. The thought of starry-eyed innocents sitting at my feet, looking up at me adoringly, in a trance, and kissing the hem of my garment makes me want to puke. You should be reading this book because *you*, as screenwriters, directors, producers, development executives, critics, historians, students in those disciplines, and just plain movie fans want to learn about screenplays. While this book is addressed, often literally so, to screenwriters and would-be screenwriters, keep in mind that movies are a collaborative medium. Others who collaborate with screenwriters, not only directors, actors, and producers, but audiences as well, may learn much to help them in their collaborative roles.

There are two major ways you can learn from this book.

The first is from my observations about the scripts and the films. I have been a practicing film historian specializing in the history of screenwriting for forty years, and I have been teaching screenwriting at Los Angeles City College since 1972. This has led me to analyze more scripts and films than I can count. Between my screenwriting course and a course in film structure, I have taken many students through many films. A few of the scripts and films I have written about here (the Good ones, of course) I have done detailed class analyses of. I can guarantee you will not agree with all of my conclusions (*I* might not agree with some of my conclusions the next time I see the films), but these comments will give you something to think about. And I can guarantee that for every long section you think is too long, there is somebody who thinks it is too short. And vice versa on the short ones. Among the people who read the first draft, there was absolutely no agreement on the issue of the length of the sections. You may not be surprised to learn that there are several films in the Short Takes sections that I had hoped to deal with in more detail. If you think I have shortchanged a film, make your own analysis.

As you may have already gathered, I like a book you can argue with. That is one reason this book is very informal in style. The few books that have tried to do this sort of thing before ended up forcing the scripts to fit into the author's formal rules. The analysis in this book is done on the go, just as you will do it when you watch a movie. Which is why the analysis is done, especially in the longer sections, as I am telling you the story of the film, rather than saving it for a grand summing up. There are no Great Rules of Screenwriting here. Screenwriting is, as the creation of any art form, a very situational process. What works in one place may not work in another, as some discussions here will show you. This is known as creative logic, which I will tell you about later.

The other thing you should learn from this book, and more important than my observations on films, is how to look at scripts and films on your own and develop your own abilities to do so. I am not going to be there in the future, whispering in your ear every time you read a script or see a movie. Okay, metaphorically I may be, after you read this book, but not literally. Joseph Conrad, the novelist, said that above all, he wanted to make people *see*. D.W. Griffith said the same thing about his movies. I want you not only to see, but to think about what you see.

You may have noticed that I keep referring to both scripts and films. Yes, if you live in Los Angeles or another big city, you may have access to libraries with screenplays in them, some of which are mentioned in the book. Or you may be able to buy copies of scripts on eBay or other sources on the web, or else read them on the web. But in many cases, you will only have the film and/or the DVD to look at, and I am assuming you will look at the films before, while, or after you read the book. With very few exceptions, DVD commentary tracks do not include the writers; I long for the day when each writer gets his own commentary track to complain about how the director messed up his script. In any case, you are going to learn how to look at a film from the standpoint of screenwriting. In some cases, I will be discussing one or more drafts of the screenplay and how it developed, although the discussion of *Kinsey* (2004) is the only one where I had access to script material not generally available to the public. If I am teaching you how to analyze scripts on your own, I feel obligated to teach you how to do it primarily with the materials available to you. Since many readers may not be screenwriters, I will also bring in a discussion of the other collaborators and their contributions that either brought out the best in the script or (often) harmed it. As for those of you who are or want to be screenwriters, keep in mind that the great American writer Ernest Hemingway once eloquently noted that you can learn to write only by putting your ass in the chair and writing. But you can add to the knowledge of your craft from studying both its past and present.

Since I am both a screenwriting instructor and a film historian, my younger students very often look puzzled when I mention a film, even a famous one, made before they were born. For this book I am assuming you have a basic awareness of American film history. So if you have not seen *The Birth of a Nation* (1915), *Intolerance* (1916), *The General* (1927), *The Grapes of Wrath* (1940), *His Girl Friday* (1940), *Citizen Kane* (1941), *Double Indemnity* (1944), *On the Waterfront* (1954), *Dr. Strangelove* (1964), and *The Godfather* (1972), put this book down right now and go see them. I have tried in this book to stick to films made within the last twenty-five years, since I had my say on earlier scripts in my 1982 book *Screenwriting*. There are a few classics, however, that I've discussed simply because they are so good, and even people writing for the screen today may actually learn something from them. I do include, for example, *Rear Window* (1954) and *Lawrence of Arabia* (1962) not only because they are great scripts that are frequently stolen from today, but because both films are generally thought of as directors' films. You may get an inkling of how important a good script is even for great directors like David Lean and Alfred Hitchcock.

There are twenty-one films I will write about in considerable detail. To cover the widest variety and number of scripts, and the divergent approaches to them, I will also do shorter bits on thirty-two scripts. In addition to some chapters dealing with more than one film (three trilogies are discussed), there will be a Short Takes chapter at the end of each section. The writing in both the long and the short sections will be interactive, in the sense that I may explain some element of the film in detail, or just tell you to listen and watch for certain things the next time you see the film. I will quote lines of dialogue, but not long speeches, usually because you ought to *listen* to them, not just *read* them. Although if you insist on reading them, and do not have access to a copy of the script, you can check the "memorable quotes" sections for each film on the Internet Movie Database (IMDb). You might find it frustrating when I stop for a discussion just as you are caught up in the story of the film. I figure that since many of you have listened to a lot of commentary tracks on DVDs, you can probably handle that.

You will also find that when I write about a film, I will discuss the length of the film in minutes, since it gives you a sense of how the film works over its running time. Sometimes I refer to the pages of the screenplay as well, either the original screenplay or the published edition. As you may already know, a general rule of thumb is that one page of screenplay runs about a minute on screen, although that is not absolute (and I will mention some exceptions to that). Sometimes I will write a lot about the dialogue, quoting various lines. Sometimes I will hardly mention the dialogue at all. Sometimes the director and actors will get mentioned, sometimes not. If my approach varies from screenplay to screenplay, it is because *your* approach to learning from a script will also vary. Sometimes you will have only the film, sometimes only the script. You will have to develop your own variety of approaches.

The obvious question I am sure you have already asked is, why these films? I can tell you that of the several people who have read the various drafts of this book, there has been absolutely NO agreement on which films should be included or left out. One reader loved the chapter on *Lawrence of Arabia*; another thought it should be dropped. One reader (a publisher, no less) thought I should deal only with the Good and not the other two categories; another reader loved the Not-Quite-So-Good and Bad sections the most. And one reader provided me with a full page, single-spaced list of other films she thought I should do *as well as* the ones in the book. So please don't waste your time kvetching about my choices; just focus on what you can learn from the ones I have selected.

I picked each film because I felt you could learn something useful about screenwriting from it, even the ones in the Not-Quite-So-Good and Bad categories. After all, that's why medical schools study disease and why business schools study the Edsel and New Coke. Part of the purpose of including the less-than-perfect scripts is to train you to look for problems, so that you can do that in your own scripts. I assure you your first drafts will not be perfect. As I tell my students, that's why God made second drafts. And third drafts, and...

I have picked a wide variety of films, especially of the kinds being made today. So you will get science fiction movies (*Star Wars: Episode I, II,* and *III* [1999ff]), horror movies (*Jurassic Park I, II,* and *III* [1993ff]), horny teenager movies (the *American Pie* films [1999ff]), romantic comedies (*Bull Durham* [1988]), and even historical films (*Titanic* [1997]). In addition to the large-budget films, I also deal with several limited-budget films (*Kinsey* [2004], and more in the Short Takes sections). For those of you who are beginning writers (and producers and directors), you will probably be better off trying to break into the business writing and directing your own low-budget film. Low-budget films depend even more than their big-budget brethren on good screenwriting, since they cannot hide bad scripts with special effects, sets, star performances, etc. You may be able to show off your writing talents better in a low-budget film.

One thing that has always struck me about the really talented people I have known is how open they are to learning new things. Here are three stories to illustrate the importance of trying to learn.

Nunnally Johnson, the great screenwriter of *The Grapes of Wrath*, told me once in the sixties that he had to go see the film version of Neil Simon's *The Odd Couple* (1968) twice. He said he was laughing so hard the first time, he wasn't able to figure out how Simon did it.

Another time, Nunnally and I sat down to watch a television showing of John Ford's 1964 film *Cheyenne Autumn*. Nunnally was writing a big western for producer Jack Warner and hadn't seen Ford's film before. He turned it off after half an hour, saying, "You can't learn anything from something like that." He did *not* mean it was too good. I, on the other hand, as you will see in the Bad section, believe you can learn plenty from the bad ones. I have tried, by the way, not to be too snarky about the scripts that are not good. They were written by mostly talented, certainly hard-working writers who just happened to make mistakes. It happens to all of us, and we can learn not only from our mistakes but others' as well.

In 1945 in England, Noel Coward wrote and David Lean directed a beautiful film called *Brief Encounter*. In it, Laura, a married woman, falls in love with Alec, who is also married. They resist consummating the relationship. One day Alec says he has a friend who is out of town and will let Alec use his apartment. They go to the apartment, but before anything happens, the friend arrives and Laura runs out.

When the film came to America, Billy Wilder saw it and, being Billy Wilder, wondered about the friend. Why does he lend his apartment out for this sort of thing? Does he do it a lot? How does he feel when he gets home and the sheets are mussed and his liquor has been drunk? Wilder realized he had no story, only a character and a situation, so he just filed it away (never throw anything out).

In the early fifties, producer Walter Wanger, the husband of movie star Joan Bennett, discovered she was having an affair with an agent, Jennings Lang. Wanger shot Lang in a delicate area. Wanger went to prison, where he realized prison conditions were a great subject for a film. When Wanger got out of the slammer, he made *Riot in Cell Block 11* (1954). As screenwriter Phoebe Ephron, fatally ill in the hospital, told her daughter Nora, "Take notes. Everything is copy."

Meanwhile, in the trial it came out that because Bennett was a movie star, she and Lang had not gone to a hotel, but conducted their affair in the apartment of a junior agent at Lang's firm. Wilder thought, "Of course. That's the guy from *Brief Encounter*." Years later, he and I.A.L. Diamond wrote a script about a junior executive who lends his apartment to senior executives for their assignations. It was the 1960 film *The Apartment*, which won Wilder and Diamond the Academy Award for Best Original Screenplay.

The story is not over yet. Twenty-eight years later, I was conducting a seminar on the history of screenwriting at the American Film Institute. One night my guest was Edward Anhalt, who had written *The Young Lions* (1958), starring Marlon Brando. In the course of talking about working with Brando, Anhalt mentioned that it was *Brando's* apartment where Bennett and Lang canoodled. The junior agent had taken the rap to protect Brando. The junior agent was shipped off to the London office. He later became a producer, and one of his films starred. . .Marlon Brando. If Billy Wilder had gotten his facts straight, he would have had no movie.

So even when you make mistakes, pay attention.

"Take notes. Everything is copy."

I

The Good

1
LAWRENCE OF ARABIA

> **LAWRENCE OF ARABIA** (1962. Based on *Seven Pillars of Wisdom* by T.E. Lawrence. Screenplay by Michael Wilson and Robert Bolt. 216 minutes in the 1989 restoration)

THOMAS Edward Lawrence was a young British scholar of the Middle East serving with the British Army during World War I. Sent to help the British-supported Arab revolt against the Turkish Empire, Lawrence successfully led the Arab guerilla fighters against the Turks. At the end of the war, hardly anybody outside of military circles knew who Lawrence was.

Lawrence's fame came from an American journalist–filmmaker, Lowell Thomas, who filmed Lawrence's superior, General Allenby, as well as Lawrence. In his 1919 lecture tour, Thomas discovered that audiences were more fascinated with Lawrence than Allenby. Lawrence became one of the first stars of documentary film.

Thomas wrote a book about his experiences, and Lawrence wrote one as well, called *Seven Pillars of Wisdom*. From the mid-twenties on, there were several unsuccessful attempts to make a film about Lawrence. The 1962 film began with producer Sam Spiegel. He needed to persuade Lawrence's brother, A.W. Lawrence, who handled the literary estate of his brother, to sell him the movie rights to *Seven Pillars*. Spiegel hired Michael Wilson, the blacklisted screenwriter who had done the final drafts on Spiegel's previous film, *The Bridge on the River Kwai* (1957), to prepare a treatment for the film. The brother approved of the treatment and sold the rights to Spiegel.

Wilson went to work on the screenplay. As historian Adrian Turner has made clear, Wilson's script provided the general structure of the film as it came to be. Wilson, however, gave a darker view of Lawrence, more knowing and more cynical, than the film shows. The Arab characters had very little dignity. Wilson tried to keep as many characters from Lawrence's book as possible, as well as material from Thomas's book, and the script was an overcrowded 311 pages. And, as Spiegel's director David Lean said in one of his notes, it included "Too many train raids."

Wilson's third draft, the final one he worked on, was 273 pages and focused more on politics and less on the aspects of Lawrence's character that Lean wanted to concentrate on. As in the earlier drafts, the dialogue was adequate, but rather flat. The writer hired to replace Wilson was Robert Bolt, who had just had a successful play in London, *A Man for All Seasons*. He had never written a screenplay. Wilson, then still blacklisted, was denied a screen credit; his name was finally added in the prints made in 2002 for the fortieth anniversary of the film, and in the DVD made from that print. What follows is a discussion of the film, with references to the contributions of Wilson and Bolt.

The film opens with the main titles on an overhead shot of a man working on a motorcycle, with no title setting the time or the place. At the end of the credits, the man gets on the motorcycle and rides off. We now see some of his face, but he has goggles on, so we cannot identify him. The shots of the road from the point of view of the motorcycle bring us almost physically into the film, less on the DVD but very much so in the 70 mm prints. The motorcycle skids off the road, the man is thrown off, and his goggles are hanging on a branch. In the screenplay, they merely "slither along [the road] to the CAMERA." This opening scene has pulled us into the film, and it has also raised the question the rest of the film will deal with, if not answer completely: if we take the mask of the goggles away, who is this man?

The first obvious answer is in the next shot. We see a bust of the man, with one of the many names he will have in the film, T.E. Lawrence. Two men are looking up at the bust, and one, Colonel Brighton, says, "He was the most extraordinary man I ever met." A Cleric standing next to him asks, "Did you know him well?"

"I knew him."

"Well, *nil nisi bonum* [the start of a Latin phrase meaning 'say nothing but good of the dead'], but did he really...deserve a place...in here?" In four lines, Bolt has suggested the differences of opinion about Lawrence that will carry through the film. The working draft screenplay's version is one of the few scenes substantially different from the film. In the script, we see some of the ceremony before Brighton goes up to the bust, so the Cleric's line after his *"nil nisi..."* is that he wonders if there isn't "something...disproportionate in all this." Only then do we get Brighton's comment that he was a "remarkable chap." Why is the rewritten scene an improvement?

"Here" turns out to be St. Paul's Cathedral in London. As people come down the steps after what we assume (again, no titles or notices on the Cathedral door, but the people are in formal dress) is a memorial service, a reporter approaches Lord Allenby and asks for a few words on Lawrence. Allenby replies, "What, more words?" By 1962, there had been a *lot* of books and articles about Lawrence, and there were more to come. What Bolt is telling the audience in three words is: do not look for an explanation of Lawrence in the dialogue. This is not a movie about words, and there will be no psychiatrist at the end of the film "explaining" Lawrence. Many critics in 1962 and since have complained that the film does not "explain" Lawrence's character. It doesn't; it shows us, which is what screenwriting ought to be about. We will see many examples of both explaining and showing in the films discussed later in this book. One of the smartest comments in the original reviews was one critic's line that Lawrence was most himself not in close-up, but in the long shots when he is riding a camel across the desert. When are your characters most themselves?

Allenby then gives a by-the-book answer about Lawrence's involvement in the war, and when the reporter pushes him for more, Allenby replies, "No. No, I didn't know him *well*, you know." Ironic, since Allenby knew him as well as anybody. The reporter then goes to Jackson Bentley, the highly fictionalized version of Lowell Thomas. Bentley tells the reporter that Lawrence was "a poet, a scholar, and a mighty warrior," then after the reporter leaves, Bentley adds to his friend, "and also the most shameless exhibitionist since Barnum and Bailey." Bentley's combination of fake sincerity and cynicism is established in two lines. His last line is overheard by the Medical Officer, who takes "the gravest possible exception" to his comments. Bentley asks if he knew him, and the Medical Officer says that he once had the honor to shake his hand in Damascus. It is obvious we are going to see Brighton, Allenby, and Bentley again, since they are played by recognizable actors (Anthony Quayle, Jack Hawkins, and Arthur Kennedy). The Cleric we will not see again, but what about the Medical Officer? Yes, we will, but not for another 3 hours and 20 minutes or so, and then not in the way this scene suggests. I am sure there must be one, but I cannot recall ever having read a review or commentary that mentions the use of this character at the beginning and the end of the film. Should you do something like that in a script? Yes, if it is consistent with the theme of the piece and/or gives your work texture.

Next, Bolt drops the reporter and goes to General Murray, who says to a friend that Lawrence had "some minor function on my staff in Cairo."

Before we go to Cairo, a few comments about what we have seen so far. First of all, "so far" has been very fast. The main titles, the ride, and the crash run 3 minutes, 30 seconds, and the St. Paul's sequence is about 1 minute, 50 seconds. Most epic films tend to start off slowly (see some of the films discussed in the later chapter on *Lawrence* Wannabes), but *Lawrence* starts *fast*, pulling us into the picture and raising in several ways (visually, through oblique dialogue, the structure of the scene with the reporter) the central question of the film: who is Lawrence? The next time you watch the film, keep a notepad beside you and mark down the number of times somebody in the film asks Lawrence, "Who are you?"

Second, this sequence was much longer (approximately nine pages) in Wilson's script. There was more discussion among the people at St. Paul's; Sherif Ali was with the bust; Lowell Thomas, before he was transformed into Bentley, was seen on his yacht reacting to the news of Lawrence's death; and other details. Wilson's model was obviously the News on the March episode at the beginning of *Citizen Kane*, which runs ten minutes. What Bolt has done is condense that into just what is *needed* to get the film moving, so that in a little over five minutes from the start of the 3 hour, 36 minute film, we are in Cairo in 1916.

The scene is the map room. We know it is Cairo because Murray's line has told us where we are going. The camels outside the window help as well. An Arab paper Lawrence can read shows he not only knows the language, but is more aware of what is going on in the world than his fellow soldiers. He plays the match game that Bolt devised: lighting a match, then snuffing it out with his bare fingers. This is the first indication of Lawrence's masochism. When one of the other soldiers tries it, he yelps in pain and says that it hurts. Lawrence replies, "The trick, William Potter, is not minding that it hurts."

Ordered to see General Murray, Lawrence goes through the Officers' Mess. We learn that a) Lawrence does not seem at ease with the other officers, and b) he is something of a physical klutz. When he tries to quote the ancient military leader Themistocles to Murray, Murray replies, "I know you've been well educated, it says so in your dossier." The Themistocles reference is virtually the only one of Wilson's many classical history references remaining in the film.

One idea I beat my screenwriting students over the head with is that when you are writing screenplays, you are writing for performance. That is, the actors are going to have to say and do what you write, and you had better make those things interesting for the actors to say and do and the audience to hear and watch. I will refer to this many times about many films in this book. Murray is only in the film for about five minutes, but Bolt gives actor Donald Wolfit a juicy role. In this scene, Murray is bombastic, distracted, and focused on his own conventional military thinking that he needs artillery. He is willing to give Lawrence to Dryden of the Arab bureau as much to get him out of his hair as because he thinks it is a good idea. And, he adds, "It might even make a man out of him," touching again on the question of identity. Then he is out of the picture, literally, but audiences remember him when he is referred to later in the film.

If Lawrence is not at home with Murray, he is with Dryden. Dryden is a composite figure, based on several bureaucrats and politicians, just as Brighton is based on several military officers. By turning Brighton and Dryden into single characters, Bolt has human, actable characters to express the ideas of a number of people, which give the characters they play some depth. The two scenes with Murray and Dryden tell us as much as we need to know at this point in the story about the political situation between the British and the Arabs. Unlike Murray, Dryden is smooth, sophisticated, sometimes cynical, and very manipulative. In other words, a perfect character for Claude Rains to play. What Dryden wants him to do is to go into the desert, meet with Prince Feisal, the leader of the Arabs, and learn his intentions. Lawrence insists it will be fun, and Dryden warns him that "Only two kinds of creatures get fun in the desert: Bedouins and gods, and you're neither. Take it from me, for ordinary men, it's a burning, fiery furnace." The words "burning" and "fiery" set the audience up for the desert we are about to see. Lawrence lights a match, and when we think he is going to do his trick, he blows it out, and we get one of the most famous cuts in film: to a desert horizon at sunrise. Bolt wrote it as a dissolve, but Lean, who had been a cutter earlier in his career, went for the straight cut. We are approximately thirteen minutes into the movie.

In *Seven Pillars*, Lawrence's trip to see Feisal is mostly by boat, and while the boat is mentioned in some later dialogue, this is a movie about the desert, and we now have scenes that let the director, cinematographer, and composer do what they do best. Bolt gives Lean scenes to stage, cinematographer Freddie Young vistas to shoot, and composer Maurice Jarre wordless scenes to accompany his romantic themes. When I say writing for the screen is writing for performance, it is also for the performance of the other collaborators on the film, including the CGI (computer-generated imagery) technicians in modern films discussed later, such as the *Jurassic Park* and *Star Wars* films.

Lawrence's guide in these scenes is Tafas, whose function in the film is simple: to ask Lawrence some basic questions about his background.

They come to a well. A mysterious figure appears in the distance. In the *far* distance. He rides his camel to the well, through a mirage. One of the great entrances in the history of movies is not wasted on a minor character. He is Sherif Ali, and he shoots Tafas for drinking at the well of his tribe. The shooting happens much quicker in the film than in Bolt's script, where it reads almost like a western shoot-out. David Lean had as his "Oriental advisor" Anthony Nutting, who had been with the British Foreign Service in the Middle East. Nutting objected strenuously to Ali killing Tafas, saying that Arabs did not kill each other over wells. He begged Lean and Bolt to get rid of Tafas in some other way. While Ali's action in the film may not be politically correct, it is dramatic. It gets rid of a minor character we do not need anymore, and allows Ali to replace Tafas as a more complex sounding board for Lawrence. It establishes Ali as a passionate man in the most dramatic terms. It puts him into conflict with Lawrence immediately. And it puts Lawrence in danger because Ali leaves him alone in the desert.

Until the death of Tafas, Lawrence's journey has been lighthearted, gorgeous to look at, and fun. Tafas's death is the first sign that it will be more, but immediately afterward, the lighter tone returns. Lawrence is amusing himself, singing "The Man Who Broke the Bank at Monte Carlo" as his voice echoes off the walls of a steep canyon, a scene not in the screenplay. The echo of the music is interrupted by Brighton, applauding. He is the British military advisor to Prince Feisal, serious, a bit put off by Lawrence's larking about, and not quite sure what Lawrence is doing there. He starts to explain the situation when they hear explosions and notice biplanes in the sky. They ride toward them and we get the first big action sequence of the film, 35 minutes in. The planes are Turkish and attacking Feisal's camp. The camp is in chaos, and Feisal himself is on a horse, riding back and forth after the planes, trying to attack them with his sword. It is not so much that Feisal thinks he can bring them down, but more a demonstration of his frustration. In the screenplay, it was a gun. Why is a sword better for the scene?

In *Seven Pillars* Lawrence meets Feisal in a town, talks to him, and goes back to Cairo, then eventually returns somewhat reluctantly to Feisal's camp. In Wilson's script Lawrence meets Feisal at the camp, and only after they meet do the planes attack. Bolt's version is shorter, more visually striking, and a better entrance for Feisal than either Lawrence or Wilson provided. In the film Feisal agrees with Brighton that they must move out of the range of the Turkish planes, and Lawrence joins the party, with no return trip to Cairo.

After the visual splendors of the last twenty-five minutes, there is now a nine-minute dialogue scene inside Feisal's tent. Feisal, like Brighton and Dryden, is a combination of characters from real life. The head of the Arab revolt was Prince Hussein, and Feisal and Ali were two of his four sons. Feisal in the film has the age, power, and title of Prince Hussein, and is no longer Ali's brother, so there is a greater distinction between the two. Not only is he older than Lawrence and Ali, but wiser as well. In this scene he rules the action because, as one character says, we are "in Feisal's tent." He is sharp, sophisticated, curious, and rules with a delicate touch. He listens to Brighton and appears to agree with him that he must retreat to Yenbo, farther from the front lines, but he wants to hear what Lawrence has to say. The screenwriters give Lawrence a line straight from *Seven Pillars*, although in reference to a different place, that Yenbo is "far from Damascus." This is the first time Damascus has been mentioned, and there is no discussion of its importance, but from the way every-one talks about it, we know it *is* important to the Arabs. Feisal says he would not have to go to Yenbo if the British would provide him with artillery, a reflection on Murray's outdated obsession with artillery. Brighton says they could give him artillery if the Arabs could take Aqaba, a town on the Gulf of Aqaba. Feisal says the British navy could take Aqaba, but Brighton points out that the Turks have large cannons that would destroy any navy ships in the Gulf. As the meeting breaks up, Feisal talks to Lawrence alone about the history of the Arabs, how they had miles of lighted road in Cordoba when London was a vil-lage, which leads to his wonderfully evocative line, "I long for the vanished gardens of Cordoba." He is suspicious of British interests in Arabia and thinks Lawrence may be another "desert-loving English-man." But we can see that he also buys into Lawrence's romantic view that more can be done. Bolt makes Feisal the example of the best of the Arab culture, something Wilson apparently never got in his drafts. Another reason the tent scene works so well is that Bolt beautifully balances a multi-character scene, in which it is clear what is going on between Feisal, Brighton, Ali, Lawrence, and an elder wise man. Can you write a multi-character scene this good?

Lawrence goes for a nighttime walk in the sand. The focus is on Lawrence thinking, but we get no voiceover indication of what he is thinking. We can see that he is, and Peter O'Toole as Lawrence in his acting, Lean in his staging of the walk, and Jarre is his musical accom-paniment focus on the process rather than the content. We see and feel

Lawrence's intensity. The payoff of the scene is Lawrence's simple pro-
nouncement, "Aqaba, by land."

A word here on the showing of Lawrence's character so far in the
script. Mostly we have been watching his reactions to what is going
on and the people he deals with. Movie acting is as much about reacting as acting, and screenwriting is as much about writing reactions as
actions. Watch the reactions Bolt has given Lawrence to the different
characters and situations. Through both his actions and his reactions,
we have seen him begin to redefine himself, a process re-enforced by
dialogue that raises the question of who he is. The dialogue is never in
long monologues, but in the apparently casual conversations. Listen for
it the next time you watch the film.

So Lawrence decides to go to Aqaba by land. The obvious next scene
is him telling Feisal. We do not see it. First of all, it would be a repeat
of the scene in Feisal's tent. Second, it would be the expected scene. Instead he tells Ali, trying to enlist him in the venture, in a two-character
scene, rather than a multi-character scene. As they get ready to go with
several of Feisal's men, Feisal appears. Ali has told him of Lawrence's
plan. We know from the tent scene that Feisal too has been charmed by
Lawrence's vision, so it is no surprise that he lets them go. At 53 minutes into the picture, they start for Aqaba. The journey and the attack
will take another 53 minutes.

The next scenes alternate between the raiding party crossing the
desert and stopping to rest. At the first oasis, Gasim, one of the men,
catches Farraj and Daud, two Arab boys we have seen earlier, sneaking
into camp. Lawrence lets them stay as his attendants. Then they must
cross the Nefud, the emptiest part of the desert and the reason it was
assumed that a land attack on Aqaba was impossible. During the night
crossing, Gasim (see how neatly Bolt had introduced him casually in
the oasis scene?) falls from his camel. When this is discovered in the
morning, Lawrence, against the advice of everyone, rides back to try to
rescue him in the heat of the day. He succeeds, and the Arabs begin to
think he is more than just a mad Englishman. Lawrence and Ali have
a quiet dialogue scene around the campfire, similar to an earlier scene
with Tafas, but whereas the discussion in that scene was Lawrence's
background generally, here it is about Lawrence's illegitimacy.

Ali burns Lawrence's English uniform, and Lawrence is given
Arabian clothes. Where the beautiful white outfit came from on the
edge of the Nefud is never dealt with, but as we will see later, especially
in the *Jurassic Park* movies, if the audience is caught up in the story,
they will not sweat the small stuff. Lawrence rides off to try out his
new clothes (the costume has given him the look of a Bedouin, which

Dryden had said he was not), and he admires himself in the mirror of his new knife. That gesture is not in the script, but came out of Lean's asking O'Toole to think about what Lawrence would do in the situation. The gesture will show up again later. Lawrence is spotted swanning about by Auda abu Tayi, the fiercest of the Arab warriors, again a composite of several real people. Auda threatens Lawrence's raiding party because they are drinking at his well, but he invites them to "Dine with me tonight in Wadi Rumm," his camp. The scene that follows, all the riders galloping into Wadi Rumm, was cut shortly after the film opened, but then replaced in the 1989 restoration. One reason to cut the entrance will be discussed shortly.

The scene in Auda's tent is different from the scene in Feisal's tent. Auda is larger, noisier, more bombastic than Feisal. Feisal's tent is closed; Auda's is open to his people, whom he plays to throughout the scene. The heart of the scene is Lawrence, amused by Auda, figuring out how to persuade him to come to Aqaba. Watch in the scene how Lawrence tries several different approaches, finally finding the one that will appeal to Auda.

What Lawrence told Ali back in Feisal's camp—that if a group came out of the Nefud, others would join—proves to be true. What we have next in the film is Lawrence and his group, now with hundreds of Auda's men, leaving Wadi Rumm. The columns of men and camels ride slowly through the wide canyon as the Arab women on the sides of the canyon ululate (the women were not in the script). It is a much more striking scene than the arrival in the camp, both visually and aurally, with the sound of the women. The action of the two scenes is somewhat similar, and having the two so close together diminishes the impact of the departure. It is stronger when it stands alone.

We have had so many crossing-the-desert scenes by this time that any more before the attack on Aqaba would be redundant. So we go to the night before the attack. They have maintained the element of surprise as they look down on the town. Until a shot rings out in the Arab camp. There has been a shooting between two men of different tribes. The tribe of the dead man wants revenge, which would start a fight between the tribes, and the mission would be over. But if they do not get revenge, the mission will also be over. Lawrence steps in and sets up a compromise: if he kills the man, justice will be served, and the attack can go on. There will be no repercussions. Guess who the man he must kill is? Gasim. In *Seven Pillars*, it was Gasim he rescued, but not in the Nefud, and it was not Gasim he had to shoot. The writers have changed it because this way it puts more pressure on Lawrence and will come back to haunt him. In other words, repercussions.

The attack on Aqaba is a splendid piece of action filming and totally untrue. There was no camel charge on Aqaba. The Turks remaining in the town surrendered quietly after two days of negotiation. But that would not make a very interesting climax to the fifty-minute trek to Aqaba, would it? Nor would an attack on a truck convoy coming out of Aqaba, which was in Bolt's screenplay before the charge. Wilson's script was slightly more accurate. The heavily defended area was not the town of Aqaba, but Aba el Lissan, the gateway to the canyon that led to Aqaba. It was there that the Arab charge took place, and Wilson placed it there. I do not know if Wilson used one of the stranger details from that attack: Lawrence was so caught up in the shooting that he accidentally shot and killed his own camel in the middle of the attack. Since it is Aqaba that has been talked about in the film leading up to the raid, the attack on it is a better release after the suspense of the trek. And Lawrence stays on his camel all the way through.

At the end of the attack, the radios in Aqaba are broken, so the next journey is to tell the English that Aqaba has fallen. Lawrence decides (he has been driving the action, not just reacting to it, since he decided to go to Aqaba) to go across Sinai to Cairo, taking Daud and Farraj. But on the journey, Daud is sucked into quicksand and dies, which is another death on Lawrence's conscience. This journey is darker and less sweeping than the one to Aqaba. By the time Lawrence and Farraj get to the Suez Canal, Lawrence is emotionally exhausted.

They catch a ride to Cairo in a truck, and Lawrence notices a man on a motorcycle behind them in the traffic, a foreshadowing of his death. They go first to the Officers' Mess, where the officers are upset to see two people in Arab dress. The officers do not know quite what to make of Lawrence, even after he tells them he has taken Aqaba. (Adrian Turner has both Wilson's and Bolt's version of this scene in his book and you can see why Spiegel and Lean went with Bolt; as I have been indicating, he can be more dramatic in fewer and more distinctive words.)

Lawrence is taken to see Allenby, who is, as we have suspected from his St. Paul's scene, smarter than Murray. He understands the value of Lawrence in a way Murray could not. But he is still a military man. When Lawrence defends his decision to take Aqaba by asking, "Shouldn't officers use their initiative at all times?" Allenby quickly sets him straight: "Not really. It's awfully dangerous, Lawrence." Allenby seems sympathetic when Lawrence confesses that he is upset by the deaths of Gasim and Daud as well as the other killing, but when Lawrence adds, "I enjoyed it [the killing]," Allenby dismisses it with "Rubbish. Rubbish and you know it. You're tired," although this line is not spoken as clearly in the film as it might be. There are limits to Allenby's sensitivity.

Allenby, Lawrence, Dryden, and Brighton move to the patio to continue the discussion, where they are watched by the other officers, who now admire Lawrence. Seeing their general listening to him changes their attitude toward Lawrence. Allenby agrees with Lawrence's plans for additional guerilla activities. In fact, Allenby agrees to everything Lawrence asks for, including artillery. Walking along the corridor after they have left Lawrence, Dryden points out that artillery will make the Arabs independent, and Allenby immediately says that he won't let them have it. This is now 2 hours, 15 minutes into the film, half an hour after the raid on Aqaba, and where the Intermission begins.

Wilson's screenplay continued on before the Intermission. Lawrence returns to Arabia, attacks a train, has his picture taken by Lowell Thomas, and leads the Arabs in a defeat of the Turks at the lost city of Petra. Lean, in his scouting for locations, was determined to have a scene at Petra, but eventually he was unable to work out the technical problems of shooting there. Steven Spielberg later shot there for the final exterior sequences of *Indiana Jones and the Last Crusade* (1989), a film that owes more than Petra to *Lawrence*. Look at the opening scene of *The Last Crusade* if you don't believe me.

Wilson's scene at Petra, which was his final scene before the Intermission, has Lawrence going up the steps to the cliffs overlooking the temple as the Arabs chant their name for him: "Aurens! Aurens!" He has become a god to them, and perhaps to himself. We will see how that is taken into Bolt's script.

Part II of the film begins with the re-introduction of Bentley, who has come to Aqaba to find Lawrence. He meets Feisal first, and Feisal sizes up Bentley, as he had of Lawrence. It happens quicker in this scene because it has already been established that this is what Feisal does. Once you establish something (a character, a process, etc.) in your script, you do not have to re-establish it each time. This can save you a *lot* of time. Bentley then cheerfully admits he is after a good story. Feisal realizes he can use Bentley just as Bentley is using him. He makes the point that the Arabs treat their prisoners according to the Geneva Code while the Turks do not. When Bentley asks if this is Lawrence's influence, Feisal is bothered that he thinks so. He says, "With Major Lawrence [Allenby promoted Lawrence from Lieutenant at the end of Part I; he will be promoted to Colonel just before the end of the film; one detail in the progression of the film], mercy is a passion. With me, it is merely good manners. You may judge which motive is the more reliable."

Lawrence has promised Allenby that he will disrupt the railroad, and we now have the first, and most spectacular, of the train raids. Lawrence sets off an explosion under the tracks and the engine slides off, into and along the sand. In *Seven Pillars* the most elaborate of the train raids is the blowing up of a bridge with a train on it. Much more impressive than what's in the film, so why did the filmmakers not use it? It wouldn't have cost that much more. The answer is simple: in Lean and Spiegel's previous film, the enormously successful *The Bridge on the River Kwai*, the big climax is, yes, the blowing up of a bridge with a train on it. Putting the same scene in *Lawrence* would have been repetitious, although in *Kwai*, Lean seems to have had no qualms about repeating the collapsing-bridge-and-train from Buster Keaton's 1927 film *The General*.

The Arabs sweep down to the wrecked train and begin killing and looting. Bentley is taking pictures, and he encourages Lawrence to climb up to the top of the train, where he parades like a god, the other thing Dryden said he was not. This is Bolt and Lean's version of Wilson's Petra sequence, and it is psychologically more complex. With Wilson it was Lawrence putting himself above the Arabs. In the film Lawrence is encouraged by Bentley to perform, but he also throws himself into it. He is, at the end of the scene, wounded by a Turkish officer, proving he is not the god he has momentarily seemed to be. Bolt has combined three scenes from Wilson's screenplay (the attack on the train and his wounding, Thomas taking his first pictures of Lawrence, and the Petra scene) into one condensed scene.

The first time David Lean met (reluctantly, assuming he would be a typical Foreign Ministry type) Anthony Nutting, he asked him what it was he liked about the desert. Nutting's reply: "It's clean." Lean was delighted and knew he had to get it into the film. But where? If it is in the first desert scenes, it is just stating the obvious. If it is in a scene with one of the Arabs, then it sounds like Lawrence is just sucking up to them. Bolt's solution was more ingenious. After the train attack, Bentley interviews Lawrence. Bentley has two questions. The first is what the Arabs hope to gain from the war. Lawrence tells him they want their freedom, and that he is going to give it to them. Bentley is taken aback by Lawrence's ego. He regains his composure and asks what it is that "attracts you personally to the desert?" Lawrence, in Bolt's stage direction, "looks the disreputable figure up and down with insulting deliberation and says, 'It's clean.'" Robert Towne, the author of *Chinatown* (1974), in a June 1991 article in *Esquire*, said that the dialogue's very simplicity made it great screenwriting. On the other hand, *Mad Magazine*, in its April 1964 parody, pointed out the ridiculousness of the line by having "Florence of Arabia" say it while he was up to his armpits in blood at the massacre of the Turks.

The "clean" scene is followed by Auda saying he needs to find something "honorable" to steal. Cut to a train carrying a beautiful white horse. The explosion is set up so that we think this will duplicate the first train raid, but here the train is not knocked off the tracks. The focus is not on the train, but on the action of the characters. Auda takes the horse and leaves. In the next train raid, we do not even see the train. Farraj is killed when he misplaces a blasting cap and it explodes in his clothes. The shift in the three train scenes matches the flow of the film altogether: from the romance and action of Part I to the grimmer realities of the war. The three scenes are not simply action set pieces, but transitional scenes.

Lawrence and his few remaining followers are in a cave in winter. Lawrence announces that he is taking the Arab revolt in Deraa, and if none of the Arabs appear to join him, he will do it himself. Lawrence and Ali, the latter reluctantly, go into Deraa, and Lawrence is captured by the Turks. It is 27 minutes into Part II, 2 hours and 42 minutes into the film.

We are now introduced to the only Turkish character we will get to know in the film, the Turkish Bey, or leader, of Deraa. Simply the fact that he is the leader of the Turks makes him a threat to Lawrence, which gives the scene a tension without anything else being said. We assume he is going to figure out that it is Lawrence his men have captured, but he does not. His appearance is even more polished than any of the British officers we have seen, and his interest in Lawrence is of a more personal nature. He has Lawrence whipped, and the implication of the scene (this was 1962, so it is only an implication) is that he rapes Lawrence. After all the discussion of the brutality of the Turks, he is subtle and sophisticated. He is five minutes of quiet threat, late in a picture that is long and filled with action. José Ferrer plays the Bey. He arrived on location on Monday, shot his one exterior scene on Tuesday, shot the office scene on Wednesday and Thursday, waited on Friday until it was confirmed there were no problems with the negative, and left on Saturday. He said later that he was asked about this performance as much as any other performance he gave. That is an example of writing a great cameo role.

Lawrence has, as he tells Ali, "come to the end of myself." He feels he must return to the English, now in Jerusalem. He does, but he does not fit in there any more than he did at the beginning of the film. Lawrence meets with Allenby and Feisal, who bring up the Sykes–Picot Treaty, in which the English and French have agreed on how they will divide

Arabia between them after the war. Lawrence is shocked, although in real life he knew about the Treaty before he went to Feisal the first time. It is used here to put more pressure on his character in the following scene. Allenby is preparing the "Big Push" on Damascus and needs Lawrence to lead a group on his right flank. According to *Seven Pillars*, all Allenby had to do was explain the situation and Lawrence went back. Not very dramatic. In the film, the drama is in Allenby figuring out how to appeal to Lawrence. As written in Bolt's screenplay, Allenby talks to Lawrence about leadership, common humanity, and Lawrence's interest in poetry, mentioning that there have been poet-generals. Lawrence demurs at being considered extraordinary. As now cut, the discussion begins with Allenby's next line, which sums up his attitude toward Lawrence, whether real or a put-on: "I believe your name will be a household name when you'd have to go to the War Museum to find out who Allenby was. You are the most extraordinary man I've ever met." The preliminaries have been cut to get to the heart of the scene, especially crucial since we are now 3 hours, 5 minutes into the film. We know who Allenby and Lawrence are, as much as we ever know about them, and want to see them get on with the discussion and the film. Which in some ways is too bad, because there is some beautiful writing in the cut sections. Lean cut it at least partially because he felt he had not gotten what he should have out of the script. Imagine that: a director admitting he is not perfect.

Bolt does interrupt the scene with a brief scene in the outer office, in which Bentley is trying to find out what is going on and Dryden is avoiding telling him. It is the only scene in the picture between Dryden and Bentley. Their characters are so similar that we do not get the kind of dynamics between them we do with others. Lawrence agrees to go back, but only if he can get the fiercest fighters to join him. Allenby promises him all the money he needs, but Lawrence replies, "The best of them won't come for money. They'll come for *me*." Allenby's massaging of Lawrence's ego has worked.

"The best of them" turn out to be the worst thieves and killers Lawrence can find, which Ali objects to. But Lawrence delights in his "bodyguard." They ride off, a scene reminiscent of the exodus from Wadi Rumm, but different from the stately beauty of the earlier scene in the frenzy of the action. They later come across the retreating Turkish army. Talal, one of the bodyguards, came from the village the Turks had just destroyed, and he encourages Lawrence not to take prisoners. Ali is worried that it will turn into a bloodbath and suggests they not waste time getting to Damascus. This conflict is defined at the beginning of the scene in the shortest possible exchange of dialogue: Talal's

"No prisoners!" followed by Ali's "Damascus, Aurens." Talal gallops toward the Turks, is shot, and Lawrence yells, "No prisoners!" The attack is on and far bloodier than anything we have seen. When it is over, Lawrence again looks at himself in the knife, but is also appalled at what he sees. Even Bentley is shocked. He has gone from delight at having photographed Lawrence at the first train raid to disgust at the blood. This is the last scene with Bentley in the film. The massacre of the Turks takes place 55 minutes into Part II.

The Arabs win the race to Damascus, but we do not see their arrival. We don't need to. It is Allenby we see get there after the Arabs, so we watch Allenby's reactions to the information that is brought to him about the conditions in the city. The meeting of the Arab Council in the town hall is chaos. The tribal feuds that Lawrence seemed to overcome during the war now return. The Arabs suggest they need English engineers to run the machinery and Lawrence points out that if they take English engineers, they will get English government. The Arabs start to leave the city. Auda and Ali leave Lawrence to go back to the desert, which Auda thinks is the only place Lawrence will be happy. Lawrence stays and the next morning sees the bad conditions in the Turkish hospital: no water, no medicine, and overcrowding. A British truck arrives, and who gets out but the Medical Officer. Remember him from over three hours ago? He does not, however, gladly shake Lawrence's hand; he assumes that Lawrence is an Arab and slaps him. This is the only meeting with the Medical Officer in *Seven Pillars*, but Bolt has expanded that to the St. Paul's scene and a scene that comes after this.

Lawrence meets with Allenby, Dryden, Brighton, and Feisal, who has arrived in Damascus. Feisal smoothly tells Lawrence that while young men make war, it is now time for the older, wiser men to make the peace, an echo of the first discussion in Feisal's tent. Lawrence is to be sent home and leaves. Outside Lawrence meets the Medical Officer, who now recognizes him as *the* Lawrence and wants to shake his hand. Lawrence suggests that they have met before, but the Medical Officer assures him he would have remembered it. This connects to the Medical Officer's first scene, which dealt with the different ways people perceived Lawrence, which connects also with the scene that follows.

Back in Allenby's office, discussing Lawrence's contribution, Feisal says, "Aurens is a sword with two edges. We are equally glad to be rid of him, are we not?" Allenby replies, "I thought *I* was a hard man, sir." Feisal says, "You are merely a general. I must be a king."

A word here on the dialogue. I have quoted many lines because Bolt's dialogue does so many things so well. It gives us the characters, with a different voice for each character, as we will see in other good scripts, notably *Fargo* (1996). It is superbly playable by the actors. It condenses what needs to be said into the shortest amount of words. It is often witty. I have also quoted so much of it here so you will know why you should not pay any attention to film critics. Bosley Crowther, the chief film critic for the *New York Times* for over twenty years, called the dialogue in *Lawrence of Arabia* "surprisingly lusterless."

The last we see of Lawrence, he is in a car being driven across the desert. The driver tells him he is going "home." A man on a motorcycle rides by, a second foreshadowing. The last shot is a close-up of Lawrence, but through the dusty windshield, so we do not see his face any clearer than we did in the opening scene with the goggles.

Wait a minute. We started the film over three and a half hours ago by going into a flashback. Shouldn't we now come out of the flashback? Let me explain to you the difference between real logic and creative logic. Real logic is not picking a British actress to play a Southern belle; creative logic is Vivien Leigh in *Gone with the Wind* (1939). Real logic (as well as film history) is that we should come out of the flashback and find out what Rosebud is; creative logic is that in this movie there is no Rosebud and the man on the motorcycle is enough.

Lawrence of Arabia was made more than forty years ago, and the question you should ask yourself is, could a script like this be written and made now? Yes, it certainly could be written now, although the homosexual rape might be handled with less subtlety. Could it be made? In the early nineties, the answer was probably not, since the cost would have been prohibitive. Since then one of the side effects of the development of CGI has been an increase in the number of historical films being made. These included such Academy Award winners as *Braveheart* (1995), *Titanic* (1997), and *Gladiator* (2000), as well as such recent films as *Troy, King Arthur, Alexander* (all 2004), and *Kingdom of Heaven* (2005). Not all of them have been great, as we will discuss later, but enough have made enough money to make it worthwhile to produce such films. Of course, with CGI you miss the sheer physicality of real people and real places that *Lawrence* has, but to quote the British novelist L.P. Hartley, the past is another country and they do things differently there.

Sources
The Margaret Herrick Library of the Academy of Motion Picture Arts and Sciences has some script materials from *Lawrence of Arabia*. One is Michael Wilson's December 10, 1959, treatment, which is mostly a summary of *Seven Pillars of Wisdom* and the political situation in Arabia. There are then two working drafts of the shooting script with, curiously, neither writer listed

on the title page. Version A is the one I looked at in detail; Version B is slightly condensed from A. These versions were obviously worked out with Lean since there are detailed camera instructions, most of which appear not to have been followed in the shooting, at least to judge by the final version of the film.

Adrian Turner's *The Making of David Lean's "Lawrence of Arabia"* (Dragon's World, 1994) has the most detail about the development of the screenplay of all the books on the film. Turner is especially good on Michael Wilson's contributions. L. Robert Morris and Lawrence Raskin's *Lawrence of Arabia: The 30th Anniversary Pictorial History* (Doubleday, 1992) has more about the physical production of the film than you would probably ever want to know, but it also has detailed information on the cuts that were made after the film opened and how the film was restored in 1989. T.E. Lawrence's *Seven Pillars of Wisdom* (originally published publicly by Jonathan Cape in 1935, paperback edition by Penguin, 1962ff) is Lawrence's version of how it all happened, which is interesting to compare with the film.

2

BULL DURHAM

BULL DURHAM (1988. Screenplay by Ron Shelton. 108 minutes)

BEFORE he became a screenwriter, Ron Shelton played minor league baseball. The first screenplay he wrote, *A Player to Be Named Later*, told the story of "Crash" Davis, a journeyman catcher brought in to the Durham Bulls to help train a recently signed pitcher, Ebby Calvin "Nuke" LaLoosh. The script did not sell, but Shelton went on to write other scripts that were produced. *A Player to Be Named Later* was only about baseball, and Shelton recognized that he needed a character to bring the non-baseball audience into the story. He had known a number of women fans around the minor leagues, so he created a character based on them, Annie Savoy, and the script became *Bull Durham*.

After still photographs of famous and not-so-famous baseball players, we hear Annie say in a voiceover narration, "I believe in the church of baseball," one of the great opening lines in the history of movies. Why is it great? Yes, it tells us the movie is going to be about baseball, but other options would do that as well: "I am a really big baseball fan" or "Gosh, I like baseball a whole lot." The "church of baseball" line says it in the most interesting way possible. It is not literal, "on the nose" in the industry expression. It suggests that whoever is talking has a striking way of looking at things. She then tells us (we still have not seen her) that she has tried "all the major religions, and most of the minor ones. I've worshipped Buddha, Allah, Brahma, Vishnu, Siva, trees, mushrooms, and Isadora Duncan." She is not only interesting but something of a flake. She thinks "there's no guilt in baseball, and it's never boring…which makes it like sex. There's never been a ballplayer slept with me who didn't have the best year of his career." We now know that the movie will be about sex as well as baseball, and that she will probably sleep with a player. We also see her for the first time here as she is getting dressed to go to the game, and since it is Susan Sarandon, we believe a player will have his best year when he sleeps with her. She says, still in voiceover, that she gives them "life wisdom," reads Walt Whitman and Emily Dickinson to them, although, as she points out in one of the truest philosophical statements ever uttered in a movie, "'Course, a guy'll listen to anything if he thinks it's foreplay." By the time she finishes her monologue, she has walked through the town and come into the ballpark. I have always contended that if she was doing this same monologue about the church of auto mechanics and turned into a garage instead, we would follow her there because she has been established in the first three minutes of the film as a character we want to spend time with.

Most screenwriting textbooks will tell you not to start your film with a monologue. They are right in terms of real logic. In terms of creative logic, listen to Bonaserra's monologue at the beginning of *The Godfather* (1972) or Annie's monologue here. Both set up the themes and ideas of the film and establish one of its major characters. In *The Godfather* the character is Don Corleone, and he is established by how Bonasera approaches him. In *Bull Durham* it is Annie and how she says what she says. Some people have complained that what Shelton has created is a female fantasy figure for men. Well, duh. She's a woman who likes baseball and sex; of course she's a fantasy figure for men. But he has also given her idiosyncrasies that take her way beyond the category of fantasy figure. We find out late in the picture that she teaches at a junior college. She can be pushy, but she is also perfectly willing to admit that sometimes she is full of crap.

At the ballpark we get, and will throughout the movie, the atmosphere of minor league baseball. I will mention a few of these details as they show up in the film, but there are a lot more. Look for them on your own. And then think about how you can use the details of the world your film is set in to give it texture. For now, there is the older male radio announcer, who will give us exposition and transitions throughout the film (as announcers nearly always do in sports movies; learn your clichés, they're your friends). He is talking about the new pitcher just brought up, whom the Coach is looking for. The Coach finds him having sex with a girl in the locker room. The Coach is more upset that Ebby is wasting his energy than that it is on sex. He tells the girl, Millie, that he does not want her in the locker room and she says that if he bans her, her father will take back the scoreboard he donated. This is *minor* league baseball.

In the middle of this, Ebby says he thinks he needs a nickname. Just as Shelton first "got" Annie when he heard her say "I believe in the church of baseball," he got Ebby when he heard him thinking about his nickname. What are your characters telling you about themselves in what they say to you?

Millie sits with Annie and they watch Ebby throw the ball all over the park. Millie captures his speed on the radar gun—she is not just a bimbo and she loves baseball as much as Annie does. Unlike the women in too many American movies, these two have interests beyond sex. When Annie asks her about Ebby, Millie replies, "Well, he fucks like he pitches—sorta all over the place." What did Annie already tell us the film is about?

The Coach and his assistant Larry are in the office after the game. A man walks in and when asked who he is, replies, "A player to be named later," a phrase famous in sports trades for someone not a star who is thrown in as part of a deal to get a star. It is Crash Davis, it is 9 minutes into the film, and he wants to know what he is doing here. The Coach tells him about Ebby, and Larry, whose dialogue throughout the film is mostly incomprehensible baseball chatter, describes Ebby as having "a million dollar arm and a five cent head." Maybe Larry heard that from somebody else, but it is to Shelton's credit that he gives the line to Larry the first time we hear it. It is the sort of sharp line that stars usually insist they get, and here it establishes that Larry is not as dumb as he sometimes appears. It also confirms what we have already seen of Ebby.

Crash is not happy. He quits, leaves, then comes back in the room. "Who we play tomorrow?" Leaving the locker room, he hears Ebby giving an interview about his first game: "It's out there. It's radical in a tubular way." We think Crash's disgust at this is just a simple reaction, but we will come back to it later in the film. Shelton is very good at what appear to be casual actions that set up scenes later in the picture.

Crash and Ebby are both introduced to Annie in a bar and Ebby invites Crash outside to fight. Instead of just another movie bar fight, Crash flips a baseball to Ebby and asks him to try to hit him with it. Ebby, knowing his speed, is reluctant, but Crash, knowing his wildness, pressures him, and the throw goes wide. Crash tells him he is his new catcher and "You just got lesson number one. Don't think; it can only hurt the ball club." The progression of the film will be Crash and Annie giving Ebby a lot of lessons about baseball and life, and because he learns them, we have a comedy. If he didn't, it would be a drama.

Annie takes both Ebby and Crash home with her (19 minutes in). She explains that she takes on one player for the season. Crash refuses to "try out" after twelve years in baseball, which leads Annie to ask him what he believes in, and he replies with a wonderful speech that covers everything from Astroturf to "long, slow, deep, soft, wet kisses that last three days." Listen to this speech. Several times. If you have to write monologues for your characters, this one and Annie's opening speech are as good a set of models as any. In both, Shelton gives the actors a variety of things to talk about so they can vary the rhythm of their delivery. Crash leaves, Annie sighs, "Oh, my," and then ties up Ebby and reads Walt Whitman to him.

In a wordless street scene, Crash picks a long, cylindrical carton out of the trash, holds it like a baseball bat, and looks at his stance in the front window of a store. This again is casual, something any player might do, but it also prepares us, purely visually, for his run at the minor league home run record. In the next baseball game, we get Crash at bat, and Shelton finally gives us, both in spoken dialogue and Crash's thoughts in voiceover, an idea of what batters think about when they are at bat. Crash is surprised when Annie intrudes in his thoughts.

Annie sends him a note about his batting, and they meet the next day at the batting cage. He offers to get together with her, and it is obvious from previous scenes that they are interested in each other, but she replies, "Despite my rejection of most Judeo-Christian ethics, I am, within the framework of the baseball season, monogamous." This line picks up on what she has said about herself in the opening monologue. They both agree they will help Ebby, to whom, after their first night together, Annie has given the nickname Nuke.

Nuke is pitching and rejects what Crash wants him to throw. Crash lets him throw what he wants, but tells the batter, who knocks it into the sign with the mechanical bull. Crash tells Nuke he's told the batter. This scene is about six minutes long, since we are watching the process of Nuke's education. A process takes place over time, just like a movie, which is why processes are great subjects for movies. Look at "heist," "mission," and "trek" movies: they all show a process.

As Annie's contribution to the process, she gives Nuke her garter belt to wear under his uniform on the road trip. He doesn't wear it and the team loses. On the trip we learn that Crash had actually been in The Show, as the major leagues are called. He tells the players about it. Listen to the authenticity of the details in this speech, which is not only about baseball, but about Crash and about sex. In other words, all the things the movie is about.

They get home from the trip and Annie gives Nuke more advice, including that he try to breathe through his eyelids. He starts to wear the garter belt. Crash sees it on him, asks for an explanation, then tells him, "The rose goes in the front, big guy." Nuke is beginning to follow Crash's instructions. When he doesn't, Crash again tells the batter what the pitch will be, and Nuke realizes immediately he has told him. Nuke is getting a *little* smarter. The process continues.

On the team bus, Crash instructs Nuke on interview sports clichés, since "They're your friends": "We gotta play it one day at a time...I'm just happy to be here. I just hope I can help the ball club." This is a very short scene, but one audiences remember. Like Crash's batting scene, it shows us something we have wondered about: do those clichés we hear in interviews come naturally, or do the players work at it? Shelton did not include this in the earlier bus scene where Crash discusses The Show. It could fit logically there, but is better as a separate scene. You get two short scenes instead of one longer scene, and each scene has more impact on its own. Don't always try to hit home runs; singles and doubles are part of the game, too.

Jimmy, a younger player, was seen earlier in the locker room announcing that he was starting prayer meetings. At the end of this road trip, Millie greets the bus and talks to Jimmy. Given what we know about Jimmy and Millie, this promises wonderful scenes, all in keeping with the main themes of the film: baseball, sex, and, secondarily, religion. But Jimmy and Millie are minor characters in the film, and as fun as those scenes might be, we won't have time for them. We are a little over an hour into the 108-minute film, and we will see how Shelton makes this late setup pay off in the rest of the film.

At Annie's suggestion, Nuke has channeled his sexuality into baseball on the road trip. The Bulls have gone on a winning streak and Nuke wants to protect the streak. Annie gets him to try to undo her garter belt, on the pretense that it is an exercise in hand–eye coordination. But Nuke holds out. As Crash tells her when she complains to him, "I told him that a player on a streak has to respect the streak. . . . And you should know that!... Come on, Annie, think of something clever to say, huh? Something full of magic, religion, bullshit. Come on, dazzle me." She replies simply, "I want you." But they do not make love. We are 73 minutes into the film.

Nuke is having trouble pitching, partly because his father is at the game. We then get another of Shelton's great "inside baseball" scenes: the discussion on the mound. What do they talk about? In this case, the fact that Jimmy and Millie are engaged. This is the first we have heard of it; sometimes you can leave out potentially interesting scenes and let the audience use their imagination. This is particularly helpful when you have to keep the script moving. When one of the players says he is going to tell Jimmy about Millie's past, Crash, showing the leadership he was brought to the team for, makes it clear that if anybody does tell him, he will have to answer to Crash. Then the chicken bones that José, the Latino player, has been using to get the curse off his bat have not worked, and they need a live rooster. And Nuke's attempt to breathe through his eyelids is not working. The Coach sends Larry out to see what's going on. Now, what do we know about Larry? He does not seem that bright and speaks mostly in chatter, but he has his moments. Listen to his suggestions for their problems: "Okay, well, uh...candlesticks always make a nice gift, and uh, maybe you could find out where she's registered, and maybe a place-setting or maybe a silverware pattern." The game continues. Would Larry's speech be as entertaining coming from the Coach? And the next time you watch the film, listen for Larry's line earlier in the film that *very* indirectly sets him up for this speech.

Annie and Millie are preparing Millie's wedding dress while listening to the game on the radio. When Millie asks Annie if she thinks it is right that she wear white, Annie says, "Honey, we all deserve to wear white." The game includes an argument between Crash and the umpire. This is not as good as the other "inside baseball" scenes because it doesn't tell us anything fresh, except that, not surprisingly, Millie knows which particular dirty word gets Crash an automatic ejection.

Nuke and his dad visit Annie and Nuke gets the phone call: he is going to The Show. We are approximately 80 minutes into the film. He is suddenly humble, something we have not seen before. Perhaps we should have had more of a hint of it before, but we can believe it in the context because we have watched the learning process Nuke has gone through, both in baseball and "life wisdom," to get to this point. Shelton gives us a delicate goodbye scene, which is a surprise and a change of pace from the previous Nuke and Annie scenes. At first Nuke assumes he will see her again, but watch how Shelton has Annie make it clear that they will not, without actually saying so.

Nuke finds Crash in a pool hall, drunk and more melancholy than we have ever seen him. The tone of the whole scene is in a much lower key than any other in the film. The rest of the film has been Preston Sturges, one of Shelton's favorite screenwriters, on baseball. The pool hall scene is John Huston of *Fat City* (1972, screenplay by Leonard Gardner): a sense of loss and time passing. The scene works because it gives a hint of depth to the material, without turning the film into high drama. The proprietor of the pool hall, Sandy, once hit .375 in the minors, and this gets Crash talking about the difference between the minors and the majors. He tells Nuke that while he, Crash, is smart, Nuke has talent, and that makes all the difference in the game. Nuke punches Crash, but

Crash, still teaching, makes sure it's not Nuke's pitching hand he hits him with. A similar but lighter scene the next morning in the locker room, more prose than poetry, has Crash apologizing for his behavior.

Jimmy and Millie get married on the field before the game, giving us an ending for their story as well as more minor league baseball atmosphere. After the game, the Coach lets Crash know he is being let go, since Nuke is gone. Crash is devastated, which Shelton the writer lets us know by giving Shelton the director a long close-up of Crash's face when he gets the news. The pool hall scene has set up Crash's reaction in this scene. It is 90 minutes into the film.

Crash goes to Annie's house, and after letting her know he's been released, they begin to make love in a scene with virtually no dialogue. This is either awfully early in the film for them to get together, or awfully late. Many romances keep the couple apart, physically or emotionally, until the very last scene. Many get them together much earlier. The creative logic here (and Shelton is right) is that since we have known from the beginning that these two are attracted to each other and are made for each other, we will want to see how they *are* together. It helps that Shelton provides unusual actions for them, which makes the scene more vivid than a conventional lovemaking montage. One of my biggest complaints with sex scenes in movies is that they tend to be very generic—soft-focus close-ups of the body doubles' body parts, with conventional romantic music on the soundtrack. Shelton is precise: *this* is what *these* two *specific* people do in their intimate moments. The details are funny as well, so audiences remember this scene as being longer than it actually is. From when Crash shows up at Annie's door until he leaves, only five minutes pass.

As Annie notes in a voiceover speech, "Baseball may be a religion full of magic, cosmic truth, and the fundamental ontological riddles of our time, but it's also a job." Crash has gone to the Ashville team, where we learn from Annie's voiceover that he got the final home run he needed to set a minor league record. We see Crash get the hit, but we get the *meaning* of it from Annie's voiceover. She mentions in passing that she hardly ever thinks of Nuke.

Ah, yes, Nuke. What happened to him? What do we need at this point in the film to finish off his story? We need to see how he is doing in The Show, but this is a modestly budgeted movie that probably cannot afford a major league game. What have we seen in Nuke's scenes that can be used here? Shelton's choices are the interview clichés. What seemed like an atmospheric detail, and a short one at that, now comes back. Nuke is being interviewed in an empty (for budgetary reasons) major league stadium, and he is spouting the very clichés that Crash taught him. Funny, and just off-center enough to make a great, and quick, payoff for him as a character.

And Crash and Annie? After the season is over, he returns to her. He tells her that the Coach had told him that he would make a good manager, and that there might be a minor league job in Visalia next year. Annie starts to talk, but Crash says he just wants to "be." Annie replies, "I can do that, too." They do not get into the specifics, like whether she is going to move, if she will be able to get a job out in California, etc. We do not need to know that, just that they are, even temporarily, together.

Annie ends the film with a voiceover quote from Walt Whitman about baseball. It is 103 minutes into the film, and time for five minutes of credits. Now, I love Whitman, but frankly, folks, he is not on par with Ron Shelton as a screenwriter. Whitman's lines are no match for "I believe in the church of baseball."

Sources
Most of the background on the script came from an appearance by Ron Shelton at a seminar at the American Film Institute in 1988. An excellent review of the script by Mary Dalton and Davis March, "Rough Trade in the Gender Wars," appeared in the November/December 1998 issue of *Creative Screenwriting*. The article includes a lengthy script extract of a scene, cut from the film, in which Annie explains how she got hooked on baseball. Read it and see if you can figure out why it was cut.

3

REAR WINDOW

REAR WINDOW (1954. Based on the short story "It Had to be Murder" by Cornell Woolrich. Screenplay by John Michael Hayes. 112 minutes)

SOMETIMES in my Screenwriting class at Los Angeles City College, I run a film in segments over the semester, and we discuss the screenplay as we go. Sometimes I don't decide on the film before school starts. Once I had a student ask on the first day why he had to learn screenwriting, since he did not want to tell stories, but "create pure cinema, like Hitchcock." I instantly knew I had to show *Rear Window* that semester. I did, and the student never uttered the words "pure cinema, like Hitchcock" again.

Cornell Woolrich's short story was written in 1942, and later Broadway stage director Joshua Logan thought about making it his first film. Logan wrote a thirteen-page treatment, which was not used by anybody later connected with the film *Rear Window*, for the simple reason that it never solved the problems of Woolrich's original. The 15,000-word story has a possible *idea* for a movie—a man in a leg cast spends his time looking out his apartment's rear window and figures out that a murder has been committed in one of the other apartments—but Woolrich told it in very effective prose rather than in cinematic terms. Looking at how it got developed into a film, you can appreciate how to take a good *idea* and develop it into a top-notch *screenplay*.

Woolrich tells the story in the first person. Jeff, the narrator, tells us what he sees, which is essential for the screen, but he also does *not* tell us things we would see if we were watching. For example, on the first page of the story, Jeff says, "The idea was, my movements were strictly limited just around this time." We do not learn until the last lines of the story that Jeff is in a leg cast, but in a film, there would be no realistic way for us not to see that immediately.

The way Woolrich has set up the apartment and the adjoining courtyard, the window of the apartment where the murder takes place is perpendicular to Jeff's apartment, which means that every time he looks into that apartment, he has to move to his bay window and lean out. Woolrich doesn't *tell* us this every time Jeff looks, but in a film, we would constantly have to *watch* Jeff lean, which would get repetitive.

Woolrich also uses Jeff's narration to tell us what he thinks, particularly as Jeff begins to figure out what may have happened in the other apartment. Jeff's thoughts make the story flow from one relatively minor incident to another. Jeff first sees a discrepancy between Thorwald's apartment and the landlord in the empty apartment above Thorwald's, but it is not until eight pages later in the story that Jeff realizes what that means: the difference in height when both men were walking into the kitchens of their respective apartments probably means that Thorwald has buried the body of his wife in the floor of the upstairs apartment as it is being remodeled.

Woolrich's story does not have many characters. There is Jeff, his houseman Sam, Thorwald, and Boyne (a cop Jeff calls early in the story). Woolrich mentions the inhabitants of only two other apartments, and then only in passing: a young man and woman who go out dancing a lot, and a woman with a young child.

Joshua Logan's treatment adds a girlfriend for Jeff, an actress named Trink. At one point in the story, she goes into Thorwald's apartment, but when he discovers her there, she manages to talk her way out with her improvisational acting skills. Logan does not begin to explore the ways Trink or Sam could be used to have Jeff explain what he thinks is going on. At one point, Logan has Jeff tell Trink "of the various people he has been watching," but Logan gives no idea of who they are.

Eventually Logan's agent persuaded him to sell the story to Hitchcock, who took "Rear Window" off their hands at a profit. The screenwriter next hired to write *Rear Window* was John Michael Hayes, a radio writer who had moved into screenwriting in 1951. Hayes had a few preliminary meetings with Hitchcock, mostly to impress Hitchcock with how much Hayes knew about Hitchcock's other films, then Hayes went off and wrote a treatment. When the treatment was shown to James Stewart, he agreed to star in the film.

One can understand why. The treatment solves virtually all of the problems in adapting Woolrich's story to the screen, and is so detailed in setting out the action that large sections of it appear unchanged in the screenplay. Hayes is so precise that in the first scene with Boyne, the cop friend, Hayes numbers each of the reasons why Jeff thinks a murder has been committed. Hayes tells us in the treatment what Jeff sees, what he thinks he knows, when he knows it, when he learns it's not true, and when he knows for sure. In Woolrich's story there is a growing certainly on Jeff's part, but in Hayes's treatment there are constant reversals: Jeff thinks this, then someone proves it is not true, then something else is revealed that convinces Jeff something has happened. This basic dramatic structure gives the film dramatic twists and turns that the story does not have.

The major work that Hayes has done in the treatment is the development of the characters. Woolrich's Jeff has no defining characteristics other than his interest in the murder. Here is Hayes's description of Jeff from the treatment, which appears in every draft of the script that follows: "He is L.B. JEFFERIES. A tall, lean, energetic thirty-five, his face, long and serious-looking at rest, is in other circumstances capable of humor, passion, naive wonder and the kind of intensity that bespeaks inner convictions of moral strength and basic honesty."

No wonder Stewart signed on after reading the treatment. What star wouldn't? And note how Hayes appealed to the actor's vanity: Stewart was forty-five when he was offered the part. Hayes's description is one of the best introductions of a star character in a script I have ever read. You should type it out and attach it to your computer to use as a model. Nothing draws a star so much as a wonderful character to play, and if the character shows "moral strength and basic honesty," so much the better.

Hayes also gives Jeff an occupation. He is a news photographer, which is carefully established in the visual opening of the treatment and film by showing us pictures Jeff has taken, including the last one, which got him a broken leg. Consider the advantage of making Jeff a photographer: it means he professionally watches, so we do not feel quite as uneasy as we might at his watching his neighbors. Woolrich had to work a little at excusing his Jeff's voyeurism in a section ending: "Well, what should I do, sit there with my eyes tightly shuttered?"

Jeff as a photographer is one of the best examples in film of the use of a character's occupation. Hayes could use a device he had wanted to use for some time, but recognized would never work on radio. When Thorwald comes to Jeff's apartment, Jeff disorients him by setting off flashbulbs in his face. Jeff also has telephoto lenses lying around the house, so Hayes can increase the intensity as the film goes along by having Jeff move from simply watching to watching with binoculars to watching through a long-focus camera lens, thus providing changing image sizes for visual variety. Woolrich's Jeff has to ask about "that spyglass we used to have, when we were bumming around on the cabin-cruiser that season." Neither the cabin-cruiser or "that season" are ever mentioned again in the story.

A very welcome change made by Hayes is in the person of Jeff's caretaker. Woolrich's Sam is a very clichéd black houseman. Hayes gives us Stella, a middle-aged female nurse. Stella's ability to say outrageous things makes a comic counterpoint to the civility of Jeff and his girlfriend Lisa. Late in the script they are watching Thorwald wash his bathroom walls, and Stella says, "Must have splattered a lot," to which Lisa objects. Stella replies, "Well, why not? That's what we're all thinking." Stella is also more of an equal to Jeff than Sam was, which eliminates any need for putting Woolrich's prose into a voiceover for Jeff.

Hayes never saw Logan's treatment, so his creation of the character of Lisa was inspired by two other circumstances. First, he knew that Hitchcock was expecting that Grace Kelly would star in the film, so the part was written for her. Like Stewart and the treatment, it was the script that persuaded Kelly to do this film instead of *On the Waterfront*. Second, Hayes's wife Mel had been a fashion model, and so he made Lisa a department store buyer, someone intimately connected with the fashion world. The thrust of the Jeff–Lisa story in the treatment and the film is that Jeff does not want to marry Lisa because he feels she would not fit into his world. Making her someone concerned with the world of fashion both lets us understand her interests and gives her a way to suggest an alternative to his life: fashion photography. It also lets Kelly dress really well in the film, which is not a minor consideration; as a screenwriter, you have to think all these things through.

In the treatment Lisa is not as involved in the murder story as she is in the script or film. Her perception that Mrs. Thorwald would not have left her handbag and her jewelry is not in the treatment, nor is her finding the wedding ring that clinches that the murder has taken place. In the treatment she goes into Thorwald's apartment to locate a crime magazine that Jeff assumes will provide a more general clue to the murder. The change in the script to have her looking for the wedding ring is all for the better, both for the character of Lisa and for the suspense in the scene in Thorwald's apartment.

The Jeff–Lisa relationship is more detailed and developed in the treatment than in the script and film. In the treatment Hayes extends the discussions about whether they should get married throughout the story. In the scripts these discussions are eliminated, and while some dialogue remains, much of it has been cut. When Lisa returns from delivering the note to Thorwald's apartment, she asks Jeff how she did, and in the script he has a speech about how she is a "real professional," which was cut from the film in favor of a close-up of an admiring Jeff.

That close-up is a prime example of how the material moved away from literary dialogue and into the realm of visual storytelling. This is the sort of thing Hayes learned from Hitchcock. Hayes has said, of the process of working on this script with Hitchcock, "We met infrequently while I was writing the script [unlike other projects, where they met every day], but afterwards we sat down and broke it down shot for shot, and he showed me how to do some things much better." Hayes told one interviewer, "Hitchcock taught me how to tell a story with the camera and tell it silently."

By adding the characters of Stella and Lisa, Hayes has been able to both reduce the amount of relative time Boyne, the detective, appears and also make his impact greater. In the story Jeff calls Boyne on page 12 of 33. In Hayes's treatment, he does not show up until page 36 (of 75). By then Jeff has discussed what he thinks is going on with both Stella, who is perfectly willing to believe the worst, and Lisa, who takes longer to come around. Boyne's arrival pushes the story forward because the law is now involved, which means he can and does check out facts, which for most of the second half of the treatment prove that Jeff has been mistaken. As in the original story, Boyne has two cops surreptitiously enter Thorwald's apartment, where they find nothing incriminating. Someone obviously pointed out to Hayes that this was now against the law, and in the screenplay, Coyne, as he has now been renamed (and renamed again in the film as Doyle), gets mad at Jeff for even suggesting such a thing.

The character of Lars Thorwald has also been developed from the story to the treatment, primarily by adding scenes at the beginning that show us that the marriage is not a happy one and that Mrs. Thorwald is a shrew. It makes us willing, along with Jeff, to think there might be something wrong when we do not see or hear her after he has killed her, since we have seen and heard her very distinctly before. As a screenwriter you have to learn to use what we do *not* see and hear as well as what we do.

Hayes's most colorful additions to the Woolrich story are the people he puts in the other apartments, which give the film a richness the story simply does not have. They also give us something different to look at and something for Jeff to react to. Above the Thorwald apartment, which is now across from Jeff's apartment so he does not have to turn his neck in every scene, is a young couple, just married, who have the shades down constantly, although we see the husband getting more and more irritated every time his bride calls him back to bed. In the first draft of the script Hayes has a great payoff that did not survive into the second draft or the film. The bride calls the groom one more time, and he replies, "Start without me." Then he turns away from the window and we see that she is sitting at a table ready to play chess.

In the film the couple is moved to the building off to Jeff's left so he can just occasionally glance at the drawn window shades. By the first draft screenplay, Thorwald has been moved upstairs to the couple's old apartment, which will make it easier for us to see what is going on in his place, always helpful in a film.

Thorwald's old apartment is now taken over by Miss Lonely Hearts, whom Hayes also introduces in the treatment. She is a spinster, and in the script and film she ends up with the composer who has been working on a piece of music in another apartment, though in the treatment her fate is more interesting. Hayes introduced a married couple who did not make it into the script. In the treatment the husband of the couple goes out of his own apartment and into the apartment of another woman, with whom he is having an affair. In the treatment, the last we see of the man's wife is her sitting and knitting with Miss Lonely Hearts. Hayes writes, "The spinster's hand lingers on her arm. Jeff looks away, leaving them to whatever companionship they have found in their private worlds of loveless disappointment."

Hayes has given each of the additional characters a storyline progression, which helps give a sense of both completeness and structure to the film. Miss Torso, a dancer, is seen having several men in and out of her apartment, but only at the end do we see her true love, a soldier.

Hayes's treatment was completed on September 12, 1953, and he was given the approval to start the screenplay. He completed the 167-page draft by October 30, 1953. One reason the script went as quickly as it did was that much of the description of the characters and the action was taken over into the screenplay verbatim. The storyline has also been strengthened, primarily by involving Lisa more in solving the mystery. The shooting script was completed on December 1, 1953, and it is not substantially different from the October 30 draft. The December draft is only five pages shorter than the first draft, and some additional minor changes were made dated January 5, 1954. According to notes in the Paramount story files, production opened on November 27, 1953, and closed in January 1954.

If the 162-page length of the shooting script seems long for a film that only runs 112 minutes, keep in mind that Hayes has written out *everything* the actors are to do, down to the smallest reaction. When you watch *Rear Window* next, pay attention to how much Hayes and Hitchcock get out of the reaction shots. Even moments in the film that seem to have been improvised are not. Early in the film Jeff gets an itch inside his cast. It is such a vividly immediate moment that it feels like Stewart was caught on camera by accident, or else it just happened on the set and someone decided to keep in the film. It's not. Here is Hayes's description of the action:

> Jeff's attention is suddenly diverted to himself. His leg, under the cast, begins itching. He squirms, tries to move the leg a little. It gives no relief. He scratches the outside of the cast, but the itch gets worse. He reaches for a long, Chinese back-scratcher lying on the window sill. Carefully, and with considerable ingenuity, he works it under the cast. He scratches, and a look of sublime relief comes over his face. Satisfied, he takes the scratcher out.

Hayes also balances the dialogue with the action, as in the scene where Stella gives Jeff his breakfast and then begins to speculate about what Thorwald has done with his wife. Jeff begins to eat, but Stella's wondering about where he cut her up, and deciding the bathtub would be the only place to hold the blood, makes Jeff unable to eat.

Hayes uses his characters, especially Stella and Lisa, as sounding boards for Jeff's ideas. What makes these scenes work on film is that the discussions are put in terms of the characters and their relationships. After the first scene with Lisa, in which she and Jeff get into an argument, she later comes back determined to seduce him. He is busy thinking about what he has seen the previous night in Thorwald's apartment. She is kissing him as they talk, but he keeps talking about what might have happened. Believe me, it is more fun to watch James Stewart and Grace Kelly neck than it would have been to listen to a voiceover of one of Woolrich's interior monologues.

For all the details in the script, there were changes from the script to the film. One of the biggest changes is in the climatic moment when Thorwald is trying to drop Jeff out his window. In the script the people in the courtyard apartments come out to see what's going on. Virtually none of this survives in the film, which speeds up the ending considerably, crucial at the end of a film, when the audience is restless and wants to get it over with. Speeding up the ending may not have been the only reason this material was cut. It may simply have reminded everyone of the one really bad scene in the script and the film. One of Hayes's more inventive changes unfortunately led him to write that scene. In the Woolrich story Jeff notices the difference in height between the floors of the two apartments. In the treatment, Jeff notices the difference in height between the flowers in Thorwald's garden a few weeks ago—he happened to take photographs then (see another advantage of his occupation?)—and their height now. The flowers are *shorter*. In the treatment Jeff just happens to notice the flowers. In the screenplay he first thinks to notice them when a dog in the courtyard, who has been seen digging in the plot, is discovered dead. The screams of the owner of the dog bring everybody—except Thorwald—to their windows to look. The owner's long speech is the sort of diatribe more at home in a Stanley Kramer message picture of the period than in a romantic thriller. Hayes at least had the good sense to put the reaction shots of the other people in semi-long or medium shots, which does not break the visual scheme (we see virtually everything in the film from the view of Jeff's apartment) too much. Unfortunately the sequence was shot in close-ups of the neighbors, which only emphasizes the preachy writing.

Other than that, Alfred Hitchcock's direction is virtually flawless, but by now you can see why I tend to refer to this film as John Michael Hayes's *Rear Window* rather than the more conventional Alfred Hitchcock's *Rear Window*. The "pure cinema" of, for example, Hitchcock's direction of the scene of Lisa in Thorwald's apartment works only because of the context of the story that Hayes has carefully built up.

Rear Window has been borrowed from a lot, usually badly. The 1998 television remake of *Rear Window* drops all of Hayes's interesting characterization and much of the shifting drama of his script. In its place is the socially admirable but dramatically inert material on how Christopher Reeve, playing the lead after his accident, can cope with the help of assorted equipment and friends.

In the early nineties it would not have been possible to do a remake of *Rear Window* for the theatrical market, since there was so little action (i.e., bloodletting). That changed due to three factors. First, M. Night Shyamalan's 1999 box office blockbuster *The Sixth Sense* showed that there was a market for movies that were more suspense than action. Second, the call for reduced violence in films after the 1999 Columbine shootings led Hollywood to focus more on suspense than gore, with the occasional exception such as *Saw* (2004ff). And third, surprise, the less gory films have done better at the box office, since they appeal to women as well as men. The best recent rip-off of *Rear Window* has been the 2007 smash hit *Disturbia*, which owes its success to those three factors. And the fact that it is smart enough to borrow the crucial structural element of Hayes's screenplay: the constant reversals that Kale, the Jeff character, has as to whether the next door neighbor is a murderer or not.

Sources

For a longer, more detailed version of this chapter, see my article *"Rear Window*: A John Michael Hayes Film" in the Winter 1997 issue of *Creative Screenwriting*.

The original story is found in "William Irish" (Woolrich's pen name), *After-Dinner Story* (J.J. Lippincott Company, 1944). The story was reprinted in William Kittredge & Steven M. Krauzer, *Stories into Film* (Harper-Colophon, 1979). The page numbers I used are from *Stories into Film*, where the story runs from pages 134 to 167.

There are several sources of information on and interviews with Hayes. I have relied on four. The earliest interview appears in J.D. Marshall, *Blueprint on Babylon* (Phoenix House, 1978). Hayes was then interviewed for Donald Spoto, *The Dark Side of Genius: The Life of Alfred Hitchcock* (Little, Brown, 1983), and *Backstory 3: Interviews with Screenwriters of the 60s* (University of California Press, 1997). Most recently, Steven DeRosa's *Writing with Hitchcock* (Faber and Faber, 2001) is an excellent look at the working relationship between Hitchcock and Hayes on the four films they worked on together.

A copy of Logan's February 1952 treatment is in the Alfred Hitchcock Papers of the Academy of Motion Picture Arts and Sciences Special Collections at the Margaret Herrick Library. The Hitchcock collection does *not* have John Michael Hayes's treatment or first-draft screenplay. Faye Thompson of Special Collections realized they might be in the Paramount Story Collection, also in the Herrick Special Collections, which they are. Given that Hitchcock's entire reference to François Truffaut about Hayes and his contribution to the film was "John Michael Hayes is a radio writer and he wrote the dialogue" (François Truffaut, *Hitchcock/Truffaut* [Touchstone, 1985, a reprint of the 1967 original], pg. 222), it is not surprising that one has to look elsewhere for the evidence of Hayes's work.

4

FARGO

FARGO (1996. Screenplay by Ethan and Joel Coen. 95 minutes)

ETHAN and Joel Coen made an impact as screenwriters with "cult films" like *Blood Simple* (1984) and *Raising Arizona* (1987). They are cult because the Coens condescended to their characters, showing all of them at their worst. The "cool" people who make films cult hits liked that attitude; the regular moviegoing public did not, probably because they felt *they* were being condescended to. Then the Coens made *Fargo*, their biggest commercial success, which features a character who is actually likeable. Did they learn from their success? Well, their films following *Fargo* fell back into condescension and were not commercial successes. Until recently.

The titles of *Fargo* are over a car with a trailer going through the snow. We are not in Los Angeles. The car pulls up to a bar in Fargo, North Dakota. Jerry Lundegaard, the car's driver, meets two men, Carl Showalter and Gaear Grimsrud, in the bar. They immediately get into an argument about whether Jerry is late, which, in addition to giving the actors attitudes to play, sets the tone for the meeting. While these three are discussing the kidnapping of Jerry's wife, they are clearly not criminal masterminds. We are in a recognizable world in which people screw up, and that tells us that their kidnapping is probably not going to go well. In certain heist films, we are watching near-geniuses at work, and our pleasure will come in how well they bring off their plans. Here the pleasure will be in watching the variety of ways they screw up. That does not mean they will not be dangerous. The Coens understand something that the writers of the television series *The Rockford Files* (1974–1980) knew: just because a criminal is an idiot does not make him less dangerous; it may make him *more* dangerous.

Jerry is back in Minneapolis, having dinner with his wife Jean and her father Wade. Jerry is even more fidgety than he was in the bar, and in even less control of the situation. He is very much under the thumb of Wade, a dense, bombastic older man who turns down Jerry's idea of investing in parking lots.

Carl and Gaear are in a car, presumably heading toward Minneapolis. Carl is the talker of the two, as we saw in the opening scene. The Coens have given him wonderful short arias that Steve Buscemi (Carl) beautifully performs. Peter Stormare (Gaear) is mostly silent, reacting to Carl's speeches. His reactions, and sometime lack of them, provoke Carl. The Coens have written two very different characters (how did these two get together in the first place?—we never learn) who play off each other. We keep wanting to see what Carl will say *this* time, and how Gaear will react or not react.

Jerry works as a car salesman, and the Coens show us every cliché we know about car salesmen. Jerry insists that he is "trying to work with you here," then says he has to talk to the boss, goes into another room, waits, and comes back with a deal. This is Jerry in his element, doing something he is semi-good at. Meanwhile, Carl and Gaear stop at a motel and have sex with two hookers. By going back and forth between Jerry and the kidnappers, we are *seeing* the difference in their lives. Nobody discusses the life of criminals or the sterility of middle-class life; it is just shown.

Morning at the Lundegaard house. Wade calls Jerry to say he is interested in Jerry's deal, the one he had turned down before. When Jerry gets to the garage, he finds Shep Proudfoot, the mechanic who set him up with the kidnappers. Jerry needs to tell them the deal is off, but Shep has no idea how to contact them. We find out Jerry has borrowed $320,000, apparently using cars on the lot for collateral. The reason he wanted his wife kidnapped becomes clear—he needs the ransom to pay off his loans—but now if Wade is going to front his deal, he can call off the kidnapping and they can all live happily ever after. Fat chance. We are 17 minutes into the movie. We have been introduced to Jerry, Wade, Jean, and the kidnappers, the plot has already had a couple of reversals, and we have the texture of two very different ways of living.

The kidnapping goes wrong. Jean is not quite the wimp we thought from her first scene. In the chase she falls down stairs. Is she dead? We do not know, and won't know for two more scenes. Sometimes you can hold off telling us information, which can peak our interest. Meanwhile, Wade tells Jerry he is not going to give him the $720,000 he needs for the deal. Wade is investing in it on his own, not as a partner with Jerry. Jerry leaves and goes to his car in the parking lot. In a scene with no dialogue (a car salesman at a loss for words!), he starts to scrape the ice off his windshield, then throws a fit. Jerry finds the kidnapping scene at home, then *practices* the phone call he is going to make to Wade. What does this tell you about Jerry's character?

A sign tells us we are now in Brainerd, Minnesota, the home of Paul Bunyan, the mythical giant lumberjack of the Great North. In the car, Jean is alive in the backseat under a cover. Carl has forgotten to put on the temporary registration tags on the car. (Yes, it's the same car Jerry had on the trailer in the first scene as part of the deal for the kidnappers.) A cop pulls them over. If Carl and Gaear were smart, they could talk their way out of the situation. Carl maybe could have on his own, but Gaear shoots the cop. Stupid, but dangerous. And when another car drives by, Gaear chases the car, which crashes. Gaear kills the two occupants. Stupid, but very dangerous.

We are now 32 minutes into the 96-minute film. The only thing that has not happened yet: the star of the movie has not shown up.

What? YOU CAN'T DO THAT! You'd better have the star show up in the first few pages of your script, or else a star will not continue reading the script. If you are paying for a star, you had better make sure he or she is in most—if not all—of the scenes. But here is an advantage of not writing an obvious star vehicle: you do not have to cater to the star's ego. It helps in this case, of course, that one of the writers was married to the actress they wanted for the lead.

What we have so far is a typical Coen Brothers film, with *no character we have any sympathetic identification with*. We are caught up in the story, but there is still the Coens' condescension toward the characters. But the Coens are now going to raise their game to a different level, as our friend the sports cliché goes. So naturally they give us pictures and paintings of birds next. The phone rings, and one of the couple sleeping in the bed answers it. We might assume that the crime report would be for the man, but it is the woman, Marge Gunderson, who takes the call. It is not until later in the scene, when she and her husband Norm are having breakfast, that we realize she is very pregnant. Marge bundles up for the cold, goes out, and comes back in a minute later to tell her husband that her car needs a jump start. It is a warm domestic scene, unlike the scenes with the kidnappers and especially the domestic scenes at Jerry's. Showing, not telling.

Marge arrives at the highway crime scene. She listens to the deputy Lou, but says to him, "I'm not sure I agree with you a hundred percent on your police work, there, Lou." She looks over the situation and knows *exactly* what has happened. Her first "cop" scene establishes Marge as smarter than anyone else in the film, but also nicer, as in her comment to

Lou. We like her immediately, and we want to see her bring the idiots to justice. And we know there are going to be some laughs along the way, but not at her expense. She appears to lean over to look for a clue, but as she explains to Lou, "Oh, I just think I'm gonna barf…Well, that passed. Now I'm hungry again." The star has, finally, arrived on the scene.

Before you insist this is just the Coen Brothers being cool, transgressive, un-Hollywood, etc., consider this: the television series *Columbo* (1971–1993) did the same thing (introduced the detective long after we had seen the crime) *twenty-five years* before *Fargo*.

Jerry talks to Wade about the ransom, which is now $1 million. Notice how the ransom increases as the film continues. It is Wade's daughter, so Wade insists on carrying it himself and negotiating with the kidnappers.

Carl and Gaear take Jean to a cabin in the woods, but even though blindfolded, she tries, and fails, to run away. We assume that her feistiness is going to get her killed eventually. You can show a lot about your characters by the *bad* decisions they make, and this script is a textbook of those.

Marge interviews the hookers the kidnappers visited. They are not that helpful, although one remembers that one of the guys wasn't circumcised. Look and listen to how this scene takes clichéd characters and makes them fresh: their lack of attention, what they do pay attention to, their naïveté, and their reference to their high school.

Carl is upset at the poor TV reception in the cabin, and we cut to Marge and Norm watching TV in their house. Marge gets a call from Mike, an old boyfriend, who has seen her on the news and suggests they get together if she ever gets to Minneapolis. Who is Mike and what does he have to do with the story? It will be some time before we find out. We are about halfway through the film.

At work Jerry gets a call from Carl, who now wants more money after the deaths in Brainerd. Another caller asking about Jerry's loan needs the vehicle numbers of the cars (probably fictional) that he has used for collateral. The world is closing in on Jerry. Marge has arrived in Minneapolis because a phone number that the kidnappers called has been traced to Jerry's garage. She checks into a hotel, then talks to… Jerry. This is the scene we have been waiting for, that the Cohen Brothers have held off on until now, an hour into the film. She wants to know if any vehicles are missing. He does his usual song and dance. We can see that she is not particularly suspicious of him *now*, but we also get the sense that she is taking the measure of him in case he turns out to be more crucial to the case.

Marge meets Mike. We have heard her talk to him; we have seen her decide to go to Minneapolis to investigate the phone number herself rather than send a deputy. What the writers have not prepared us for is that Mike obviously still has a thing for Marge. She puts him off a bit, but listens sympathetically as he tells her about the death of his wife. (We learn later from somebody else that he was never married.) What is Mike doing in this movie? He has no relation to the mystery story, and nothing happens beyond this scene. Any development executive would tell you to drop the scene. I think it performs an important function. Marge is so smart, so nice, so warm, so *perfect*, that we need to see a little human weakness, vanity in this case, to make her as well rounded as she is. This will in turn help us understand her comments at the end of the film.

Shep beats the hell out of Carl for putting him in danger by calling him, giving the cops his number. Carl calls Jerry and wants even more money. Wade takes the money, and a gun. Carl kills Wade, and Wade manages to shoot Carl in the jaw. Carl takes the case with the money, bleeding as he goes.

We are now 73 minutes in to the film. Next is a long scene featuring two characters we have not seen before and will not see again. An officer is interviewing a part-time bartender. The bartender had talked to a guy, most likely Gaear, who mentioned that he was out at the lake. This scene could be a typical example of why mystery stories do not work as well as thrillers on film. In thrillers, somebody is trying to do something, while in mysteries, somebody (cop, private eye, little old lady, whoever) is going around talking to people, trying to get information. Talk, talk, talk. To make those scenes work, you either have to make them dramatic (see the next Marge–Jerry scene), or else give us enough interesting texture to make us want to watch. In this case, the Coen Brothers give us texture; only when the bartender is asked to describe the guy do we realize he is talking about Carl. How? He describes him the same way the hooker did: "A little guy. Kinda funny lookin'." No mention of circumcision.

The bartender–officer scene is also an excellent example of something the Coen Brothers do in the entire film. Like Bolt in *Lawrence of Arabia*, they give each character his or her own voice. You could not put one of Marge's lines in Carl's mouth, or vice versa. Jerry sounds completely different from everybody else in the film. You have seen films where everybody sounds exactly alike. That is usually because the writer has not had both the imagination and the feel for the characters to make them sound different.

Carl drives back to the lake, burying most of the money by a fence post near the road. In the snow, so there is no way he will know which fence post. Then, at 80 minutes into the film, we get the Main

Event: Marge versus Jerry, Frances McDormand versus William H. Macy. Watch this scene and see if you can figure out *when* Marge *knows*. If the first Marge–Jerry scene is mostly Jerry's, this one is both of theirs, a great duet, a beautiful example of writing for performance. And, as with most extremely well written scenes, all the director (Joel Coen; he's the one married to McDormand) has to do is point the camera at the actors and get out of the way. Great screenwriting makes it so much easier to make a director look good, if the director is smart enough to realize it.

Gaear is in the cabin, watching a soap opera on the bad TV, the closest we have seen him come to domesticity. Jean is already dead. With Gaear around, it would be a surprise if Jean were still alive. She has been nothing but trouble for them from the beginning, and there has been no indication they were warming to her. She is a relatively minor figure in the story, and we are late in the picture, so we do not need an elaborate death scene for her.

Carl arrives, still bleeding. He wants to take the car and get away, but Gaear won't let him. Carl says, "No fuckin' way! You fuckin' notice this? I got fuckin' shot in the face! I went and got the fuckin' money! I got shot pickin' it up! I've been up for thirty-six fuckin' hours! I'm taking that fuckin' car! That fucker's mine!" Gaear goes after him with an ax.

A few words here about language and violence. First, the language. When you listen to *Fargo*, you will realize that it is primarily Carl and Gaear who use foul language, and even then not all the time. A general piece of advice given to actors is that if you are playing a drunk, just establish that in the beginning and then do not make a point of it afterward. The same is true of language: a little of it goes a long way. I know, I know, I have heard it a hundred million times from my screenwriting students: "But that's the way people talk." Well, some of them. Carl and Gaear and Shep do, but the others in the film don't (the part-time bartender quotes Carl as calling him a "jerk," but then adds, "only he doesn't use the word 'jerk'"). And even if people do, that language can get very tiresome in a film, which is a more concentrated experience than life. Well, it can get tiresome in life as well. I think generally the Coen Brothers strike a nice balance here, as opposed to Oliver Stone's screenplay for *Scarface* (1983). Tony Montana and the others use the f-word so much that when Elvira asks him, late in the picture, to stop saying "fuck," the audience I saw the picture with cheered.

With the development of the MPAA Rating Code in the late sixties, violence on film became more explicit, as in *Bonnie and Clyde* (1967), *The Wild Bunch* (1969), and *The Godfather* (1972). The question, as with language, is: when does the violence become excessive? Again, I think the Coen Brothers manage the balance nicely in this film. We have the shooting of the cop, the car wreck, the gunfight between Wade and Carl, and Carl bleeding from being shot. The Coens show that violence has consequences, which so many "action" films do not. _Fargo_ is not a film about violence, but about violent people. We believe _these_ people, as established in the "regular" scenes, would behave as they do in the violent ones.

Which brings us to the woodchipper. Marge gets to the cabin first and finds Gaear running the woodchipper, which is spewing red "wood." Marge, always at the top of her game, says to Gaear, "And I guess that was your accomplice in the woodchipper." The woodchipper is brutal, but the gore is not explicit. The Coens let us use our imagination, which can be worse than anything they might show. The woodchipper is funny, but in a grim way. The woodchipper is what you would find in Minnesota at a cabin by the lake in the middle of winter. All of which is why the woodchipper is so memorable in the film. Pick the right details and people will remember them forever.

Marge arrests Gaear and puts him in her police car. She says to him, "There's more to life than a little money, ya know. Don'tcha know that? And here you are. And it's a beautiful day." Nice little speech. Sums up her vision of the world. Most writers would be happy to leave it at that. The Coens don't. She then adds, "Well, I just don't understand it." That line makes the script and the movie great. Why?

Marge is a cop. She sees everyday crime and violence in her life. She even knows, although she would never say so out loud, that she is not immune to temptation, which is what the Mike scene was all about and why it is there—to support this one line. But what Gaear and Carl have done is so far beyond what even she, with all her experience, can comprehend that all she can say is that she does not understand how they could behave that way. That line completes the movie.

But wait, there's more. One is a plot point, one a thematic one. The plot point is the speedy arrest of Jerry at a motel. We do not get another Marge–Jerry scene; how could you top the last one? We just need to know, and probably need to see, that Jerry has been caught. True to his nature, he tries to weasel out the back window when the cops show up, but they, as well as everyone else in the picture, have outsmarted him.

The thematic scene comes when Marge gets into bed with Norm. Domestic order has been restored, as we generally see in most crime stories: the criminals are caught and everything is back to normal. The audience is soothed, which they need here after the violence. Marge is back with Norm, who has good news from the real world (as opposed to the grotesque world of woodchippers and blood): his painting of a mallard (remember those bird pictures in his first scene? They have been referred to in other scenes with Marge as well) has been chosen to go on a three-cent stamp. He is a little put off that it is only a three-cent stamp, but Marge reminds him that people need them to make up full postage sometimes. Marge sums up by saying, "We're doing pretty good."

Not only did the Coen Brothers win an Academy Award for their screenplay, but Frances McDormand, who as Marge is onscreen in only 60 of the film's 96 minutes, won for Best Actress. Let's hope stars learn to read all the way through the scripts they are sent. And that the Coen Brothers eventually write another sympathetic character. Which of course they did with the Sheriff Ed Tom Bell (Tommy Lee Jones) and Llewelyn Moss (Josh Brolin) in *No Country for Old Men* (2007). And it was their biggest commercial success since *Fargo*.

5

KINSEY

KINSEY (2004. Screenplay by Bill Condon. 118 minutes)

Aᴸғʀᴇᴅ Kinsey first came to scientific notice as an entomologist studying the gall wasp. What made him famous were his studies in the forties and fifties of human sexuality. It took until 2004 for a film to be made about him. It has always been difficult to do films in America that treat sex seriously.

For her 1994 film *Quiz Show*, producer Gail Mutrux's research included David Halberstam's book *The Fifties*. The book contained a chapter on Kinsey, and she thought there could be an interesting film about him. In 1999 she brought Bill Condon, who had just won an Academy Award for his screenplay of *Gods and Monsters* (1998), onto the project. Mutrux later told the *Los Angeles Times*, "Both of us saw the movie in the same way: 'Sex in the name of science.' Kinsey's research was a way of exploring his own sexuality. It wasn't until later that I became aware of the bisexuality, the wife-swapping, the purported self-mutilation, which made things more dramatic and complicated. Kinsey was more than a workaholic who died because he pushed himself. He was a tragic hero."

Kinsey's personal sexual activities were brought to light primarily in a highly critical, rather homophobic 1997 biography, but the following year a more balanced and nuanced look by Jonathan Gathorne-Hardy was published. It was *Kinsey: Sex the Measure of All Things*, the rights to which were purchased by Mutrux in 1999. The script was not an adaptation of the book, but Condon used the book for research.

Condon went through several drafts of the screenplay, as might be expected, given the complex and controversial nature of the material. For the purposes of this chapter, we will be looking at the second, sixth, and final drafts of the screenplay, so you can see how Condon developed the material.

The second draft. (125 pages)

The screenplay opens in 1955, a year before Kinsey's death, with Grafton Noone taking Kinsey and his wife Clara on a tour of the sexual highspots of Rome. The Kinseys are described (page 2; the numbers in parenthesis will be the page numbers) as an "older, dowdier version of Ozzie and Harriet." If you look up Grafton Noone in the Gathorne-Hardy biography, you will not find him. He is a completely fictional character. Condon said in an interview in *Creative Screenwriting* that Noone (no one) was based on an occasional helper of Kinsey's, Clarence Tripp, but there are at least three other people Kinsey dealt with who were involved in the various activities combined in Noone.

We have seen in *Lawrence of Arabia* how composite characters can be useful in condensing several similar characters into one. The problem is that Noone takes too large a role in the screenplay. After the Rome sequence, we see Noone being interviewed by an unseen interviewer about Kinsey and his life. This gets a lot of information in the form of a voiceover from the interviews. Too often this material feels like a lecture, and cutting away from Kinsey to go back to the interview disrupts the story.

In an early scene (7–8) we get the young Kinsey, age nine, and other slightly older children in the basement of a house, encouraging a "well-developed" twelve-year-old girl to take off her clothes. The scene is interrupted by Kinsey's father, who gives his son a stern lecture. Given how visually explicit this scene is in terms of the girl's nudity, I am surprised it stayed in the screenplay through at least the sixth draft, since there would be no way to film it as is.

We then (8–9) get Kinsey as a nineteen-year-old Boy Scout on a field trip with Kenneth Hand, whom Kinsey was romantically attracted to, although that is not made clear in this draft. After more interview material with Noone, we pick up Kinsey as a twenty-seven-year-old, lecturing at Indiana University on the gall wasp. What stays the same through all the drafts is Kinsey's observation that what he has learned from gall wasps is that they are all completely different, an attitude he will later bring to his sex research.

Clara, who will become his wife, is in the class, and later (14) approaches him while he is eating out on the grass. In this draft it is at a zoology department picnic, and she has a few lines with another professor before approaching Kinsey. Their wedding night (19–20) is unsatisfactory and painful for her. They see Dr. Reed, who says it is a simple problem (Clara's hymen "shows an inordinate thickness"), and he says he can fix it today (21). Condon then cuts back to the interviewer and Noone at a diner in 2000, and Noone explains that part of the problem was the large size of Kinsey's penis. Noone takes a paper napkin and draws an image of the size. The waitress asks if she can keep the napkin. It is a funny scene, but it takes up a full page. You will see later how Condon gets across the same information in a much quicker and funnier way, with characters who are more central to the story.

We now (22–23) jump ahead to 1938, with a scene of Kinsey gardening in almost the nude. A younger and older couple drop in and are shocked. Kinsey tells the younger couple about pamphlets he has that recommend the diaphragm. The scene establishes Kinsey as someone who advises students about sex, but the gardening and the older couple detract from the point. Another scene immediately after repeats the point with a group of graduate students.

One page 26 we are introduced to the new president of Indiana University, Herman B Wells. Wells hosts a reception for Kinsey in honor of his new book. Wells, unlike some college presidents, seems to know what Kinsey's book is all about, although Kinsey notes, "I thought you might have actually read the book, until I saw those crib notes you were palming." Now, if you were writing Wells, who is going to be supportive of Kinsey in the rest of the film, how would you have him react to Kinsey's comment? Condon writes, "Wells lets out a booming laugh."

So it is no surprise later in the scene that Wells mentions to Dr. Thurman Rice, the head of the medical school, that "Some reform-minded undergraduates...are campaigning for a sex course." Rice insists he covers that in his hygiene class, but Kinsey, overhearing, calls it "the most useless course on campus." Kinsey insists that students learn about female anatomy by "sneaking into the cadaver room at your precious medical school." It is a shocking line, and not without some historical truth to it, although much of it was probably urban legend on the I.U. campus. It reads shocking, but hearing it may have been too shocking. Judge for yourself. It remains in the sixth draft, was dropped by the final draft, but was shot and appears in the Deleted Scenes on the Special Edition DVD, as does some other material from earlier drafts. Never throw anything away.

Wells sits in on Rice's course (29–31), watches the sex education film (in this draft it was to be made specifically for this scene), and listens to Rice. Rice tells the class that when he is "tense" at bedtime, he relaxes by closing his eyes and "thinking of all the Johns I know." This was actually said in the class years before by the distinguished then-president of the university, William Lowe Bryan. It got laughs when Bryan said it, and here it gets laughs when Rice says it, and Condon elaborates on it by having Rice, confused, saying, "Well, not only Johns. Sometimes Peters." More laughter and a student asks, "How 'bout Dicks?" This exchange survives into the film. The scene shows us exactly how out of it Rice is. Wells just "slips out of the class quietly."

Kinsey's first day teaching the sex education course (33) gives a wonderful aria for the actor who plays Kinsey. As with the "Johns" line in the previous scene, Condon uses a Kinsey line from a much later class here. Kinsey asks the class, "Who can tell me which part of the human body can enlarge one hundred times?" When a young woman gets upset at him for asking that "in a mixed [male and female] class," he replies, "I was referring to the pupil of your eye, young lady. And I think I should tell you, you are in for a terrible disappointment." The stage direction reads, "A loud explosion of laughter cuts the tension. The coed smiles good-naturedly." The reactions tell us that the class was tense, that this cuts the tension, and that the woman was not upset at what he said to her. Not bad for two sentences.

Kinsey meets (34) Clyde Martin, a student, whom he puts to work for him. Kinsey is beginning to talk to students and answer their questions about sex. We get a montage of heads of students asking questions that students of the time (the late thirties) might ask: "Does too much masturbation cause premature ejaculation?" and "Does having sex while pregnant lead to polio?" The last of the interviews (36) is with a Female Student who has a question about oral–genital sex, finally asking, "Is it wrong?" to which Kinsey replies, "If it is, then we're all in a lot of trouble." What the montage shows is how ignorant the students of the time were about sex, which helps push Kinsey into his research, out of his concern to help people understand sexuality. This leads to his having the students fill out a questionnaire. This in turn leads him to try the questionnaire in a community of homosexuals in Chicago that a student told him about. His first attempt in a bar is not successful. He talks to Jake, a young gay man, who suggests (42) that instead of using a written questionnaire, Kinsey just talk to people. This puts in motion Kinsey's development of the interview method of taking people's sexual histories. On a return trip to Chicago (43–44) Kinsey finds Jake on the street and "Excitement mixes with dread and anticipation as they move toward each other"—a discreet way of suggesting a homosexual encounter.

Kinsey tells Clara about the sex with Jake when he returns home. Clara tells him, "It's not like I'm surprised, exactly," and lists some signs that had hinted that he might have homosexual tendencies. He asks her if she had ever wondered what it would be like to sleep with another man. She says she has, but did not act on those thoughts "Because we are married. We have children." Kinsey insists those are social restraints and starts to lecture her. She finally says, "I can't talk about this any more." As it stands in this draft, it's a good if somewhat standard scene, enlivened by character details: Kinsey's desire to be completely open, Clara's hurt, and her willingness to stand up to him.

Oh yes, the children. The Kinseys did have several children, some of whom we have seen briefly in earlier scenes, but one we have not. In 1926 their four-year-old son Daniel died, and as Gathorne-Hardy wrote, "This terrible blow continued to reverberate in them for many years." You would think then that Daniel's death would have been a major plot point in a script about Kinsey. If nothing else, it would make him more sympathetic when he takes some of his more extreme actions. How many screenwriting manuals tell you to do everything you can to make your characters "sympathetic"? The problem here is that the death of a child is probably too big and too emotional an event to be used in the limited way it would have to be in a two-hour film. The film must necessarily focus on Kinsey's professional life and how it affected his personal life, as opposed to how this early personal tragedy affected his professional life. Sometimes you have to give up the good stuff. Even the *really* good stuff.

After another Noone scene in which we are *told* that Kinsey had started sleeping with Clyde Martin, Kinsey, Clara, and Martin, whom we do not know very well, are in Kinsey's office. Clara says she has decided to make the best of the situation. Martin says that he misses sleeping with women and asks Kinsey if it will be all right if he asks Clara to sleep with him. Kinsey "for once, has nothing to say." Clara says, "Well…I think I'd like that. I'd like it very much" (48). But we do not see them together in bed.

Thurman Rice attends one of Kinsey's classes, is appalled, and goes to Wells to object. Rice threatens to stir things up, we see a minister preaching against Kinsey, and then Wells listening to the complaints of the Board of Trustees. Wells defends Kinsey's research, but agrees to do something. He sends Kinsey a letter saying he can continue the research or teach the class, but not both. Kinsey is outraged, but Clara points out that Wells is being rather shrewd, since the choice gives Rice and the others a scrap, while putting the university behind Kinsey's research. We see in these scenes the character of all four of people, which expands on what we know and moves the story forward. We also learn about Wells's character as we often do in a film: indirectly, by what others, in this case Clara, say about them. Versions of these scenes survive in the sixth draft, but not the final draft, although variations of the sixth draft version were shot and appear in the Deleted Scenes. The scenes probably took up too much time, but it is a shame they were cut.

From pages 54 to 59 we see Kinsey put together his crew of interviewers, particularly Wardell Pomeroy and Paul Gebhard. Pomeroy is established as having a very extensive sex life, and Gebhard is established as having a more academic résumé than the others. From pages 60 to 64 Kinsey trains them in the interviewing techniques: putting the subjects at ease, asking follow-up questions, etc. After a montage of them interviewing undergraduates, schoolteachers, et al., we get a discussion (68) of the differences in sexual behavior in social classes, a scene that is a little too much of a lecture to survive into the final draft and film.

We return to Kinsey's garden for the wedding of Clyde and Kay Martin (69–71). Kay is astonished at the explicitly sexual talk among the wives, especially Martha Pomeroy's suggestion that all wives need a "Mommy's helper": someone "who takes care of Daddy before he comes home." The "Mommy's helper" discussion is dropped from the final version of the scene.

Dr. Robert Yerkes, who studies primates and is connected with the Rockefeller Foundation, tours Kinsey's lab and collection of erotic objects. With him is Dr. Alan Gregg, also of the Foundation, which is considering giving Kinsey a grant for his research. Later the two scientists have dinner at the Kinsey house, where Clara is concerned about the food and the scientists are making sure that the research is of a high standard. The scientists are warning Kinsey, and foreshadowing for us, the potential public criticism of Kinsey's results. Clara and Kinsey discuss the dinner afterward and Kinsey is upset that he cannot just do what he wants. He says, "I don't have forever," a reference to his bad heart, which unfortunately has not been established earlier in the script. In the family garden (76–78) Kinsey announces to his team that they have received the Rockefeller grant, but we also see Gebhard flirting with Kay Martin, Clyde's wife.

A cross-country montage (79ff) includes a large variety of people telling the camera their occupations, but with no details of their sexual histories. The idea is that Kinsey was collecting material from a wide variety of people, just as he captured a wide variety of gall wasps. We do not hear what they are saying in the interviews, so we do not know how different their sexual experiences are. This montage will change by the final draft.

This sequence also leads Condon to some very generalized writing, such as "The team ingratiates itself with various communities. . . . They attend church bazaars and community dances; bingo games and bake-offs; weddings and baptisms; poolrooms and taverns." In addition to being rather general, it would also be very expensive. It was dropped by the sixth draft. The sequence does include a nice scene (80–81) where the team is having dinner in a fancy restaurant on the road and talks so loudly about sex that the other diners complain. Pomeroy then starts talking in the code they use for the interviews and a subtitle translates what he is saying. This survived to the sixth draft, but was eventually dropped, although it appears in the Deleted Scenes. Condon says in his commentary on the Deleted Scenes that the scene was too much of a "musical number," meaning it called attention to itself as a scene and stopped the show, in the wrong sort of way. He's right, but it is a funny scene. Condon was also cutting down the amount of talking about sex the members of the team do, possibly to make them more sympathetic, or at least less gross. Again, lines that may be acceptable on paper can be too much when heard out loud. If you have any question as to whether your dialogue is too much, read it out loud to your mother. She'll tell you.

Kinsey's office has expanded (82–83), and we learn that World War II is over when a secretary tells Kinsey. He obviously was not paying attention, a nice detail about his obsessiveness with his work. The secretary also mentions that his father has called. At the house after his mother's funeral, Kinsey convinces his father to let him interview him for his study (84–86). The real Kinsey hardly saw his father after he left for college, and his father went to Nevada for a quickie divorce when he became enamored of another woman. The divorce could have been handled in a line or two of dialogue, but the interview is a better scene. First of all, it finishes off the relationship with the father. Second, it is a very creepy scene, and I mean that in the best way. We know that Kinsey's father was restrictive about sex, but here we find out what was done to him as a child that helped make him that way. At the end of the scene, the father says, "Sounds to me like you're wasting your time. Nobody wants to know about these things." Finally, it is a great, playable scene. There are multiple subtexts for the actors to play. The scene remains in the final film virtually verbatim as it appears in this draft.

The first Kinsey book, *Sexual Behavior in the Human Male* (1948), is published (87). Wells talks to the Board of Trustees, warning them it is coming and telling them what's in it. He asks for a formal show of support and gets it, although one Dowager hopes that it will not bring too much publicity. Wells says, "With any luck, the general public won't even notice." We hear the sound of a bomb exploding and cut to a newspaper cartoon comparing the book to the explosion of the atomic bomb. There is a montage of the impact of the book, including a *New Yorker* cartoon, a Bob Hope joke on the radio, a scene from *I Love Lucy*, and a woman who gives up reading the book and reads an illustrated condensed version in *Good Housekeeping* instead. By the final draft the Hope and *Lucy* clips have disappeared, probably because they would have been too expensive to obtain the rights to, but the *Good Housekeeping* scene remains. We do see Kinsey speaking to a large crowd at the University of California at Berkeley, and talking to reporters after the speech. One of the reporters asks Clara how her life has changed and she replies, "I hardly ever see him since he took up sex."

Noone now shows up in the story (92) and is put to work in Kinsey's lab photographing women having orgasms. One women, Alice, is in her sixties and has multiple orgasms quickly. We see the film of Alice with Kinsey as the team discusses the film. They watch other films, and Kinsey tells Noone he will have to break up Kay and Gebhard's affair because Martin is being hurt.

The Customs Board intercepts a box of erotica being sent to Kinsey. Kinsey is in Wells's office as Wells is on the phone, listening to the governor of the state complain (99). After listening for a minute, Wells says, "Governor, you're so mad I can't reason with you. When you calm down, we'll discuss it." And he hangs up. Could that possibly be real, the president of a state-supported university hanging up on the governor, upon whom the university funding depends? Yes, it is. It's in Wells's memoirs as well as Gathorne-Hardy. And Condon keeps it not only because it is a great bit, but also because it tells us a lot about Herman Wells and his character. Wells then warns Kinsey about the potential problems his work will cause with the Rockefeller Foundation as well as the state.

The second book, *Sexual Behavior in the Human Female* (1953), is published in another, more restrained montage of reactions (101), including existing footage of Billy Graham preaching against the book. This montage was eventually eliminated, probably for reasons of cost and time, as well as the fact that it duplicates much of the first book's montage. And the script and film are going to deal in more substantial scenes with what the reaction to the female volume *meant*. The film cuts to the next scene (102), Kinsey reading a review and complaining to Clara that he cannot understand why people hate the book. Clara gives the definitive answer: "You told them their grandmothers and daughters are masturbating, having extramarital sex, sex with each other. What did you expect?"

Then Condon gives us a great scene that was dropped by the sixth draft. J. Edgar Hoover, the head of the FBI, calls Kinsey (103–105). Hoover mentions that Senator Joseph McCarthy, whom Hoover hates ("but he's got the country's ear"), is claiming there are homosexuals in the State Department. What Hoover wants Kinsey to do is help him identify the true homosexuals in the State Department, so "we'll do a better job of protecting the falsely accused." Kinsey turns him down. Given Hoover's reported homosexuality, the scene could simply be too strange and too funny for the movie. Like the restaurant scene, it would stop the film in its tracks. It does not appear to have been shot, since it doesn't show up in the Deleted Scenes. Sometimes you have to give up the good stuff.

Kinsey finds Martin and Gebhard fighting in the office (105–107) over Gebhard's affair with Kay. Kinsey orders Gebhard to stop the affair, since he gets Gebhard to admit he is never going to leave his wife and children. Then we find out (108–109) that Noone is in love with Kay as well. After Kinsey faints during a lecture and is taken to the hospital, the FBI visit him and we learn that Kay had told them about the sexual activities of Kinsey's group. We later find out that Noone married Kay after she and Martin were divorced. All of this is handled too quickly to have the impact it should. The crucial relationships for the Kinsey story are Gebhard having the affair with Kay and getting into the fight with Martin. It shows how impossible it was, in spite of what Kinsey thought, to keep emotions, especially love, out of sex. Noone's relationship with Kay seems tacked on, especially this late in the script. He was not a part of the group until late in the story, and we do not have the emotional and intellectual investment in him that we have in the others, and in Kinsey and his work.

Congress grills Dr. Gregg of the Rockefeller Foundation on its support of Kinsey. After stating that Kinsey's work will help the Communists weaken the country, a congressman asks if the Foundation should be in the business of sex research. Gregg replies, "I think it's probably something the Foundation shouldn't have anything to do with" (114). Kinsey watches this on television.

Wells asks the Trustees to support the research, pointing out that the university is running a budget surplus from the increase in students that Kinsey's work has attracted to the campus. The Trustees vote against it. Wells says, "That's it, then." We have seen him exercise his considerable political skills, but there are limits for him, which he recognizes.

Kinsey meets with Huntington Hartford, the millionaire A&P heir, and his social circle of rich friends. Since Hartford has been married four times, he does not feel he can support the controversial research. No one else there offers any help (115–118). Noone sums up Kinsey's contribution (121–122).

Kinsey is in San Francisco, in the apartment of a Woman in her late fifties. He has taken her sexual history, which involves having been married and realizing she had lesbian feelings for a friend. She was on the edge of suicide, which leads Kinsey to say, "It's just another reminder of how little things have changed in our society." The Woman replies that things have gotten much better. He says, "Really? What happened?" "Why, you did, of course." The Woman tells him that she had the courage after reading his books to come out to her friend, and that they have lived together happily ever since. She shakes his hand and says, "You saved my life, sir." The incident with the Woman is not mentioned in Gathorne-Hardy's biography, but it is typical of the thousands of letters that Kinsey received as his work became public, and it sums up, better than Noone's speeches in the previous scene, his contributions toward the opening up of American society. When I read the reviews and saw the film, I assumed that this was always intended as the last scene, since it is so powerful and moving. But it is not, not even in the second draft.

The final scene in the draft shows Kinsey and Clara in the Muir Woods, north of San Francisco, where they are dwarfed by the redwood trees. They watch two porcupines about to mate. Clara says, "Maybe we should alert Congress." She hopes they are in love, and Kinsey says that he hopes so, too. He starts to leave and when she asks, "What's the hurry?" he replies, "There's a lot of work to do," which becomes the final line of the film, and a charge to the audience to continue his work. This draft ends with the porcupines mating.

This second draft is passable, but particularly with the inclusion of Grafton Noone, it is both very literal (in his de facto narration) and unfocused (Noone takes up more time than he is worth in the story). In the documentary on the making of the film on the Special Edition DVD, Condon says that the Noone character and his narration would have given the film less immediacy and was distracting. Condon will continue to find ways to tell the story better.

The sixth draft. (123 pages)

The first thing you notice is that Grafton Noone is gone. Completely.

As is Rome, which was always going to be an expensive location shoot.

We begin now in darkness, with Kinsey instructing Clyde Martin on how to take a sexual history. Kinsey's first line is "Try not to frown." Then we continue in the lab room and see Martin, with Kinsey as an off-screen voice, for the first two pages. He is instructing Martin on taking his (Kinsey's) sexual history, one training method Kinsey used. The discussion here between the two deals with how the interview works, as well as the biographical information we get about Kinsey (date of birth, marital status, relationship with his mother). This scene gives us several things. The most obvious is exposition on Kinsey. Since Martin is going to be more of a major character in this draft than he was in the second, we get introduced visually to him as well as watch him perform. We see that Kinsey is the teacher, Martin the student. And by postponing Kinsey's "appearance" until the top of page 3, there is some sense of mystery about him.

There is something else, even more important, about the new opening. It tells us what the film is about, that we are going to be looking at sex as much from the outside as the inside. Kinsey's constant interrupting not only establishes Kinsey's character, but prepares us to step outside the action and observe it as Kinsey and his team did. This helps Condon when he later comes to deal with the sexual histories and the films Kinsey made. Unlike most movies, which make every effort to seduce us into the story, this film is going to let us remain at least partially removed from whatever elements of the material we may want to distance ourselves from.

We finally see Kinsey for a brief moment when Martin asks him about his relationship with his father. Then we are into a flashback in which the father is preaching in a Methodist church basement about the evils of sex. The father is creepy, but now a little funny, as he preaches against "the most scandalous invention of all, the Talon slide fastener, otherwise known as the zipper, which provides every man and boy a speedy access to moral oblivion." Condon is giving the father more color than he had in the second draft, and also setting him up for his next two scenes.

We now see Pomeroy learning to interview Kinsey, which uses some material from page 56 of the second draft. We get to see and know the team members much earlier than in the second draft, so Condon won't have to take up time introducing them when they come into the story. On page 6 we again get the flashback of the girl undressing with the father arriving, but without the lecture. We know from the "zipper" scene what the lecture will be and do not need to hear it. Then on page 7 we get Gebhard interviewing Kinsey, using material from pages 56–57 of the second draft. The Kenneth Hand scene now includes the fact that Kinsey is studying at Stevens (which, we do not know from the script, is where his father teaches) at the insistence of his father, who thinks he should be an engineer. We still do not get much of a sense of the attraction between Kinsey and Hand. We go back to Martin, Pomeroy, and Gebhard firing short questions at Kinsey, but without his answers, suggesting the end of that montage. The interviews will continue as a counterpoint throughout this draft and the film, although as Condon notes in the documentary on the making of the film, he cuts back on the use of the interview material as the film progresses because it was taking us out of the story too much. Balance and flow are crucial.

We now (10–13) get a new scene. His father gets the twenty-year-old Kinsey to go into a store and ask to buy cigarettes. When the grocer gives them to him, the father charges in and calls him a criminal for selling to an underage boy. The grocer, instead of being intimated, grabs a broom and shoos the father out of the store. It is almost a slapstick scene, and carries on the idea that the father is funny as well as creepy. Why a scene that has nothing to do with sex? Because it connects Kinsey's father's restrictive attitudes to the larger world. However, it wouldn't work if it were not a funny and interesting scene on its own. Condon needs both elements to make it work. Kinsey is embarrassed by his father's behavior, and tells him he is dropping out of Stevens and going to Bowdoin to study biology.

We now jump to the lecture on gall wasps (13) and meeting Clara (15–17), but we also get a new scene of Kinsey playing Beethoven on the piano and showing Clara his classical music collection, then Martin interviewing Kinsey as to whether he was a virgin when they got married. The music scenes add texture to the relationship, and Condon is using the interviews to get across information in ways that complement what we are seeing and hearing, not just explaining it, as with the second-draft Noone material.

Kinsey's proposal to Clara and their first night together are much the same, but then we have a scene of Kinsey taking Clara to meet his parents. Kinsey's brother is the apple of his father's eye, and Clara telling the father that Kinsey has published a textbook fails to impress him (22). The father says to them, "I assume you plan to start a family soon," which probably provokes Clara's line later in bed, "…he's much worse than I expected." The doctor is now Dr. Reynolds, who still diagnoses the thick hymen, but then he asks Kinsey how big his penis is when it is erect. The doctor holds up a twelve-inch ruler. "Here? Here? Or here?" The stage direction reads, "Clara points to the largest size, then adds a inch." Now isn't that a better way to establish the size than the one-page scene with Noone and the waitress? And it gives the actress playing Clara a wonderful sight gag and reaction shot. And the doctor gets a good comeback line as well: "I'm surprised you didn't pass out" (26). Kinsey and Clara consummate the marriage, and Condon has added a line to the scene from the second draft: "They fall back, amazed and elated." Reaction shots, folks.

We now get Pomeroy, Gebhard, and Martin taking both Kinsey's and Clara's sexual histories. The scene (26–28) shows how in synch Kinsey and Clara are (similar answers) and reminds us of the three members of the team. There follows a montage of the Kinsey family, with Christmas card photos of them all, including the kids as they grow up. This leads into a montage of the family on camping trips in Canada, which was ultimately dropped, most likely because of the expense. What survives in the film is a series of photographs.

Next (29–31) is a new scene. Ben and Emily, young married graduate students, have come to Kinsey to talk about their problem. Ben says, "We heard you had good advice for some of the biology students...," which establishes that Kinsey has been talking to other students. Kinsey replies, with what Condon calls "a warm smile," saying, "Sexual difficulty among newly-married people is more common than you think. It's nothing to be ashamed of." Kinsey makes suggestions, including oral–genital sex. This scene is a combination of the dropped "garden" scene and the end of the montage of students asking questions from the second draft, but it takes those further. When Kinsey suggests oral sex, Ben says that his brother told him that could cause problems "later on. With having babies." Kinsey doesn't think it's true, but Ben asks how he knows, if there has been any actual research. When Kinsey admits he does not know, Ben asks, "Then how can you be sure?" This establishes that Kinsey wants to help people and that there has not been research, as well as providing him with the motivation to do research. Kinsey reads to Clara from some current sex manuals that show what he is up against. Both of these scenes establish the ignorance that was prevalent at the time, and do it in a dramatic way.

We now have the reception in Wells's house, the argument with Rice, and Wells sitting in on Rice's class, which now uses existing footage from a film of the period about venereal disease called *The Innocent Party*. Wells still slips out of the class at the end of the scene. We see the setup of Kinsey's new class, which we did not in the earlier draft. A Staff Secretary is telling students that the class is only for faculty members and their wives, grad students, seniors, and married undergraduates. Martin gets into the class by grabbing a girl and pretending to be engaged to her.

The montage of student questions is now shorter than before and leads directly to Kinsey in class reading some other questions, which leads, as in the second draft, to Kinsey handing out the questionnaires. In Kinsey's garden, Martin is now there helping him. The two men discuss the results with Clara. Kinsey says he needs more, and Martin suggests he do it as interviews rather than a questionnaire. This scene helps focus on both Martin and Clara and their relationships with Kinsey. The scenes with Clara and Martin in this draft in general have increased their importance to the story and developed their characters from the second draft. This is helpful because of the relationship that is going to develop between the two of them later. This is a writer seeing what he needs to do to develop the basic material in the most useful way.

Condon has also developed what was a brief scene in the second draft, in which Kinsey is discussing his work with his teenage children and being very open about it. He is more open here, although his son Bruce is not particularly interested, and in the second of the two back-to-back family scenes Bruce asks if they could talk about something else.

In the Chicago scenes (48–54), it is now not Kinsey's first time there, and he is accompanied by Martin. At their hotel Martin and Kinsey talk about his scale, 0 being completely straight, 6 being completely gay. They compare what they think their own numbers are (Martin a 3, Kinsey a 1 or 2), and then Martin asks him if he has ever done anything about it. Martin kisses Kinsey, pulls away, then Kinsey pulls him back. It is a more explicit scene than the Kinsey–Jake scene in the second draft, and there is more at stake, since Martin has been a major character from the beginning of this draft. Therefore the next scene, from the second draft, where Kinsey confesses to Clara, carries greater emotional weight. Condon has developed the scene more and added an interesting line for Clara. Kinsey asks her, "When I took your history, didn't you admit to having sexual feelings for other men?" and she replies, "Don't…don't you dare use that against me" (55). Clara also suggests that if it were known that Kinsey engaged in homosexual activities, people would say his research was biased.

After the scene between Rice and Wells, Clara and Martin talk (59–62). She says she didn't like him at first, but if it had to happen, she is glad it was with him. He thinks she has handled it remarkably well. Kinsey shows up and the scene continues as in the second draft. Her final line is now "Well…I think I might like that. Prok [everybody's nickname for Kinsey], what do you think?" which is a more complicated response than her line in the second draft. This is followed by Gebhard taking Clara's history about her extramarital affairs. We see Clara in bed with Martin, but she has to get up when Kinsey calls her from downstairs because the Rockefeller Foundation is about to visit. As she reaches for her blouse, she says to Martin, "It's just a very full day." This is a great *character* line for Clara. It is warm, delicate, surprisingly casual given the circumstances, and yet showing where her priorities are.

The Rockefeller Foundation in this draft is just Dr. Gregg. Dr. Yerkes has disappeared completely, either because Condon felt that one man was enough, or because he couldn't get the rights to portray Yerkes. Condon's solution is to add Herman Wells to the scenes, including the tour of the collection and the dinner at the Kinseys'. This gives a new twist to Kinsey's line at the end of the collection scene, which is still as it was in the second draft: "There's plenty of time to take your sex histories before dinner. Who'd like to go first?" With Gregg and Yerkes it was funny, but with Gregg and Wells it's even funnier, because we know Wells by now. The dinner scene is developed further, with a greater contrast between Kinsey talking about his work and Clara talking about the food. At the end of the scene, Wells brings up the question of the combination of teaching and research, and then we get the scene of Clara saying Wells is shrewd. This cuts to another "interview training" scene, starting with Clara, then Pomeroy talking about prostitutes, which uses material from pages 62–64 of the second draft. Then we get a montage of interviews, which was four pages in the second draft, and is now down to three. The college students have been dropped and it is just the grownups. This is still followed by the discussion of social classes (74), the montage on the road, and the restaurant scene. Clyde Martin's wedding in the garden is next, with the discussion among the wives.

In this draft Kinsey learns that the war is over in a phone call from Kenneth Braun. Who is he? We didn't see him at all in the second draft, but he is the most infamous of Kinsey's subjects. He had sent material to Kinsey for years, but Kinsey had not yet met him. The few lines here set him up for a later scene of Kinsey and Pomeroy taking his sexual history. After Kinsey's mother's funeral, taking the sexual history of his father, and Wells warning the Trustees about the first book, we get Kinsey's son Bruce on a college campus saying he's not related to *that* Kinsey. The montage of reaction to the book has been condensed from the second draft. The speech at Berkeley is now just a photograph of the actual event (much less expensive). The scene with the reporters is now at Grand Central Station (possibly because, in keeping the budget down, the decision may have already been made to shoot the film on the East Coast, rather than an extensive location shoot in Indiana). Condon at this point has the same "Ozzie and Harriet" description he used in the opening of the second draft. Kinsey ends the scene with the reporters with a rant against sex crime laws, which translates into a newspaper headline: "Kinsey Says Rapists Are Victims." Gregg, of the Rockefeller Foundation, is upset at the headline and objects to Kinsey flaunting his connection to the Foundation, which is a change from Gregg's earlier support, and foreshadows what happens later. Gregg brings up the rumors that Kinsey is photographing women in aroused states. Kinsey claims the films are "just some photographic studies of mammalian behavior," which Gregg seems to accept (93).

We have scenes from the second draft of Alice, who is now renamed Barbara, and the group watching the films. The party scene from page 77 of the second draft is placed here, with no reference to winning the Foundation grant, and we see Gebhard flirting with Alice Martin (Kay in the earlier draft, changed to Alice here and in later drafts, just as Alice, the subject of the films, was changed to Barbara). We go back to the films the group had made, with Kinsey dictating over them, including a comment on how some women find it "impossible to share such an intimate relationship with more than one partner," which becomes a voiceover as Clara is typing up the dictation. The films also include a shot of Gebhard and Alice Martin having sex, "and something more, a visible emotional connection" (97). By moving the party scene to this later place, there is now a more distinct line from it to the problems the Gebhard–Alice relationship caused.

Now we meet Kenneth Braun. Kinsey and Pomeroy take his sexual history, which is prodigious. And Braun has kept records. As he points out in the beginning of the scene to Kinsey, "We're actually a lot alike, you know." It is a creepy moment, and the scene gets creepier as Braun goes into details, done in a verbal montage, of his sexual biography. Pomeroy, who we have seen is the most highly sexual of the Kinsey team, is so turned off he has to leave, even though Kinsey's training is for interviewers to be non-judgmental. Even Kinsey is challenged by Braun, both directly and indirectly, to keep his detachment.

Kinsey admits this to Clara in the next scene, where they talk about Braun. Clara suggests not using the material, but he says he has to, since Braun has given them data no one else has. Clara, foreseeing what will be one of the major complaints by the later anti-Kinsey critics, says, "You're playing with your reputation, Prok. If people knew where this information came from…"(102). We then get the Customs Board scene and Wells hanging up on the governor. Wells makes a reference to Hoover still being mad that Kinsey wouldn't help him, although the Hoover scene is no longer in the script. The reaction to the female volume is condensed, without the clips of Billy Graham, but with a nightclub comic making jokes. Next is Clara's explanation of why people hate the book, then the fight between Gebhard and Martin. Kinsey collapses at a lecture, is at the hospital but without the FBI agents, then watches Gregg before Congress on television at home. Wells's meeting with the Trustees is now intercut with Clara coming home and finding Kinsey in the bathtub, bleeding from having pierced his foreskin. His explanation is, "How can I question people about their activities unless I know what they are talking about?" He thinks that he has gone too fast in his research, that people weren't ready for it, and that now he has "ruined it for everybody" (114). Some of the dialogue here is similar to a scene on page 118 of the second draft, but it is put in a much more dramatic setting. Next are the Huntington Hartford scenes, followed by a new scene of Gebhard, Martin, and Pomeroy talking after Kinsey's death about how they are going to continue Kinsey's work, which they did. This scene was shot and appears in the Deleted Scenes. Condon says he simply had too many ending scenes. Next is the scene with the Woman, the same as in the second draft. The final scene is now played not in the Muir Woods but in the woods of New Jersey, still watching birds and the porcupines and talking about love. The shift in locale was also a question of budgeting, given that the film would be shot on the East Coast. Kinsey's last line is now, "Come on. There's a lot of work to do."

The sixth draft helped bring the story into focus, particularly with the dropping of Grafton Noone, but also in developing the characters of Clara and Martin. Some of the grosser discussions of sex by the researchers have been eliminated, and more will go by the final film.

The final draft. (108 pages)

The final draft, in essence the shooting script, follows the sixth draft, but with reductions (most likely for budget reasons), and with greater focusing of the scenes. As I have mentioned above, sometimes Condon was able to squeeze in shooting scenes from earlier drafts. You should note, however, that none of them show up in the film, only in the Deleted Scenes, which suggests he was right to cut them, however painful it may have been to do so.

We still start in darkness, but with voiceovers. The first line now is Kinsey's: "Don't sit so far away. Anything that creates a distance should be avoided," which was slightly later in the sixth draft. The line is of course ironic because Condon is using the interviews as a distancing device.

Kinsey's father's "zipper" speech is still here, but the details of Pomeroy's sex life have been cut in the following interview scene, although some of it was shot and appears in the Deleted Scenes. Many of the Deleted Scenes are from the interview material, which, according to the documentary, was shot in a two-day rush at the end of the filming. The interview references to Kinsey's puberty have been changed to emphasize his early interest in biology. This is an example of Condon figuring out in the rewriting process how to make the material more subtle and textured. The scene with the older girl has been dropped completely. In the Kenneth Hand scene, "An uncomfortable silence as Kenneth continues to peer through the binoculars" (8 in the sixth draft, 7 here) has been changed to "An uncomfortable silence as Kenneth returns Al's gaze," establishing Kinsey's tentative homosexual feelings. The grocery store scene has an establishing shot of Kinsey and his dad arriving, but the scene is now all inside the store (12). In the sixth draft the second half was outside, with local kids watching. Now there are no extras, and the establishing shot can be done MOS (without sound), so it will be easier to set up and shoot. On a low-budget film, everything counts.

The interviews are now used to tell us that Kinsey went to Bowdoin, Harvard, and then Indiana University. Clara's meeting with Kinsey now does not take place at a picnic (fewer extras and props). The scientific talk before he proposes to her in the sixth draft has been cut, and when she comes into the lab to agree to marry him, she now says, "If you'll have me…" In the sixth draft she just showed up, but since she had been hesitant to marry him, we need the line to let us know she will. The post-marriage interview (25–26) is cut from two pages to one, and a new interview scene shows that Kinsey counts time by how many gall wasps he has collected, just as he is later obsessed with numbers of sexual histories, while Clara tells time by the birth of the children. We hear the ways they connect and the ways they do not. When Kinsey reads some of the contemporary sex manuals to Clara, after he talks to Ben and Emily, he reads a line about the dangers of oral sex, to which she replies, "Well, I must be in grave danger then" (30), a variation of a line from the second draft. The film in Rice's class is now existing footage, but different from the footage named in the sixth draft. Obviously Condon and his researchers were looking for the best bits to use. The final one is a grim piece about venereal disease. Wells leaving Rice's class has been dropped.

The question about polio has been dropped from the student montage, probably because the younger generation of viewers does not remember the scourge of polio in the thirties and forties. This is a problem of doing a historical film for a national audience that does not have a strong grasp of history, a problem we saw some solutions to with *Lawrence*, and will return to later with several other historical films. The polio question has been replaced by the almost-surreal "I think about my cat. A lot." After Kinsey confesses his affair with Martin in Chicago to Clara, her line about how people would dismiss his research if they knew has been dropped, although it appears in the Deleted Scenes. It may well have given aid and comfort to those anti-Kinsey people who were likely to, and did, attack the film. It may also be that Condon, an openly gay filmmaker, felt the line might be used against him as well. Or perhaps he felt there is enough homophobia in the country without giving it voice.

Rice complaining about Kinsey's class and Wells's decision to give Kinsey the option of teaching or research have all been cut, but appear in the Deleted Scenes. The cut speeds up the film, though the missing scenes are nice character scenes and focus on Kinsey's obsessions, but perhaps it was felt that that was clear enough. In the interviews with the grownups, a middle-aged female Schoolteacher is asked about masturbation. In the earlier drafts, her reply was, "I invented it, son, and if I could have patented it, I'd have made a million dollars." Now it is just "I invented it, son" (65), but the longer version is in the Deleted Scenes, and is, frankly, funnier.

The cross-country montage has dropped most of the people announcing their occupation (fewer actors reduce the budget, and this was always going to be a film with a lot of speaking parts), and now a smaller number of people just talk about their sexual histories (67–69). The montage begins with a red line connecting the faces across a map of the United States, then ends up with Bloomington (home of Indiana University) on the map. Clyde Martin's wedding to Alice has been condensed, and the "Mommy's helper" lines have been cut. Braun does not call in the office scene, and we do not learn the war is over, but this is in the Deleted Scenes. Condon mentions in his commentary that he thought he needed to introduce Braun before his big scene, but he was right to cut this since he didn't need it. The funeral and taking his father's history are still in place, as is Wells's talk to the Trustees, but his line about the general public not noticing now includes not only the sound of a bomb, but a live-action shot of the explosion of an atomic bomb (77). The Grand Central Station scene is still in, followed by the headline about rapists, then the scene with Barbara, Gebhard flirting with Alice Martin, and Kinsey dictating material about women and infidelity. The Braun scene stands on its own, and unfortunately the Kinsey–Clara discussion after it has been cut, so we do not get Kinsey's defense of using the material. The montage of reactions to the female volume have been cut, although a few are retained in the film. All we get is Kinsey reading a reaction, and Clara's line about what he has told them about the women in their lives (92).

Kinsey watches Gregg's testimony at home, and Wells and the Trustees are intercut with the bathtub scene (99). The post-death discussion with the team has been dropped. The scene with the Woman is now followed by a scene of Martin interviewing Kinsey in 1942, where Kinsey admits that there is no way to measure love, "and without measurements there can be no science." Kinsey admits he has been thinking about the problem lately and says, "When it comes to love, we're all in the dark."

We are then (107) back in...surprise, Muir Woods. Condon fought for the extra money to shoot the scene there, and after he shot the sixth draft version, both he and the studio realized it was not strong enough to end the picture on. An irony is that this Muir Woods scene is like neither of the equivalent scenes in the second and sixth drafts. Kinsey and Clara are talking about the Sequoias and Kinsey mentions a tribe in Africa that "believe that trees are imperfect men, eternally bemoaning their imprisonment—the roots that keep them stuck in one place." Then he adds, "But I've never seen a discontented tree. Look at this one. The way it's gripping the ground—I believe it really loves it." Think about the subtle ways that that connects with what we have seen and what we know about Kinsey. His last line is now, "There's a lot of work to do."

The film.

When I first saw the film *Kinsey* in November 2004, I went with some trepidation. What I have not yet told you is that I was born and brought up in Bloomington, Indiana, during the Kinsey years. I knew slightly two of the people portrayed in the film. Wardell Pomeroy was the father of a school classmate of mine, and Herman B. Wells was my distant cousin. The reports from my friends in Bloomington, who had seen the film before its release, were that a lot of people were not happy with the film, particularly the way Wells was portrayed. They thought he came off as a clown.

The opening works in the ways I have indicated above: it lets us know we are going to be talking about sex in a detached way, but also bringing us immediately into the characters and the interview process. I had reservations about Chris O'Donnell as Pomeroy, simply because he was so young and lightweight, and the Pomeroy I knew had a gravitas about him that O'Donnell simply does not have. When I later read the Gathorne-Hardy book, I realized that Condon was casting O'Donnell because of the descriptions of Pomeroy when he first came onto the team: young and movie-star handsome. When I knew Pomeroy, and I knew him only slightly, he was older and more serious. O'Donnell caught that in the scene with Braun, when he leaves, although I think Condon was using him in a different way there. Throughout the script drafts, Pomeroy's intense sexuality had been emphasized, and his leaving the Braun interview was supposed to show how even someone as sexually active as he was could be turned off by Braun's extremes. Since Pomeroy's sexuality was not as emphasized in the film, his leaving does not work as intended in the film. Many of the interview scenes in the Deleted Scenes are of O'Donnell. Condon says in his commentary that he felt bad that he had to cut so much of O'Donnell's scenes, and watching the scenes you can see why. He really caught Condon's vision of Pomeroy. Getting your best scenes cut drives character actors crazy, but when a filmmaker is cutting the film, the first responsibility is to the film.

I did not know Paul Gebhard, so I had no particular view of Timothy Hutton in the role. In February 2005, PBS ran the documentary *Kinsey* on their *American Experience*, which included interviews with Gebhard, who comes across as rather jovial, a quality that Hutton did not get.

The Kenneth Hand scene works because Condon as the director emphasizes the looks—and not just the one in the final draft—between Hand and Al, which provides a jolt for the audience, even if they know Kinsey's story. The grocery store scene establishes Kinsey's father as odd in a funny way, which is a bit unsettling. He is played by John Lithgow, and Lithgow's over-the-top performances in his television series *3rd Rock from the Sun* (1996–2001) had made me wonder if he had lost his dramatic skills. This scene raised the question again, but the interview scene later put the question to rest. He gets everything an actor could get out of that scene.

Liam Neeson is taller and more broad-shouldered than Kinsey was, but he captures the obsessiveness of the character without making him boring, which a lesser actor might have. Condon has given Neeson a very wide palette of colors to paint Kinsey with, and Neeson merges all the details brilliantly. He also gets Kinsey's warmth, which is not emphasized in the script, but which people who knew him commented on. We can see it in the scenes in which he talks to the students Ben and Emily, and it comes across in the interview scenes as well. Neeson and Condon are not afraid to make him as difficult as he was in real life, partly because they believe in him and what he was doing. This is a beautiful example of how far you can go in showing your characters' dark sides and still make them acceptable to the viewer.

For budgetary reasons the film was shot on the East Coast, with no scenes shot at Indiana University. As a native of Bloomington, I must say that they found locations that were so right that I knew where they were supposed to be even if they were not. Clara coming up to Kinsey could easily be at the Jordan River on the I.U. campus.

Clara is played by Laura Linney, who brings out the warmth and sub-tlety of the role as Condon has written it. Her line readings of "Well...I think I might like that. Prok, what do you think?" and "It's just a very full day" are as good as you can get, as is the look on her face when she shows the doctor where Kinsey needs to be measured.

Herman B. Wells. There were three important sides to Herman's character. The first was that he was enormously likeable. Oliver Platt, who plays him in the film, gives you the social charm that Wells had, as in laughing at Kinsey's comment on Wells's cribbed notes. The sec-ond was Herman's political skills, which you see in the scenes with the Trustees, and especially when he hangs up on the governor. Wells was one of the few presidents of I.U. who could get away with that. He knew which battles to fight when and how to fight them. Platt also cap-tures this quality. The third side, which is not dealt with in the script, was his belief in the idea of academic freedom. There was a lot of pres-sure on him to get rid of Kinsey, some of it suggested in the film, and many thought a state-supported university could not afford the kind of academic freedom Ivy League schools had. Herman thought otherwise, and it was at the center of his defense of Kinsey. None of this appears in the script, and Platt cannot deliver it on his own. If you want to see an example of Herman defending Kinsey on these grounds, find the PBS documentary mentioned above, which has a newsreel clip of just that. On the other hand, Platt does add something not in the script. When he is watching Rice's class, Platt gets a wonderful expression of disdain on his face. The real Herman B. Wells would not have been so obvious in Rice's class, but it is exactly the look of disdain he could have for idiots, including those on his own faculty.

Peter Sarsgaard brings a quick wit to Clyde Martin and, more impor-tant, an almost sleepy seductiveness. We believe that he can get both Kinsey and Clara into bed with his likeable charm.

Kinsey's first sex class is, as mentioned above, an aria for Neeson, and he does it justice. Just as Condon was constantly judging and re-judging how far he could go in the dialogue, he undoubtedly also had to decide how far to go visually in terms of the slides, films, etc. that Kinsey showed and later shot. This is really more a production detail than a script detail, but as a writer you should be aware of it. Can we show the things, sexual in this case, that you are asking us to show? What sort of rating will the film get? It is amazing to me that Condon managed to get an R rating for the film, given both the verbal and vis-ual detail he has about sex, which is traditionally more strictly rated in American films than violence. The script calls for fairly specific details, some of which survive in the film, some of which do not. Condon says in the documentary that he thinks the film got an R rating because it was obviously not designed to appeal the prurient interest of the audience. Let that encourage you.

If the visuals from the slides are shocking, so is the homosexual affair between Martin and Kinsey. It happens quickly in the script and on film, but includes a kiss between two well-known male actors, which we generally do not see in mainstream American films. Its power to shock comes also from the fact that Condon does not dwell on it, either in the script or in the film. Instead we get the reactions to it, in the scenes following with Clara and Martin.

The cross-country montage works better in its final form than it did in the earlier drafts for two reasons. One, it is simpler, and sometimes simpler is just better. Two, it keeps the focus on the sexual histories, rather than just on the variety of people Kinsey talked to. We *see* the variety, we do not have to *hear* it when they announce their occupations.

The Martins' wedding scene is condensed from its original length, but we still get a sense of the life of the team, which is crucial for the later relationship between Alice and Gebhard to have the impact it does. The interview with Kinsey's father is an example of two great actors getting as much as you can out of a seemingly simple scene. It seems in the playing to be more Lithgow's scene than Neeson's, but that is partly the slight surprise at seeing Lithgow at full dramatic power after the semi-comedy of the earlier scenes. Partly it is Condon the director letting him go, knowing that Neeson has all those other scenes in which to shine.

The Kenneth Braun scene is another great scene for the actors. Braun is played by William Sadler, an actor who has been playing character parts, often villains, since 1978. He avoids the obvious choices, such as playing him deranged, or drooling, or even overtly menacing. He plays it, you should pardon the expression, straight. He is quiet, sincere, and sometimes sly in his challenges to Kinsey. Sadler, and presumably Condon, realize that what Braun says is so shocking that *acting* shocking would be gilding the lily. Sometimes restraint is best. See Eugene Levy in the later discussions of the *American Pie* films for the comic equivalent of this.

The "piercing the foreskin" scene is one of the most shocking scenes in the film, partially because it comes out of nowhere and seems so extreme, even given what we have seen and heard in the rest of the film. One thing Condon has realized is that there are going to be moments that will shock and/or disgust members of the audience. I was shocked by the bathtub scene, but then I am not into masochism. Someone who is might love the scene and wonder why there wasn't more of it in the film. People uncomfortable with male homosexuality will not like the Martin–Kinsey hotel room scene, while gay people may well be put off by the heterosexual scenes. Condon is allowing the film to be disturbing, but in the ways it should be (challenging what we think and feel about sex), since that is part of what the film is about.

The Woman is played by Lynn Redgrave and Condon has written a great cameo role for her. He knows it and plays the first half of it in one take on Redgrave, with the camera pulling back to show Kinsey. Reading the scene, it seems to be mostly exposition, but again there is the subtext of "this is the way it was," which then informs the "What happened?" "Why, you did, of course" exchange. And Redgrave knows the emotional weight to give to the "You saved my life, sir" line. The scene captures Kinsey's influence in immediate, direct, personal terms.

Even ignoring the phallic quality of the redwoods in the Muir Woods sequence, one can see why Condon pushed for the final scene there, even if the exact content kept changing. Kinsey was a scientist with an interest in nature, so it is fitting we end at one of nature's wonders. As suggested above, the speeches about the trees are a subtle summing up, and the last line is a challenge to the audience.

Unfortunately the dropping of the post-Kinsey's death scene from the sixth draft leaves a hole at the end of the film. The impression the film gives is that when Kinsey died, his research died with him, although I suppose you can interpret the last line of the film to suggest that it will go on. In fact, the Institute for Sex Research at I.U. was taken over by Paul Gebhard, who found new funding from a variety of sources, such as Hugh Hefner and the National Institute for Mental Health. Other researchers found that the vast amount of research Kinsey had collected became the base line for much of the research done later.

The final budget on the film was approximately $11 million. Through the end of March 2005 it had grossed only slightly over $10 million in the United States, with less than $3 million overseas. By the time it works its way through post-theatrical release (DVD sales, cable TV, etc.), it may break even. It was not a commercial hit, but not a flop either. Why didn't it do better?

One possible reason was the attack on the film by the anti-Kinsey people, led by Judith Reisman, who the *New Yorker* identifies as "the founder of the modern anti-Kinsey movement." Condon said a year later, "There was real money behind the campaign to vilify the movie before anyone had seen it. I didn't expect them to be so organized." The modern anti-Kinseys hold him responsible for the entire sexual revolution of the last fifty years. As the scene with the Woman at the end of the film suggests, they may have a point, but the revolution has freed so many people from their demons (while in some cases giving them new demons) that it has become part of the culture. The attack against Kinsey has caught very little traction with the majority of Americans, most of whom assume as their right a degree of personal sexual freedom that many may not even realize descends from Kinsey and his work. In her attacks on the film, Reisman was preaching to the choir, and most of them probably would never have seen the film anyway. An example of Reisman's excessive zeal is her insistence that Kinsey himself was a pedophile, as opposed to just taking sexual histories of people like Kenneth Braun who were. None of Kinsey's biographers have found any evidence that he was, which does not stop Reisman. She is quoted in the *New Yorker* as saying, "There is absolutely no reason to believe that Kinsey himself was not involved in the sexual abuse of these children." Not exactly in the great American jurisprudence tradition of "innocent until proved guilty beyond a reasonable doubt in a court of law."

A simpler and more honest answer, suggested at the beginning of this chapter, is that it is difficult for serious movies about sex to be successes in America. Our Puritan heritage makes it difficult for us to treat sex with anything other than humor (*Bull Durham*) or as part of a genre piece, particularly a thriller (*Bound*). An article in the *Hollywood Reporter* in early 2005 discussed the issue, listing the serious films about sex that had not done well, such as *Showgirls* (1995), *Striptease* (1996), *Eyes Wide Shut* (1999), and *The Brown Bunny* (2003). The problem with that list is that they were all *terrible* movies. *The People vs. Larry Flynt* (1996) was a smarter, better movie, but it also did not do well. Bill Condon was quoted in the article as saying, "There's a lot of joking about sex, but the actual idea of talking about sex makes a lot of people nervous, no doubt." He should know. Or maybe, as some in the article suggest, we would rather not be seen in a theater watching a sexy movie, especially if our parents or our kids are in the same multiplex. Or maybe we just feel more comfortable getting our sex at home, that is, on television, with such cable shows as *The L Word* (2004ff), or even on a network show like ABC's *Desperate Housewives* (2004ff).

It may also have been that *Kinsey* was too smart for the room. There are often films, and not just about sex, that are so intelligent about their characters, plots, and subjects that they simply intimidate the mainstream and even the art house audience. The richness and complexity of the characters in *Kinsey* may simply have been too much. Or perhaps the complexity of the film's views of sex and sexual behavior may have been deeper than audiences wanted to go. Or maybe they were just waiting around for it to come out on DVD so they could watch it at home.

So the challenge you can set yourself as a screenwriter is to write a great script that treats sex seriously and plays well to the American audience. Good luck.

Sources

The details of Gail Mutrux's journey to make the film are from Elaine Dutka's "Sex and the Single Film," *Los Angeles Times*, January 12, 2005. David Halberstam's book is *The Fifties* (Villard, 1993). Jonathan Gathorne-Hardy's book is *Kinsey: Sex the Measure of All Things* (Indiana University Press, 1998). James Jones's less sympathetic biography is *Alfred C. Kinsey: A Public/Private Life* (Norton, 1997). Herman B Wells's memoir, *Being Lucky: Reminiscences and Reflections* (Indiana University Press, 1980), has a fascinating section on his dealing with Kinsey. The published edition of the screenplay *Kinsey* (Newmarket Press, 2004) includes comments on the film by Gathorne-Hardy, a short biography of Kinsey by Linda Wolfe, and the shooting script, the equivalent of the final draft discussed above.

The three drafts of the *Kinsey* screenplay were provided by Bill Condon's associate, Jack Morrissey, and sent via Den Shewman, the Editor-in-Chief of *Creative Screenwriting*, who also did the interview with Condon that appears in the January/February 2005 issue of the magazine. The *New Yorker* story is "The Culture Wars: Why Know?" in the "Talk of the Town" section, December 6, 2004. The *Hollywood Reporter* story is "Actually, Sex Doesn't Sell," March 21, 2005. Condon's comment about the campaign against the film was in the "Industry" column in *Sight & Sound*, January 2006.

The PBS documentary *Kinsey* is now available on DVD.

The Special Edition DVD of *Kinsey* includes the Deleted Scenes, a funny gag reel, and a good documentary on the making of the film, *The Kinsey Report: Sex on Film*.

6
Y TU MAMÁ TAMBIÉN

> **Y TU MAMÁ TAMBIÉN** (2001. Screenplay by Alfonso Cuarón and Carlos Cuarón. 105 minutes. Mexico, Spanish with English subtitles)

ALFONSO Cuarón got his first movie camera at the age of twelve in his native Mexico, but when he wanted to study film in college, his mother insisted he study philosophy. He took philosophy in the mornings, but studied at the Centro Universitario de Studios Cinematográficos in the afternoon. His first feature, *Sólo Con Tu Pareja* (*Love in the Time of Hysteria*, 1991), caught Hollywood's attention. His first American film as a director was *A Little Princess* (1995), critically acclaimed but not particularly commercially successful. His second, *Great Expectations* (1998), failed both critically and commercially. Okay, so your script or film attracts Hollywood's attention, then they grind you into the dirt. What do you do next?

Go back to your roots, in Mexico or wherever you came from, sit down with your brother, and write a great script. The *Y Tu Mamá También* script does so many things that Hollywood would like to do but cannot seem to do well. It also does many things well that Hollywood would not touch. You will see where that got Cuarón after the discussion of the film.

Ken Dancyger, in his 2001 book *Global Scriptwriting*, suggests that worldwide screenwriting styles have been coalescing into an international model, but I am not convinced. He points out that similar subjects, such as family life, are being treated in a variety of international films, but what strikes me is that the tone and storytelling techniques are often very distinctly those of the film's native country. I think this is very true of *Y Tu Mamá También*. On the surface it is similar to an American "horny teenager" movie (see the later chapter on the *American Pie* films for examples of that genre), but it is very distinctively Mexican.

After a brief main title, the camera finds Tenoch and his girlfriend Ana fucking. No, they are not "making love" or even "having sex." They are fucking, and the film is just that blunt about it. Both Tenoch and Ana are in their late teens and do it how kids that age do it: sloppily, noisily, urgently, and with no particular skill. When they finish, Tenoch asks her not to have sex with Europeans, an indirect way of telling us that she is going off to Europe for the summer. The sex and the nudity are light and playful, in a way few American sex scenes are. We know very little about the two people.

The Cuaróns then start a voiceover narration. Most contemporary screenwriting books will tell you to avoid voiceover narration, on the obvious grounds that it will tempt you to *tell* the audience what you should be *showing* them. When narration is used in American films, it is often for reasons of nostalgia, as in *How Green Was My Valley* (1941). Or in film noir, as in *Double Indemnity* (1944). Or to add a documentary tone, as in Stanley Kubrick's 1956 film *The Killing*, although Kubrick is also using it to keep his time-jumps clear to the audience. In most American films, the film is narrated by one of the characters (e.g., *Million Dollar Baby* [2004]) so as to not take the audience out of the story.

The Cuaróns do not worry about any of that. They are using narration more in the tradition of Latin American literature. Their narrator is not one of the characters in the story, as we realize early on when he refers to the two main characters in the third person. The writers are not afraid to take us outside the story, to look at their characters from a little distance. An American film about two horny teenage guys would want us to identify with the guys to appeal to the young male demographic, but the Cuaróns want us to see the bigger picture. Yes, this is very much a movie about the immediacy of sex, but it is about many other things as well, which also makes it different from an American film. Listen to the variety of ways they use the narrator.

The narrator begins by telling us that Ana's mother did not object to Tenoch and Ana sleeping together. Surprise: we have not met her mother and we will not. But, the narrator continues, "with Julio it was different." My Spanish is not good enough to give you the original lines, so I am dependent on the English subtitles; the "translation," as it is called in the credits, is by Timothy J. Sexton. We pick up Julio in what becomes clear is the apartment of his girlfriend Cecilia's parents. We do not know yet if Cecilia is going with Ana to Europe. The narrator tells us that Cecilia's father, a doctor, had thought the relationship between Julio and Cecilia had gone too far, but her mother thought the relationship was innocent. Julio looks awkward as he waits with the father. Cecilia calls from off-screen to ask Julio to come into the room to help her find her passport. When he goes into her room, she has a quickie with him. They are just as sloppy as Tenoch and Ana were, not helped by almost being interrupted by her mother. We are only 4 minutes into the movie.

At the airport Ana's father shows up, which surprises her. The narrator tells us he is a former reporter who recently became a politician, and that he refers to Tenoch as "a preppie," although never to Ana's face. We *see* him being nice, but we *hear* about his attitudes. The narration connects us to the outside world, especially politics.

Tenoch and Julio drive back from the airport. Julio farts. Now, in an American movie about two young guys, the whole scene would be about farting. Here a fart is just a fart. Tenoch reacts to the smell, and then they talk about how Tenoch wants to switch from economics to literature, since he would like to become a writer. This would have been a perfect excuse to make an older Tenoch the narrator. In an American version he probably would have been, but the Cuaróns are not using the narrator for nostalgia. Julio mentions that his sister is at a demonstration, which leads Tenoch to say that "Left-wing chicks are hot, dude," to which Julio replies, "Totally." Tenoch cuts a fart and the two-minute scene ends. Compare this to the first Jim and Oz scene in *American Pie*.

Except the Tenoch–Julio scene doesn't exactly end there. We continue with the car in traffic while the narrator tells us that the accident they pass by had nothing to do with the political demonstrations that day. It was rather a bus hitting a migrant bricklayer, whose body will not be discovered for four days. What is that doing in a movie that appears to be about a couple of horny teenagers? One, it is, as often in the film, putting the story of the guys into a social, political, and cultural context. And two, it is bringing death into the story. This is after all a culture that celebrates the Day of the Dead.

The narrator tells us that Tenoch is one of three children of a Harvard-trained economist, who is now Secretary of State, and his wife, who studies spirituality. Tenoch was given the name of an Aztec hero since he was born at a time of growing nationalism in Mexico. This is over shots of the rather lavish house of Tenoch's parents and Tenoch and Julio smoking joints with their friend and supplier, Saba. They go outside to smoke on the balcony, where they are seen by Tenoch's mother. She appears not to notice they are smoking, but does observe that they are sad. She assures them "Your auras transcend the physical plane," demonstrating what the narrator has told us about her, helping to establish the narrator as reliable. She asks Julio if he is coming to Jessica's wedding. We have no idea who Jessica is.

We now see Tenoch and Julio at a party with their peers. The narrator tells us that they failed to pick up any girls and were afraid that would be a blueprint for the summer. He also tells us that Tenoch smashed a headlight on his car on their way home. Why tell us that and not show us? Because the Cuaróns don't *need* to show us that. The scene is simply setting them and us up for what will happen later. The narrator also tells us that Saba had group sex for the first time that night, and we catch a brief glimpse of Saba with two girls. Why not show more? This is not a pornographic movie, in spite of what some prudes would undoubtedly think, and by showing discretion here, the Cuaróns protect the impact of their other sex scenes.

At 10 minutes in, the narrator tells us that weeks have passed, the boys are bored, Tenoch's father is a member of the country club, and they can use the pool on Mondays when it is closed even to other members. Are you beginning to get the idea that Tenoch at least comes from a very privileged background? The boys swim, mostly underwater, perhaps a reference to Benjamin in *The Graduate* (1967). They shower, snap towels, make jokes about each other's dicks, and yell "faggot" at each other. They do not take what they say to each other seriously.

We assume we are at Jessica's wedding (why?), but it is the reception at Tenoch's house afterward. It is outside, with mounted horsemen performing. Tenoch and Julio are counting the number of bodyguards. Julio wanders to the bar and notices an attractive, slightly older woman, Luisa, walk by. She goes past him and he starts after her. It is 13 minutes into the film. But just as there were additional scenes between Tenoch's mother mentioning the wedding and the reception, we will not come back to Luisa for a few minutes. We cut instead to Tenoch, who is talking to Jano, his older cousin, who asks Tenoch if he still intends to write. A combination of voiceover and dialogue tell us that Jano has been out of the country and that he is now a writer. Jano tells Tenoch that it is one thing to write "cute stories" and another to "create literature." I have no evidence, but I have the suspicion that this is the Cuaróns telling both the audience and Hollywood that you may think this is just a cute story, but it is more than that. Ordinarily you should avoid nudging the audience like that, but they get away with it here because it is so subtly handled as an element of Jano's character. Tenoch's father takes the microphone and welcomes everyone, especially the President, to this "humble celebration." Bodyguards, horsemen, a guest list of hundreds, including the President? Hardly "humble."

Julio and Tenoch approach Luisa and make small talk. She is from Madrid, about ten years older than they are, and from the bride's side of the family. Luisa and Tenoch realize they are cousins by marriage, and Luisa is surprised to find "little Tenoch" grown up. She correctly, unlike her husband Jano, remembers the toy he had lost when she met him when he was a boy. The narrator gives us some of her background. Tenoch asks if she is traveling while she is in Mexico. She says Jano is about to go off to a symposium and she wants to see a beach. She mentions one, but the boys tell her it is full of "yuppie backpackers." Tenoch mentions a beach he says only he knows. He is obviously improvising, and he and Julio come up with the name Heaven's Mouth. Tenoch asks her if she would like to go there with them. She says yes and that she will tell Jano, which deflates the boys. This is obviously another one of their schemes that is not going to work out. We are 19 minutes into the film.

We now pick up Luisa in a doctor's waiting room. While Jano is off at his symposium, Luisa has had some tests done and is waiting for the results, as the narrator tells us. He does not tell us what the tests are for. They appear to be merely a setup for the scene of Luisa taking a magazine quiz in the waiting room, but this is one of many sections you will want to come back to after you finish reading this chapter the first time. The Cuaróns are pulling a bit of a Woody Allen here. You probably remember the scene in *Annie Hall* (1977) where Alvy's sneeze blows the cocaine off the table. What you may not know is that scene was shot when Allen was editing the film. In the original script there was a long party sequence in New York that, among other things, established that Alvy and Annie were going to California. After they get to California, there is the great Hollywood party scene. While editing, Allen realized that the two party scenes were repetitive. He wanted to keep the Hollywood scene, so he cut the New York one and added the "sneezing" scene, whose sole *structural* purpose is to let us know that they are going to California. In other words, the scene is about more than it seems to be, and the Cuaróns here, as elsewhere, have covered their tracks nicely. Watch this film and learn how they do this. I can guarantee you will need to do this at some point in your writing career.

The magazine test is "Are You a Fully Realized Woman?" The narrator reads some of the questions and Luisa's answers, then says as she goes into the doctor's office that her answers, according to the magazine, said she was afraid to accept her freedom. The narrator says Luisa disagreed. You can see why this works on the first level: it propels Luisa into going along with the boys.

The boys are at the pool at the country club. We now see one reason the Cuaróns established that they come on the day the pool is closed. They are each on a separate diving board, masturbating, and talking about the girls and women they are thinking of. They start with girls we assume they know, move up to Salma Hayek, and finally come at the mention of "the Spanish cousin," as Julio says, since in the throes of passion he cannot remember her name.

Luisa gets a call from Jano. He's drunk and he admits he's slept with another woman. She cannot get a word in edgewise (ach-choo). Later Luisa calls Tenoch to say she wants to go with them to Heaven's Mouth. He is flustered, agrees, and calls Julio. Without either of them saying it, we know that they are hoping they can take this attractive woman somewhere and have sex with her. It is so obvious that the Cuaróns do not have to have either of them say it. Tenoch's dad has taken his car away from him because he bashed in the headlight, so they will need to borrow Julio's sister's car. But she is using the car now (the narrator gives us a little background on Julio and his family; he is not the child of privilege Tenoch is), so they have to go to the demonstration she is at to talk to her. We get shots of them at the demonstration, but the narrator tells us the outcome of the scene: she will let them use the car for five days if she can then have it for three weeks. Why not have that scene? Julio's sister is not somebody we meet in the film, and the narrator can not only tell us the outcome in a shorter time, he will also have time to tell us that she will use the car for taking food and clothing to the poor. The Cuaróns are perfectly willing to make their two leading men seem self-absorbed and not particularly interested in the rest of the world. This accurate portrayal of these boys means the final payoff of their relationship with Luisa will have more power.

Julio and Tenoch go on a shopping spree in a large big-box super-market. What specifically would these two guys buy in preparation for such a trip? Okay, that's an easy one: snack food, beer, and condoms. They then get directions of a sort from Saba, who thinks he knows a beach that could pass for the one they have created in Luisa's mind.

At twenty-eight minutes into the film, they pick up Luisa and get on the road. Julio and Tenoch actually ask her about her life. Notice the difference between what she says in dialogue (conversational statement of facts and opinion) and what the narrator says (her previous attitudes toward Jano and his friends). He also tells us what she wanted to do. How do you show what somebody wanted to do? Here they have her tell some and the narrator tells the rest. And they include the narration over the many shots, here and later, of the car going along the highway. We are now out of the urban area of the first half-hour of the film and into rural Mexico.

Tenoch and Julio tell Luisa about their friends, including Daniel, who has come out as gay. Luisa asks them if it bothers them, and they tell her no. Remember how casual they were about the "faggot" lines in the shower? They tell her that Daniel is still part of their club, which has its own manifesto. They insist they cannot tell her what it is, but immediately tell her. It includes, among other things, that no one is allowed to sleep with another member's girlfriend. The narrator tells us that they told her stories that were mostly true, but embellished with their private mythologies. He also says the stories helped create a bond between them, which we have seen. Again, a nice balance of narration and visuals.

At 34 minutes into the film, they stop for the night and eat at a small, informal diner, quite distant from the layout at the wedding reception. Luisa asks them about their girlfriends, who they tell her are in Europe, insisting their girls would never cheat on them. Later the boys look into her motel room window. She is crying. They do not bother her.

On the road the next day, the narrator tells us we are going through the village where Tenoch's nanny was born and raised, and that he had never been there before. Could this scene have been done as dialogue? Yes, Luisa could have seen that Tenoch was sad and asked him about it, and he could have told her it was the birthplace of his nanny. But would Tenoch, given what we know about him, mention that he had never been there? Possibly, but it might seem artificial. Also, the film has established that the narrator is telling us this sort of detail, so having him do this fits the tone of the film. Julio tells her they saw her in her room the previous night. She asks if they had wanted to see her naked. As we suspected, she is more aware of what they are thinking than she had indicated. The car is stopped briefly as they pay "tribute" to the "Queen," a young woman dressed in white, possibly a bride, whom the villagers carry in a chair. This is also distant from Jessica's reception. We get long shots of the car on the road as Luisa tells us about her first boyfriend. He took her to beautiful places on his motorcycle. The boys are laughing about it until she tells them he was killed in an accident. We are 44 minutes into the film.

We see more shots of the rural countryside, with shacks, trailers, small stores, and the police searching cars along the side of the road. Why are they searching the cars? We do not know, and nobody in our car mentions it, except to suggest they hide their grass. Meanwhile Luisa, after noticing Tenoch has an erection when he wakes up, asks the boys how they make love to their girlfriends. They describe it as bluntly as we saw it in the opening scenes. Luisa suggests they try wiggling a little finger up the girl's ass. The car overheats and breaks down. At a small village Luisa finds a shrine to a young woman with the same name as hers. She calls Jano and leaves a message on their machine, saying she was wrong to leave without a note. She gives him instructions on paying the bills and picking up the laundry, suggesting going to another laundry. It all makes sense if she is just leaving him to get a divorce (ach-choo). We are 50 minutes into the film.

Taking a shower in their rundown motel, Tenoch cannot find any shampoo. He puts a towel around his waist and goes to Luisa's room to see if she has any. She is crying, then she asks him to take off the towel. She performs oral sex on him and has him go down on her. He comes quickly.

Julio is watching from the door. He runs off and the narrator tells us what he is thinking: not rage, but like the time he caught his godfather in his mother's arms. Tenoch comes down to the swimming pool where Julio is. This is *not* the country club pool; the water is covered with leaves. Julio tells Tenoch that he has fucked Ana, Tenoch's girlfriend. Notice the selection of details as to what each of the boys connect with. Notice also how the narrator is used here not just to tell us how they feel, but to tell us how they feel in comparison with other events in their lives. At dinner, Luisa thinks she is the reason the boys are upset with each other.

At 62 minutes, they are on the road again. An old woman by the shrine has given Luisa a stuffed mouse with her name on it, the same name as the girl who died. The narrator tells us that Luisa is thinking that people live on in people's minds after they die and wonders how long people will remember her, but "she preferred not to think about death." Okay, fine. The shrine has brought these thoughts to Luisa's mind, and we are in a culture that deals with death, but since she is on the road with two young guys, we can logically see why she prefers not to think about death. A big ach-choo.

Luisa climbs into the back seat with Julio. Tenoch is upset, stops the car, runs away from the car, and watches from a distance as Julio and Luisa have sex. Luisa asks them if this was not their plan, to take her away and screw her. She says she shouldn't have fucked either one. Back in the car, Tenoch tells Julio he has fucked Cecilia, Julio's girlfriend. Julio wants to fight, but Tenoch calls him a peasant, one of the few references in the dialogue to the class differences between them. Upset with them, Luisa walks off, telling them she thinks they really want to sleep with each other, and that if "you play with babies you'll end up washing diapers." Can you imagine Stifler's Mom saying that in the *American Pie* movies? Notice also how the boys have no particular response to her comment that they want to sleep with each other. After all, we have seen them joke about homosexuality and accept it with their friend Daniel.

They convince Luisa to continue with them, but she sets out her own manifesto, which includes not sleeping with either one of them and that when she sunbathes nude at the beach, she does not want them sniffing around "like dogs." As night falls, the boys are lost. They see a dirt road that might be what they are looking for, so they turn off on it and get stuck in the sand. They sleep in the car.

The next morning, 74 minutes into the film, Luisa wakes early and discovers they are at a beautiful beach. She walks into the water. This scene has no dialogue, a relief from all the arguments. Later she is sunbathing topless and the boys are indeed not sniffing around like dogs. Jesús, a fisherman in the local nature preserve, his wife Mabel, and their children offer to take our trio in his boat to the other beaches. They land on one Jesús calls—wait for it—Heaven's Mouth. In an American movie, Julio and Tenoch would have big double-take reactions. Here it is just a couple of surprised smiles that pass between them. Just because I tell you to write reactions does not mean you have to write BIG reactions. Smaller and subtler can be better. The beach is a momentary paradise for all of them. When the boat takes them back to their beach, the narrator tells us what will happen within a year to Jesús and Mabel. Notice how that information is in keeping with how the Cuaróns have used the narration throughout the film.

Tenoch, Julio, and Luisa get back to their tents and find them overrun by pigs. The narrator of course tells us what will happen with the pigs. Jesús offers to let our trio stay at his home, a collection of trailers. Luisa is on the phone, again to Jano. This time she is talking directly to him, not his machine, and the Cuaróns have written a great performance scene for Maribel Verdú, the actress playing Luisa.

We are at 84 minutes into the film and the Cuaróns now have a sevenminute scene that Alfonso has directed and shot in one single take. A word here on one-take scenes. There are many scattered throughout the history of film: Diz drunkenly proposing to Clarissa in *Mr. Smith Goes to Washington* (1939), Woodward on the phone in *All the President's Men* (1976), Sammy talking to Lillian about lesbianism in *Julia* (1977), et al. For them to work properly, you need three things: a brilliant and tightly written scene, great actors who can carry it, and a director with nerves of steel (and the ability to override producers and editors who always want to cut into it). All three are present here. Our trio is at a table near Jesús's trailer, probably all drunk. Luisa tells the boys that Jano taught her all the tricks his hookers taught him, and she is trying to pass all this on to the boys. She tells them to think of the clitoris as "your best friend," to which Tenoch replies, "What kind of friend is always hiding?" And you thought sports clichés were your friends. They have all discussed sex before, so what makes this scene different? Having been through the experiences they have had together, they now have an ease with each other. Luisa has moved from being a friend to a lover to the adult teaching them how to be adults. This scene could not come any earlier in the film. Luisa gets up from the table, walks a bit unsteadily to the jukebox, starts a song, comes back to the table, and gets the boys dancing with her.

In his direction of this scene, by the way, Alfonso Cuarón, deliberately or not, pays homage to two other great directors. The staging of the scene (sitting at the table, moving away from the table, and the camera and moving back to the table) recalls the first long take of the Thatcher–Mrs. Kane scene in *Citizen Kane* (1941), while Luisa's direct look into the camera as she returns to the table recalls Thorwald looking into the camera, at Jeff, in *Rear Window*. Just as Hitchcock implicates us as voyeurs, Cuarón makes us part of the triangle. He may have kept us slightly on the outside of the story with the narrator, but now he and Luisa/Verdú involve us in the immediacy of the moment.

In their room, Tenoch starts to kiss Luisa, and Julio comes up behind her. She kneels down and begins to perform oral sex on both of them, as far as we can tell. They are so turned on, standing side by side, that they begin to kiss each other. The scene stops there.

In the morning, Luisa is getting instructions on beaches in the area from Mabel, while in the room Tenoch and Julio wake up. They look at each other and remember what happened. There is a look of surprise and unease, but no big comedy reaction. Tenoch runs out of the room and throws up outside. They could joke about homosexuality before, but now it has happened to them. Not what they expected from this trip. Eventually the boys join Luisa for breakfast outside Jesús's cabin. She is going to explore the beaches on her own. Julio has to get the car back. The narrator tells us that the boys packed up and went home. It was an uneventful trip, he says, which means they did not discuss what happened between them. He tells us that Luisa stayed, over shots of her at the beach going into the water to swim.

We are now 96 minutes into the film and back in the city. The narrator brings us up to date on Tenoch and Julio and Mexican politics. He tells us that Julio ran into Tenoch on the way to the dentist's and "Going for a cup of coffee was easier than finding excuses to avoid it." Tenoch and Julio seem to have matured, having dealt with the real world of Mexico, Luisa, and sexuality. Tenoch tells Julio that Luisa died of cancer a month after Julio and Tenoch left her at Jesús's.

Okay, now go back and look at all the points that I have marked with an "ach-choo." Each one of them works in the ongoing context of the story, but now you can see how they can also be interpreted as being motivated by Luisa knowing she was going to die. It is a "surprise" ending better prepared for than M. Night Shyamalan's ending to *The Sixth Sense*, since the Cuaróns make every one of Luisa's actions convincing in its own terms throughout the film, as well as convincing in view of the last revelation. Shyamalan leaves in awkward moments that only make sense once we know the ending. He may well have done that deliberately to help sustain the unease he is trying to create, but I prefer the Cuaróns' smoother approach.

The narrator returns to tell us that Luisa spent her last four days in a hospital. Tenoch leaves and the narrator tells us they will never meet again. It is 99 minutes into the film, and the credits begin.

The Cuaróns have done what many American films do not, and will not, do: relate their stories to the real world. We get the sense that, like Cesare Zavattini's screenplay for the 1948 Italian film *The Bicycle Thief*, the Cuaróns have used a simple story to tell us a lot about the social, cultural, and political climate of their country. What may not occur to you until you have seen the film several times is that they have completely left out a major element of Mexican culture, one that you would have suspected they would deal with in this story. But it is not there, either in terms of character, dialogue, or visuals. I will leave it to you to figure out what it is. Meanwhile, consider that while global screenwriters may be learning about speed, pace, and narrative drive from American screenwriters, American writers can learn about writing about the real world from their global brethren.

Y Tu Mamá También was a major international art house hit, especially in America, where we have long been used to getting more sexually adventurous stories from foreign films. We assume we will get those stories from countries without our Puritan tradition. Could you make an American film that was this sexually explicit? Not for a major studio, which would not release a film with an NC-17 rating. *Y Tu Mamá También* was released without a rating, which only independent companies are willing to do. You might be able to do it if you made the film independently. Very independently.

And what happened to Alfonso Cuarón might happen to you. On the basis of the success, but not, I assume, the content of this film, and the critical acclaim for *A Little Princess*, he was hired by Warner Brothers to direct…*Harry Potter and the Prisoner of Azkaban* (2004).

Sources
The brief biography of Alfonso Cuarón is from the entry for him on IMDb written by "huckf."

The development of the sneezing scene in *Annie Hall* is from Ralph Rosenblum and Robert Karen's *When the Shooting Stops* (Viking, 1979).

Ken Dancyger's book is *Global Scriptwriting* (Focal Press, 2001).

7

SHORT TAKES ON SOME GOOD SCREENPLAYS

THE films are in chronological order of release.

> **ALL THAT JAZZ** (1979. Screenplay by Robert Alan Aurthur and Bob Fosse. 123 minutes)

I am not sure it is right and proper to make an autobiographical film based on somebody else's autobiographical film. But I heartily approve of the theory that if you are going to steal, steal from the best. Bob Fosse has done *All That Jazz* very much under the influence of Federico Fellini's *8½* (1963), and you might want to look at the Fellini film before studying *All That Jazz* to see what Aurthur and Fosse have kept and what they have changed.

The film opens with one of the best examples I know of a "getting up in the morning" scene. Everybody is tempted to write one to introduce their character, but look at the specific details the writers give us here. The big audition number that follows is a little more scripted than it looks in the film. It got more specific as the drafts progressed. In the June 1978 draft, the exchange between the two dancers who did not get picked ("Fuck him." "I did and he still didn't pick me.") has been added. Davis Newman's monologue is presented in the script in its complete form, so the actor can learn the whole thing at once. In the process of editing the film-within-a-film, we hear different bits and pieces of it at different times, but those pieces are generally not given in the script.

One of the most interesting changes from the Fellini film was to give Joe Gideon a daughter. In the screenplay she is only ten years old, which makes some of her scenes a little creepy, as when late in the script she is dressed and made up to look like a sixteen-year-old to sneak into the hospital to see her father. Sneaking into the hospital has been dropped completely in the film, and the actress hired for the part was thirteen at the time. What the character in general provides is a semi-innocent counterpoint to all the sexual activity going on around her. However in the film she is old enough to make her line "I think lesbian scenes are a turn-off" work on its own, cutting off Joe's explanation of lesbianism. Because the actress, Erzsebet Foldi, also trained as a ballet dancer, she has three numbers in the film, including a charming rehearsal scene with Joe, which is a good counterpoint to the "Airotica" number.

The dialogue is very smart, wicked in a very New York show biz way. And not surprisingly, New York-based *auteurist*-critic Andrew Sarris did not get it. In his review he wrote, "The dialogue never takes off on its own. At best, it just sits there without distracting from the visual and choreographic techniques." Listen to it and see if you agree with him.

Sources
The two drafts of the screenplay are dated April 11, 1978 (at the Herrick Library), and June 27, 1978 (at the Louis B. Mayer Library at the American Film Institute's Center for Advanced Study). The Andrew Sarris review was in *The Village Voice*, January 7, 1980.

> **E.T.: THE EXTRA-TERRESTRIAL** (1982. Screenplay by Melissa Mathison. 115 minutes)

In my 1982 book *Screenwriting*, I took Steven Spielberg's script for *Close Encounters of the Third Kind* (1977) to task on the grounds that "Every maker of sci-fi 'B' pictures in the 1950s knew that the interesting story about flying saucers occurs *after* they land." *Close Encounters* was two hours of exposition, with what was one of the major flaws in Spielberg's work at the time: a lack of interest in characterization.

He solved both of those problems five years later by getting Melissa Mathison to write the screenplay for *E.T.* The story begins with E.T. getting left behind. Very little obvious exposition, most of it visual, and right away we are hooked into the story. What is going to happen to the little guy? Well, he could meet a couple of hunters in the woods who could kill him and eat him. But then you would have a very short film. Ah, that's it, have him found by a family. Okay, this is not Eugene O'Neill's family in *Long Day's Journey into Night* (1962), but would you really want to see E.T. try to deal with the Tyrones? So we get a cute boy, Elliott; a frazzled, divorced mom, Mary; a wise-ass older brother, Michael; and a *really* cute little sister, Gertie. What Mathison does is provide the characters who are going to be the most interesting for E.T. to deal with. Pick the right characters for your situation.

Please notice that so far I have avoided mentioning the obvious: the structure of the film follows the structure of the story of Jesus. As one of the moviegoers I questioned for my book on audiences put it, "Jesus said he would be back, he just didn't say what he would look like." In other words, the details you use to tell the story, in this case the characters, are just as important as the structure.

Sources

My book was *Screenwriting* (A.S. Barnes, 1982). Joseph McBride's *Steven Spielberg: A Biography* (Simon & Schuster, 1997) has an excellent section on the development of *E.T.* What is interesting is how *little* Spielberg gave Mathison to start with. Not unlike (hmm, think about this, directors) Hitchcock did with Hayes on *Rear Window*.

My book on audiences is *American Audiences on Movies and Moviegoing* (University Press of Kentucky, 2001). It is useful for writers to read so they will have some idea how audiences actually respond to the movies they write.

UNFORGIVEN (1992. Written by David Webb Peoples. 131 minutes)

David Webb Peoples wrote the script for what became *Unforgiven* in 1976, before he became a professional screenwriter. It was optioned by Francis Ford Coppola. While the idea of a western made by the director of the *Godfather* films (1972ff) has a certain amusement value, it is probably better that Warner Brothers eventually got it to Clint Eastwood. Eastwood has always had a strong sense of scripts that were right for him, and once he finds one he tends to shoot it quickly, rather than spend time "developing it." Frances Fisher, who played the madam in the film, has said it was the only film she had worked on where all the script pages were white, i.e., original, and not the colored pages used for revisions.

Unforgiven is a rich film, filled with novelistic detail. To tell the story, do you need the character of English Bob? Probably not, but he adds texture. Do you need the scene with Little Bill Daggett's deputies sitting around the office talking about how lousy a carpenter he is? No, but it tells us a lot about Little Bill. Yes, I know I have harped (and will continue to in the future) on including only what you *need* to tell the story, but sometimes the additional material, such as the Marge and Mike scene in *Fargo*, can add to the fullness of the film. Which scenes of yours do and which do not? Good luck figuring it out. But if *everybody* tells you to take them out, take them out.

Another great strength of this script is the characterization. Two examples. One: when the cowboy who has cut Delilah's face offers her horses in return, we can see from her reaction that she would be happy with that, even if the madam is not. Two: who is the hero of this film? Well, since Eastwood is playing him, Bill Munny. But what if Eastwood had played Little Bill and Gene Hackman had played Bill Munny? Then Munny would be an intruder and Little Bill would be seen as a tough lawman keeping the peace in a tough town. That's great character writing, and think about what it suggests about what actors can bring to your script.

> **CLUELESS** (1995. Unofficially based on the novel *Emma* by Jane Austen. Screenplay by Amy Heckerling. 97 minutes)

I first fell in love with Jane Austen by watching the films made in the nineties from her novels. The wit of the characters and the rich characterizations were the mark of real writers, whether Austen or the screenwriters. Amy Heckerling, instead of keeping Austen in early nineteenth-century England, retold the story set in contemporary Beverly Hills. Well, it makes sense. Beverly Hills and its high schools are societies that are just as restricted as the England Austen wrote about. Not surprisingly, the story of a popular girl trying to run everybody else's life and continuing to geek it (*geek*, tr.v., semi-polite Americanism for "mess up") works well in the new context. In some ways, it works better, because the stakes are not quite as high for Cher as they are for Emma, and so her failures are not as devastating as they may have been for Emma, a fact that Austen seems to skim over. For an excellent example of how to shift time periods, look in *Emma* to see which objects that remind Harriet of Mr. Elton she burns, and then compare them to what Tai burns that reminds her of her Elton.

Or maybe you shouldn't. After all the wonderful films based on Austen's novels, I finally got around to reading one, *Emma*. It cured me of being a Janeite forever. The woman is one of the wordiest writers in the English language, never using five words when she can use five hundred or a thousand. You have to wade through so much verbiage to get to the wit and the characters it is hardly worth the effort. Reading the book made me appreciate even more the skill of Heckerling and the others who have done "Austen" screenplays.

> **SOMETHING TO TALK ABOUT** (1995. Written by Callie
> Khouri. 106 minutes)

Yes, Callie Khouri is better known for her Oscar-winning script *Thelma & Louise* (1991), and you should certainly study that as a good example of "changing the genders in a genre movie." But *Something to Talk About* is a little more complex. As Khouri told Jodie Burke, she struggled harder with the structure of *Something*. "*Thelma & Louise* was a great structure because it was so easy, so linear. You can have people having meaningful conversations screaming down the highway at a hundred and twenty miles per hour." With *Something* she is inventing a new structure to deal with the life of a modern American woman, which does not fit into the standard Joseph Campbell hero's journey. The main character, Grace, is working on her father's horse farm, trying to bring up her daughter and dealing with her husband's infidelity. Each of those storylines expand, sometimes crossing the others, sometimes not. What Khouri finds is a balance between the elements. Look at how she does that, and remember that you do not *have* to follow the Campbell mythology. In spite of what a *lot* of screenwriting gurus tell you.

Sources
The interview with Jodie Burke is in the published book of the screenplays, *Thelma & Louise and Something to Talk About* (Grove Press, 1996). I did a more detailed analysis of Khouri's structure of the film in "Grace Under Pressure: The New Feminine Structure," *Creative Screenwriting*, March/April 2001.

Joseph Campbell's book is *The Hero with a Thousand Faces* (Bollingen, 1972). Christopher Vogler's *The Writer's Journey: Mythic Structure for Writers*, 2nd Edition (Michael Wiese Productions, 1998) applies Campbell's theories to writing, especially screenwriting.

> **BOUND** (1996. Screenplay by Andy and Larry
> Wachowski. 108 minutes)

The only produced screenplay the Wachowski Brothers wrote before *Bound* was *Assassins* (1995). It was not, alas, an adaptation of the great

Stephen Sondheim musical of the same name, but an action picture about a hit man who wants out and is the target of a younger hit man trying to kill him...zzzz. On the basis of their script, they got a deal to write and direct *Bound*. If the price we had to pay for *Bound* is *Assassins*, well, it was worth it.

Bound sounds like basic film noir: Corky, an ex-con, gets involved with a femme fatale, Violet, who persuades Corky to help her steal some mob money from Violet's boyfriend, Caesar...zzzz. They are all obviously doomed, this being film noir...zzzz. But the Wachowskis make one crucial change and then develop that change to make *Bound* more fresh and inventive than any other contemporary film noir: Corky is a woman. Look at, among other things, how that is used and how and why it makes a difference to the film.

Over the main titles of *Bound* we hear lines of dialogue that will show up later in the film. Listen to how few lines it takes to tell us there's a plot afoot, there is money involved, and some people are not happy about it. In a flashback, it is not Caesar in an elevator who gives Corky the eye, but Violet. No dialogue is spoken between them; we just see there is an attraction, at least on Violet's part. The three of them get off on the same floor, and Corky and we all realize her apartment is next to Violet and Caesar's.

Violet comes to the door of Corky's apartment with coffee. Listen to the dialogue. There is very little in the written words that is suggestive. What the dialogue here, and in other places in the film, does is provide a subtext for the actors to play. Violet is coming on to Corky and Corky is watching her warily, so everything they say seems to have a sexual meaning. There is a long tradition of this, particularly in film noir. Listen to the "How fast was I going?" exchange between Walter and Phyllis in *Double Indemnity* (1944) or the racehorse dialogue between Vivian and Marlowe in the 1946 version of *The Big Sleep*, which was first played "straight" in the 1938 film *Straight, Place and Show*. How innocuous a piece of dialogue can you write that when played the right way sounds suggestive?

We see Corky at a lesbian bar. What details tell us that she is probably gay and she is probably an ex-con? Notice how the Wachowskis are building up to the details of Corky's past slowly. The great director John Ford once said that you should not tell the audience anything until they *need* to know it.

Corky and Violet's sexual by-play is interrupted by the arrival of Caesar. Now, if Corky were a man, Caesar would be jealous, but she's not and he's not. We know that Violet is bisexual at least, but Caesar seems not to know or not to care, which is a convenient way to suggest that he is not too bright. Throughout the script, the Wachowskis constantly use the male characters' cluelessness about Violet's sexuality to show that, no matter how tough or how smart they think they are, they are wrong.

Corky and Violet have an extended sex scene. This is a more generic sex scene than the ones in *Bull Durham*, but also more explicit, and about as explicit as you can be and still get an R rating. Explicit sex scenes are difficult to cast, direct, and act. Do not write an explicit sex scene unless you *need* it. In this case, I think the Wachowskis do need it. The sensuality has been heavy up until this scene, and the scene seals the relationship between Corky and Violet. This in turn creates a tension because of what we know of the film noir genre—that betrayal by the femme fatale is part of the plot. We have to wonder if the relationship is so intense that it will burn out, which would also be typical film noir. The Wachowskis also let this scene do the work of several, since it is the only extended sex scene in the film. We need the scene's intense sexuality to carry the Corky–Violet relationship through the violence later in the film. And once the money plot takes over, we will not have time to stop for a love scene.

Violet explains to Corky that Shelly, a mob guy she has also had sex with, has skimmed money from the mob. Violet wants out, but she cannot do it alone. She wants Corky's help. Violet explains that Caesar is going to find the money and bring it to the apartment. Corky objects to stealing from the mob, but then compares stealing to sex, tying together the two themes of the movie.

Okay, so we expect that Caesar will show up with a nice little metal briefcase filled with neatly stacked bills. How cliché. The money has blood literally all over it. The boss is coming to get the money tomorrow, so they have to clean it. They wash it, hang it up to dry, and iron it, a much more interesting visual than just a briefcase full of money. It also puts the pressure on Caesar, because he has to get the money clean, and on Violet, who has to come up with a plan as well.

Corky and Violet discuss their plan, and the Wachowskis handle the discussion in an inventive way. One problem in most heist pictures is that too much time has to be spent in discussion, laying out how the plan is supposed to work, so we will know when it begins to fall apart. What the writers do here is put Violet and Corky's discussion of what they are going to do over the visuals of the plan. We do not know for sure, at least not until well into the sequence, whether we are watching what might happen or what is happening. What they are doing is showing you both the plan and the way it works out until the points where it begins to go wrong, and then it's just what is happening. It is very effective because we do not have to remember the details of the plan, since we are in the middle of it.

Needless to say, it does go wrong, with assorted shooting and hints of betrayal. Eventually Caesar figures out Violet's connection with Corky. Will Violet betray Corky? Caesar agrees to let Violet live if she will deal with the boss, who is on his way to pick up the "money." Violet does deal with him, but then she shoots Caesar. When Micky, the boss, comes back from the wild goose chase Violet has sent him on, she convinces him that Caesar has taken the money and run. Micky believes her. If she were a true femme fatale, she would dump Corky and seduce Micky into taking care of her for the rest of her life. Instead Violet and Corky ride off together in Corky's new truck, with the money. Films noir traditionally do not have happy endings, but the Wachowskis have established from the very beginning of the film that theirs is a new, fresh take on the old genre. Sometimes a happy ending can be transgressive.

As a result of the critical and (modest) commercial success of *Bound*, the Wachowskis got the opportunity to write and direct the three *Matrix* films (1999ff). The trilogy has much more elaborate sets (*Bound* takes place in two apartments, a hallway, an elevator, a bar, and a truck in a parking lot), more action sequences, more special effects, and bigger-name actors. What the *Matrix* films do not have is *Bound*'s freshness, inventiveness, and interesting characters. So the lesson you should learn is that if you want the opportunity to make that idiotic science fiction piece you first thought up when you were twelve, you need to make a *good* movie first. If the price we have to pay for *Bound* is the *Matrix* films…

FINDING NEMO (2003. Story by Andrew Stanton. Screenplay by Andrew Stanton, Bob Peterson, and David Reynolds. 100 minutes)

I went to see *Finding Nemo* with some trepidation. Two things I knew about the picture in advance bothered me. The first was that the characters were fish, and how can you make fish interesting characters? They are ugly and they swim. The Geniuses at Pixar figured out how to make the characters interesting.

The second thing was that it took place underwater, being a story about fish. Under the water you have water, sand, maybe a bit of seaweed. How can you make that visually interesting for 100 minutes? The Geniuses at Pixar made the underwater scenes gorgeous.

Are you beginning to sense a pattern here? If you are going to write an animated film, it helps to have the Geniuses at Pixar (hereinafter GAPs) working with you. But you can also learn from what they did and did not do in this film. First of all, the GAPs tend to work with original stories, rather than adaptations. They can then develop them however they want to, and they are masters at going back and revising and rewriting. One reason the late Walt Disney was the only animator of his day to move successfully into feature animation is that he had a great sense of story. For a while in the production of *Nemo*, the barracuda attack that killed Nemo's mom was done in flashback, but they finally put the scene up front, giving the film a stronger opening and giving the father, Marlin, a more immediately believable motivation to protect Nemo. The GAPs also believe in research, which is why their ocean is so visually dazzling. Several of the staff took up scuba diving. But the GAPs are also great at realizing they are making an animated film. You could not do *Finding Nemo* as a live-action film, just as it would be difficult to do the *Toy Story* films (1995ff) with live action. If you are going to do an animated film, *use* animation. Later in the book we will come across a classic example of an animated film that would have been better as live action.

Dory, the fish with short-term memory loss, is an example of the GAPs other connection to Disney: Disney was great at characters. Dory evolved out of the research the GAPs did, which revealed that one type of fish does in fact have short-term memory problems. As Andrew Stanton was developing the character, the fish was a man. Then one night he heard Ellen DeGeneres doing one of her stream-of-consciousness routines, and Stanton developed the character with her in mind. He did not talk to her about it then, but later called her to say he would have a problem if she did not do it. DeGeneres's reaction was not "Have your people call my people," but rather, "Well, I'd better do it then." See the actors you get when you write great characters, even in animated films? Needless to say, she brings the character so much to life that even a line like her "Huh?" late in the picture gets a laugh, because from the writing and her delivery we *know* the character. Look at the way the other characters are created and listen to how the actors hired make them work.

Source
The details of the production are from Steve Daly's "Big Fish," *Entertainment Weekly*, July 18, 2003. For a look at the way the GAPs work, see Ben Rock's "Process Makes Perfect," *Creative Screenwriting*, January/February 2007.

AMERICAN SPLENDOR (2003. Based on the comic book series *American Splendor* by Harvey Pekar and the comic books series *Our Cancer Year* by Harvey Pekar and Joyce Brabner. Screenplay by Shari Springer Berman and Robert Pulcini. 101 minutes)

So you do not have access to the GAPs. You can still make at least a partially animated film. And if you insist on making a film from a comic book (or "graphic novel" if you are being pretentious about it), this is the film you ought to look at. Berman and Pulcini manage to balance three elements in their script.

First is the story of the real-life Harvey Pekar, a clerk at the Cleveland Veterans Administration who developed his own line of comic books. The film follows him as he becomes a minor celebrity, meets and marries Joyce, and lives through a cancer scare. I have talked before about how fast some scripts start. This is an example of a script starting slowly and letting us get to know the character. Look at how long it is in the film before his first comic books come out. Then how long it is until he meets Joyce. And how long it is before the cancer story takes over. That is awfully late in the film for a dramatic plot to develop, but we are living in Harvey's world, at Harvey's pace. Being a great character study also provides two great roles for Paul Giamatti as Harvey and Hope Davis as Joyce.

We also see the story told through variations in Harvey's comic books, and variations is the right word since Harvey's stories were illustrated in the comics by different artists. So we see them animated in different styles.

Since there were already multi-perspectives of Harvey in the comics, Berman and Pulcini also threw in the third element: the real Harvey. We get Harvey and his friend Toby wandering through the movie commenting on what we see. The potential problem is that this might take us out of the story—if it were not done by writers as deft as Berman and Pulcini. Watch how they manage to balance each of the three sides off each other. The real Harvey is a fascinating character, but not more so than Giamatti's version of him. The interview scenes of the real Harvey were ad-libbed, by the way, although Berman and Pulcini had put into the script "dummy" dialogue of what they thought the real Harvey might say. Sometimes they guessed right and sometimes they did not. As with Woody Allen, the "writing" of the film continued into the editing process. Pulcini was the film editor, a very convenient way to keep the writer around through the editing process.

Source

There is a published version of the shooting script (Carhil Ventures, 2003), although this seems to have been prepared to be sent to members of the WGAW during the award season rather than for retail sales. It has an introduction by the writers, explaining how they went about adapting the comics. They tended to look at all the comics as telling one long epic story, and they then used whatever incidents and details fit the structure they worked out.

> ***BON VOYAGE*** (2003. Adaptation by Jérôme Tonnerre, Jean-Paul Rappeneau, Gilles Marchand, and Julien Rappeneau. Scenario by Jean-Paul Rappeneau and Patrick Modiano. 114 minutes)

I laughed all the way through this film, so much so that other people in the audience looked at me, wondering what I was laughing about.

The film is a sweeping melodrama about a group of French people escaping Paris for Bordeaux as the Germans invade in 1940. It is gorgeous to look at, wonderfully acted, and occasionally witty. So why was I laughing out loud?

It is obvious that not *one* of the five credited writers (those are the official credits above; I have no idea what the four guys who are credited with the adaptation did, since no other source is listed) has read Syd Field. Syd Field is one of the most successful screenwriting instructors of the modern era, and his seminal book *Screenplay* has been read by millions. Field puts a great emphasis on the structure of a screenplay, bless his heart (and I mean that sincerely, really I do), but too many people read that in a mechanical way. This is true not only of screenwriters but also of "creative executives" at the studios. Which is why you can pretty much tell when a script has been written and/or rewritten to fit Field's mold of when the plot points should happen. It makes for films with a very distinctive rhythm, as we will see in some later discussions. So what I was laughing about was that the rhythm of *Bon Voyage* was *not* Field's. And the film was all the more enjoyable for that: events do not happen when they *should* but when they…well, do.

Screenwriting is not mechanical, it is organic.

And Field himself recently realized the error of his ways, as we will discover later.

Source

Syd Field's *Screenplay* (Delta, 1979).

> **LOVE ACTUALLY** (2003. Written by Richard Curtis. 135 minutes)

Richard Curtis (*Four Weddings and a Funeral* [1994], *Notting Hill* [1999]) is the most successful current screenwriter doing romantic comedies, "romcoms" in industry parlance. Although the British critics, who being British are ambivalent about success, tend to put down Curtis as shallow and artificial, he has earned his success. Yes, he makes it look easy—just like Fred Astaire made dancing look easy. You try it and see what happens. See later sections of this book for some that do not work.

In *Love Actually*, Curtis has set himself a neat trick: following nine stories in one film. He pulls it off. You think that is easy? Griffith geeked it with four in *Intolerance* back in 1916. Curtis was taking a vacation in Bali and every time he went for a walk on the beach, he came up with another story. Something you have to learn as a screenwriter is how to be prolific with your ideas; I know a lot of filmmakers who would make the same film over and over again (and several who have). Curtis came up with many more stories than he used, and the writing process became cutting them down to the ones he needed for the film. Pay attention to the ones he selected. Why these?

He also found ways to tie them together. The film is set in postcard-beautiful London at Christmastime, so there are always Christmas details popping up in scenes. Characters who we do not think would know each other turn out to, or even to be related. His theme is love, but not just romantic love, so the stories are different. David, the Prime Minister, has a romantic story, but Sarah's turns out to be about the love she has for her mentally damaged brother. The rock star Billy Mack's story is about his relationship with his manager. Daniel's is learning how to be a father to his stepson Sam. Karen and Harry's is about a marriage in trouble.

Because Curtis is covering so many stories, he does not get into the characters in great depth, one of the advantages and disadvantages of doing a multi-story film. Curtis's wit and ability to sharply delineate characters makes each character distinctive. Look at the specifics he gives to each character. For example, it would have been easy to make the American President merely a caricature of Bush, but Curtis gives him elements of Bush, Clinton, and Lyndon Johnson.

In the script, Curtis has laid out how the scenes will connect in the film, a rather striking balancing job. Look at how and when we cut back and forth, particularly as the film comes to its multiple climaxes. Nearly all of those jumps are in the script.

Source

The published edition of the screenplay (St. Martin's Griffin, 2003) includes an interview with Curtis about the writing of the film, as well as Deleted Scenes, with Curtis's comments on why they were dropped.

> ***ETERNAL SUNSHINE OF THE SPOTLESS MIND*** (2004.
> Story by Charlie Kaufman, Michel Gondry, and Pierre
> Bismuth. Screenplay by Charlie Kaufman. 108 minutes)

Yeah, right, deal with the structural complexity of this script in a short take. Well, I am not even going to try. You are on your own figuring out Kaufman's brilliance on that score. But give it a shot; you may learn a lot.

After you do that, however, and after you sit around discussing how fresh and inventive Kaufman's storytelling is (and it is), go back and look at the characters he created. I won't be cute and dismiss this film as just Kaufman's rewrite of Neil Simon's *Barefoot in the Park* (1967), but they both deal with the relationship of a quirky girl (Jane Fonda then, Kate Winslet now) and an uptight guy (Robert Redford then, Jim Carrey now). Now look at the details Kaufman gives us about the characters. What do they do? What do they want? How do they relate to each other? How do they relate to the situations they find themselves in? *Barefoot in the Park* was originally written as a stage play, and it shows. You can tell when the curtain should fall at the end of each act. Kaufman has given us these characters in cinematic terms, and it is the characters who carry us through the complex structure and make us *feel*. Kaufman may be cool, but he is human as well.

> ***MARIA FULL OF GRACE*** (2004. Written by Joshua
> Marston. 101 minutes)

This will depress you: Joshua Marston wrote the first draft of this film in forty-eight hours. And this had better impress you: he said later, "I don't think there is even one sentence that made it into the last draft." The rewrites took three years.

Marston had been traveling and collecting material for years about the drug trade from Colombians he knew. All that went into the first draft, and the research shows in the final film. But in the first draft there was too much exposition and too many details from the research.

He realized he needed to develop the characters. So he went to South American, first Ecuador, then later Colombia. He learned about the Colombian rose industry, which gave Maria a job. He talked to pregnant teens in Ecuador. He talked to people in prison who had been drug mules. Marston later wrote, "The ruling question through every rewrite was 'What is Maria experiencing? What is relevant to her subjective experience?'" What do you *need*? He said, "The whole thing was developed as an organic process." What did I tell you about screenwriting being organic and not mechanical?

If you want to break the story down into acts, Act One is Maria in Colombia deciding, for all kinds of complicated reasons (note how Marston has not made it simply a question of poverty), to become a drug mule. Act Two is the trip with three other mules, which Marston could easily have turned into a suspense set-piece that could have gotten him jobs in Hollywood for years writing action pictures. He does not do that, because he knows that would overpower the Third Act, which is what happens to Maria once she gets to New York. Look at the details of the trip and its aftermath that Marston uses.

Marston wanted the film to be political, but the problems with the earlier drafts were that they were too obviously political, with long speeches. American films generally work better in dealing with political issues if they bring the issues up in terms of story and character. *Maria* does that brilliantly.

Sources
The quotes from Marston are from an interview with Jose Martinez in *Creative Screenwriting*, July/August 2004. The material that Marston wrote, and most of the details about his research, are in his article "Full of Grace, Politically," in *Scr(i)pt*, July/August 2004.

BEFORE SUNSET (2004. Based on characters created by Richard Linklater & Kim Krizan. Story by Richard Linklater & Kim Krizan. Screenplay by Richard Linklater, Julie Delpy, and Ethan Hawke. 80 minutes)

This is a sequel to the same team's 1995 *Before Sunrise*. In that film, a young American guy, Jesse, picks up a young French girl, Celine, on a train and convinces her to get off with him in Vienna for a day. They have some adventures, make love, and in the end agree to meet back there six months later—without, alas, giving each other their addresses or phone numbers.

The sequel starts ten years later. Jesse is in Paris on a book tour. He is giving a talk at a small bookstore, explaining that his novel about the romance of an American and a French girl in Vienna is not really autobiographical. He finishes his talk…and sees Celine standing in the store. He has to leave for this plane back to America in 75 minutes. We have just used up 5 of the film's 80 minutes. Unlike the first film, there is real suspense here.

The meeting in Vienna was important to him, but what did it mean to her? Did either one of them show up? They go to have coffee. Then the writers come up with one of the most important lines in the film. Jesse says that since he will be sitting for a long time on the plane, why don't they walk? So we will not be in the coffee shop for 75 minutes. Look at the choices of locations for them to walk through. What makes this film better than the original is that Jesse and Celine are both ten years older and have experienced more. Look at the scenes that come out of the characters' experiences, such as the scene in the car. Linklater, Hawke, and Delpy had been talking about a sequel ever since the original, and all three of them wrote material for each other. The ultimate collaborative process: actors often come to know their characters even better than the writers. Look at how the character details of each are revealed over the course of the film. How do we find out what the night in Vienna meant to Celine?

In the final scene, which one critic called the most sublime movie ending in years, Celine says something to Jesse that we have heard her say several times during the movie. He replies, with a wonderful hand gesture by Hawke, "I know." Then she…doesn't do…or say…anything. Sometimes not saying or doing anything can be the most dramatic.

And let's all get together and force Linklater, Hawke, and Delpy to do another one in ten years.

SAVING FACE (2004. Screenplay by Alice Wu. 91 minutes)

Like Grace in *Something to Talk About*, Wil is juggling the elements of her life. She is a young surgeon, involved in a new relationship with a dancer, and her forty-eight-year-old widowed mother is…pregnant… and will not tell anybody who the father is. Oh yes, Wil is Chinese-American and she's gay.

Like Khouri in *Something to Talk About*, Wu beautifully juggles the mechanics of the romcom plot. You will never guess who the father of the mother's baby is because Wu has set him up to play a very different role in the story. Wil's lover goes off to Paris, without the traditional scene at the airport in which Wil would get her to stay. But Wu brings the lover back in a very satisfying way, playing off what seemed to be a minor comment early in the film. The mother story could easily run away with the film, since the character is one of the few fully developed middle-aged Asian-American women in American films, but in the writing Wu evenly balances the two as characters.

The film is also very specifically about the Chinese-American culture, as in the use of the Friday dance throughout the film, or in the mother discovering only *The Last Emperor*, *The Joy Luck Club*, and Asian pornos in the Asian section of a video store. If in the end characters who might not be as accepting as they are of Wil and her lover do accept them (the lover's doctor father says, "Well, at least she is marrying a doctor"), Wu still gives us some hesitations not unlike the final shot of *The Graduate*.

Remember: if you are going to steal, steal from the best.

II

The Not-Quite-So-Good

8

COLLATERAL

COLLATERAL (2004. Screenplay by Stuart Beattie. 133 minutes)

STUART Beattie's screenplay for *Collateral* was inspired by a cab ride. He realized that both a cab driver and a passenger are assuming the other is safe and not, say, a professional killer. But what if the passenger were a professional killer? Then what happens? It's a great idea for a "B" movie: cabbie has to deal with hit man passenger. Why only a "B" movie? Because for all of Beattie's considerable efforts, there are limits to what he does with the character of a hit man. (For more inventive looks at hit men, see *Grosse Pointe Blank* [1997], in which a hit man goes back to his high school reunion, or *You Kill Me* [2007], in which a hit man joins AA.) And Beattie runs into a problem developing the idea, particularly in the last quarter of the film. For an article in *Creative Screenwriting*, David Goldsmith looked at an earlier draft of the screenplay, and as I go through the film, I will point out the differences between the film and the earlier draft.

Beattie's draft begins with a garage for taxicabs in New York City. The film begins with Vincent walking through the crowd at Los Angeles International Airport. Beattie's screenplay was originally set in New York, but director Michael Mann changed the locale to Los Angeles. Mann knows Los Angeles better, and a side benefit is that nobody will assume this is *Son of Taxi Driver*. Fine, but why start at LAX? Because Tom Cruise (Vincent) is a STAR, and if you do not introduce him early, audiences will think they went into the wrong theater. So the film needed to justify the shots of him. The rest of the story is set up so that he cannot get into the cab at LAX. Look at the action Beattie and Mann have. Do Vincent and the man he bumps into pick up each other's briefcases?

The scene is never explained but it gets our attention and assures us we are watching the Tom Cruise movie.

At the garage Max (Beattie had at one point thought of De Niro for the part, but that would make the connections to *Taxi Driver* [1976] much too strong) takes over the cab from the previous driver. He gets in and puts up a picture of a desert island, which will be referred to later. In Beattie's script, we see him carry several different passengers, with different conversations. In the film, we get one couple, a young businessman and woman, before he picks up Annie 5 minutes into the film. Watch this scene: the way Max reacts to Annie, how Annie reacts to Max, how the relationship develops. This is a beautifully written, directed, and acted scene. Annie is played by Jada Pinkett Smith, and her performance was the best eight minutes of acting she had ever done. It makes us hope we will see this Annie again. We do, but not really.

Max gives her the picture of his island, she comes *back* to the cab *after* getting out (now that is an interesting detail) and gives Max her business card. Vincent gets into the cab, 13 minutes into the film. At first Vincent and Max seem to get on each other's nerves, especially after the Max–Annie scene. Listen to how Beattie uses some details from the Annie scene in the first couple of scenes with Vincent. Vincent tells a story about hearing of a man who died on the MTA and whose body rode for six hours before anybody realized it. Nice story, but it is a New York urban legend. The L.A. Metro has not been running long enough to collect those kinds of myths. Before their stop, Vincent offers Max $600 if Max will take him to the five stops he needs to make and then get him back to LAX in time for his morning plane. Max reluctantly agrees. Vincent goes into an apartment building, Max eats a sandwich in the cab while looking at pictures of limos for a limousine company he hopes to start, and BANG, 19 minutes into the film, a body falls on Max's windshield.

Shock! Horror! *Nineteen* minutes into the picture!!!! Cannot be done. Too soon. Syd Field's *Screenplay* says the first plot point *absolutely* cannot come until 25–27 pages into the script, which at a minute per page would be about 26 minutes. The falling body is EARLY. Which may be part of why it is a shock to audiences, even though they may never have heard of Field. As mentioned in the previous chapter, Field's paradigm is so popular in Hollywood, and so religiously followed, that an audience can tell from the rhythm of a film if it has been made under Field's spell.

So we have the body on the cab. Look at the pressure it puts on both Max and Vincent. Max is upset, Vincent is cool. Vincent orders Max to help him put the body in the trunk. Think of all the things that could go wrong with that.

Fanning, a rather shady-looking character not seen before, arrives at the apartment and sees some of the mess in the alley. He calls in to the station and *only then* do we learn he is a detective.

In the cab Vincent tells Max to stay calm. A bit difficult when they are pulled over by the police because of the big crack in the cab's windshield. The cops ask Max to open the trunk. How would *you* get our guys out of this? If the cops arrest them now, the movie is over at the 30-minute mark. If there is a shoot-out, than all the cops in town are looking for them and we have lost the structure of the film. Beattie's solution, which is used in the film, is that the cops get an urgent radio call and leave before they open the trunk. You can be more inventive than that.

The second victim: we see the cab stop and Vincent handcuffs Max to the steering wheel with plastic handcuffs. We do not see, as we did not see with the first victim, the actual shooting. Beattie and Mann are careful not to turn the film into a bloodfest, which in turn helps us connect with the characters. It also makes those scenes where we do see the violence more dramatic, and perhaps most important, it lets Tom Cruise be mostly charming for a few minutes longer. Protect your star.

Two guys steal Vincent's briefcase from the cab. Vincent arrives as they are walking away and he kills them both, quickly and emotionlessly. If we have had any questions about his professional abilities, they have been answered. Which makes us sweat for Max a little more.

Fanning and his boss are in the alley of the first shooting. The boss is warning him that the dead man is part of a federal case and Fanning should stay out of it. Since Vincent says they are ahead of schedule, he and Max drop by a jazz club Vincent has heard of. They listen to the music, then talk to the owner, Daniel. We have been lulled by Vincent's earlier comment, and Beattie's sense of structural rhythm, to assume this is just a break in the action. Look at how much character detail Beattie gives to Daniel, which helps us to believe until the last minute that this scene is not the third victim. When do we first know it is a hit? Vincent does not want Max to break his routine, so they go to the hospital to visit Max's mom, Ida.

One problem I have with many crime movies is that they seem to take place in a hermetically sealed universe where there are only cops and robbers. The 1995 film *Heat* was not only directed but also written by Michael Mann. *Heat*'s action set piece is an elaborate bank robbery/shoot-out in downtown Los Angeles. Which nobody notices. There is no TV coverage, unlike the real-life botched robbery in Los Angeles two years later. Mann missed an opportunity to open up *Heat* at that point. Beattie and Mann do not waste it here. A man takes a hit man along when he visits his mom in the hospital. What can happen? Look at the reactions of all the characters in this scene to each other. It lets some air into the universe of the film and provides beautiful acting opportunities for Cruise, Jamie Foxx (Max), and Irma P. Hall (Ida). We are 48 minutes into the film.

Max is so frustrated he throws Vincent's briefcase onto the freeway, where it is run over by traffic. Why doesn't Vincent kill Max on the spot? Because Beattie, Mann, and the actors have established through the scenes and dialogue that Vincent likes Max and is even trying to help him, since he thinks, rightly, that Max is stuck in his life and needs to break free.

When they went to see Ida in the hospital, they rode up in the elevator with Fanning. Fanning now goes to the morgue, looking for the first victim, who is still in the trunk, remember? He finds four other people shot in the same pattern. Fanning realizes that Clark, the second victim, is the "criminal lawyer turned lawyer criminal," which leads him eventually to the Federal agents on the case.

Vincent has lost his "prep" (the information on his victims, which was in his briefcase), so he sends Max into the second club of the film, telling him to pretend to be Vincent. If he does not succeed, Vincent will kill Ida, another reason for the scene with her. Getting into the jazz club was so easy we did not even see it. Here there are bouncers and security and possibly security cameras. Max is let in and led to Felix, who is surrounded by thugs. This scene, halfway into the film, is crucial, but slightly flawed, I think, in the writing. In the middle of the scene, a nervous Max begins to "be" Vincent. We do not see him mentally making the adjustment to being Vincent, who comes out of Max fully formed. Mann and Foxx appear to do the best they can, but as the saying goes, if it's not on the page, it's not on the stage. Although I will allow for the possibility that it was on the page and Mann and Foxx geeked it; if that's the case, Foxx might consider returning the otherwise deserved certificate he got for being nominated for Best Supporting Actor for his performance. Another slight problem is that the assurance Max seems to develop in this scene comes and goes in later scenes.

Felix eventually gives Max the flash drive with the information on it, which, gee, just happens to work on the trip computer in Max's cab. We will shortly have many more examples of this basic truth in other films: if the film is working for you at this point, you won't care about the convenience of that. Fanning and the federal agents get the cab's license number, figure out where the cab is going, and plan their assault.

We take our time getting there. Vincent is telling Max he should call Annie (Vincent has found Annie's card) if he survives. Beattie and

Mann build suspense with a montage of shots of cars and the city. Everybody arrives at the third club. Like the three train raids in *Lawrence*, Beattie and Mann have made the three club scenes different. The first was small jazz club. The second was not particularly crowded, except by a few thugs. The third is a noisy, packed dance club. (Do not bother to guess where the film's big shoot-out will take place.) The third club will give us more interesting stuff to watch and make it more difficult for all our major players. Everybody has to get through the crowd to get to where they want to be. Vincent shoots the victim, and the panic starts. As always in the movies, everybody runs in different directions. Fanning gets Max out of the club, Vincent shoots and kills Fanning (hey, he's Mark Ruffalo in a picture with Tom Cruise and Jamie Foxx, how long did you think he was going to last?), and hustles Max into the cab. We are 85 minutes into the film.

Max is upset and crashes the cab. Vincent gets out of the cab and runs away. When a cop comes up to the cab, he discovers—do you remember it?—the dead body in the trunk. Max sees a picture on the computer of the last victim: Annie.

Ooops. We are 95 minutes into the film and it's beginning to go wrong. Annie is the federal prosecutor in the drug case whose witnesses Vincent has been killing. But why Annie? O.K, in several countries, it is not uncommon to kill prosecutors and judges. It's not that it never happens in the United States, but only rarely. Why? Because the federal justice system is very large, very relentless, and most important...filled with very ambitious lawyers. It would be a ticket to at least the Governorship and maybe the Presidency if you could put away drug kingpins who killed a Federal Prosecutor, especially a black, woman prosecutor. Think how much of the African-American and women's vote you would get. So if the bad guys are going to target Annie, you will need to establish one of two possibilities. The first is that they are stupid, and we have seen no evidence of that. The other possibility is that somebody Annie is working with has set her up. One of those ambitious lawyers mentioned above. We do not get either in the film. Why not?

Max handcuffs the cop to the rolled-over cab, tells him where he is going, and runs off. Why handcuff him? Because Jamie Foxx is *one* of the stars of the movie, and it should be him who rescues Annie. But he could still do that by taking the cop's gun and sending him to his car radio.

Max uses his cell phone to call Annie. She has not heard about the deaths of the witnesses in her case. What? Wouldn't one of the Feds bother to call her about this? If they did, of course, there would be protection around her and Vincent could not easily get through. Which would call on him to be more inventive, which we know Vincent is capable of. Vincent is by now in Annie's building, which he seems to have keys and key cards for. Where did he get those? Okay, they were part of his prep—and wouldn't that have been in the briefcase that was run over?—but who got them for him? An obvious choice would be the ambitious lawyer who wants Annie out of the way, but as mentioned above, we do not get him or her in the film. Vincent gets into Annie's office, but she is not there.

Annie is an African-American (she, like Max, was white in Beattie's original script, by the way; snaps to Mann for casting Smith and Foxx) Federal Prosecutor. What does she do? She hides in the library. That's it. She hides. Now what would a real woman with a résumé like that do in a situation like this? I suspect she would get out the camera they use to photograph evidence, flash it in Vincent's eyes when he comes into the darkened office (steal from the best; if you do not want to steal from John Michael Hayes, have her use her Mace), use the gun she keeps in her purse (surely in her line of work she has a license to carry one) to shoot him in the groin, then ask rather impolitely who sent him (she is smart enough to know she's been set up, even if Beattie and Mann aren't), shoot him in a kneecap when he doesn't answer, ask again, shoot again, until the ambitious lawyer (see how useful this character would have been?) gets the drop on her, at which point, if you have to (and you probably do), Max can rescue her.

If this were a true "B" picture, you might be able to get away with that. But this is now a big star vehicle. The stars are Tom Cruise and Jamie Foxx. Jada Pinkett Smith is billed *below* the title. Do you want to explain to Tom Cruise that somebody billed below the title is going to kill him? And that it is a woman? Do you want to explain to Jamie Foxx that he is not going to get to rescue the woman in jeopardy? And here is my problem with the last twenty-five minutes of the film: what has been a fresh, inventive, suspenseful movie turns into a television movie-of-the-week womjeop (that's TV-speak for "woman in jeopardy") picture. We have *seen* that, and now we have paid ten dollars to see it again.

Vincent finds Annie, but Max arrives and shoots Vincent. Movie over. Whoops, no, it goes on for another *nine* minutes. This is a very common flaw in contemporary studio films: not knowing when to stop. There is a tendency to pile it on—more action, more chases, more shooting, more car crashes—long after the story has been told. The film should finish at this point: Vincent has been shot, Max and Annie are in control, the cops are on their way. But Max and Annie run. Why? All they have to do is plug Vincent a couple more times and wait for the police. But they don't. They run, and they end up on—surely you have seen this coming since the first scene with Vincent—the Metro. And Vincent, who should be either dead or in shock, follows them. And not just onto the Metro, but making a change of trains on the Metro. And then chasing them through the cars on the Metro. Finally there is a shoot-out with Max and Vincent sits down to die. Well, first he has to tell us the story of the body on the Metro again in case we've forgotten it. And then Max and Annie get off the train. Do they leave the body there? Yes. Do they call the cops? No. Max and Annie, who seemed so smart and charming in their first scene, seem to have taken complete leave of their senses in the last twenty-five minutes of the film. Do not betray your characters, no matter how many extra shoot-outs you think you can stuff in the script.

Sources

David Goldsmith's article on the earlier draft of the script, "*Collateral*: Stuart Beattie's Character-Driven Thriller," appeared in *Creative Screenwriting*, July/August 2004.

In the 2006 edition of *Screenplay*, Syd Field has removed the page-number paradigm. The sounds you have been hearing are the screams of terror from Hollywood executives who realize they are going to have to start thinking for themselves.

9

THREE *JURASSIC PARKS*

> **JURASSIC PARK** (1993. Based on the novel by Michael Crichton. Screenplay by Michael Crichton and David Koepp. 126 minutes)

NOVELIST and screenwriter Michael Crichton specializes in technology run amuck. Characterization is not his strong suit, to put it mildly. In *Jurassic Park*, the basic concept is enough to hold it together; the characterization improves in the sequels. What you can also learn from the three *Jurassic Park* films is how both the tone and the use of the basic idea can change in sequels. In Hollywood, too often sequels are merely bigger, louder, and stupider. The makers of the *Jurassic Park* films are smarter than that.

We are on Isla Nublar. Somebody we don't know is killed by something out there. The scene sets the tone for the picture. The whole point of the film is that we are going to see dinosaurs, but not showing them here creates suspense about what they will look like. The scene takes four minutes.

We shortly meet Dr. Alan Grant and his associates, and we can tell from the techno-babble that they are scientists. The techno-babble is not for our information, but to establish the characters. How much techno-babble do you need in your script? A lot less than you think.

Velociraptors are discussed, and it is established that Grant dislikes kids, much to the irritation of his girlfriend, Dr. Ellie Sattler. She wants kids, he does not. That's about it for characterization, folks. Grant is played by Sam Neill, a terrific actor, who appears to be lost in the role. Some actors, including several in this film, can make something out of nothing, but Neill did not figure out how to do it here. I was not surprised when Neill turned down *The Lost World: Jurassic Park*, and it certainly piqued my interest when he agreed to do *Jurassic Park III*. Stay tuned.

A helicopter takes Grant, Sattler, John Hammond (the builder of Jurassic Park), Gennaro (Hammond's lawyer), and Dr. Ian Malcolm to the island. Malcolm is onboard to provide comic relief. Unlike Neill, Jeff Goldblum, who plays Malcolm, has figured out not so much his character, but ways to make his line-readings interesting. Being able to read lines is a specific branch of acting, and one that is essential for actors in film and television, because very often that is *all* they are asked to do.

On the island Hammond explains the security setup, which works as exposition and whets our appetite. At 20 minutes in, the group get a first look at one of the dinosaurs amblin' past. The writers have written in reactions for the actors (writing for actors' performances), and Spielberg, who loves actors, gives them each a close-up (writing for a director's performance), which helps convince us of the reality of the dinosaurs. Grant asks Hammond how he did it, which leads to an elaborate video show in the main building. Notice how the writers have spread all the dialogue, exposition, and arguments over scenes that *show* us things. If you think you have to present the audience with a lecture, make it animated, either literally, as here, or figuratively.

At lunch we get a long discussion of the ethics of the park, a typical Crichton philosophical discussion rather than a character scene. Hammond's two grandchildren, the boy Tim and the girl Lex, arrive. We now have the 1993 equivalent of a 1940s bomber crew. If you were putting together a crew for this movie, whom would you pick? We'll get a different selection in *Jurassic Park III*.

The grandson, Tim, attaches himself to Grant, which of course makes Grant uncomfortable. Can you see Grant's "story arc" coming here? Sattler is amused, but if she wants him to want to have kids, shouldn't she be worried this will finally push him over the edge against them? The tour group (Grant, Sattler, Malcolm, Gennaro, and the kids) gets into vans and starts the tour. As the vans go through the main gate, guess which character says "What do they have in here, King Kong?" We get the setup of a lot of details that will now begin to pay off: stalled tour vans, Sattler with the dino doctor, a storm, open gates, the power being down. Could it be done quicker? Look at those scenes and see if you can cut them down.

In the stalled vans, Tim hears a repeated thudding sound and sees the water in a glass shake. This is a wonderful detail—small, precise, and surprising. And it is one people remember from the movie. Yes, the special effects are dazzling (or were at the time, though they're less so now), but sometimes simpler is better. Look for inventive details you can use. As Lex asks where the goat who was left earlier for the T-Rex to eat is, a leg of the goat falls onto the car. The T-Rex, if not the star at least a major supporting character, has arrived, just over an hour into the film. The T-Rex eats Gennaro. Didn't the fact he was a lawyer tell you he would be the first to go? Then the T-Rex knocks the kids' van off the road and down a hill. This is the big action scene we have been waiting an hour for, and its combination of action and T-Rex effects make it both suspenseful and satisfying. If you are making a movie about dinos on the rampage, you had better have at least one scene be this good.

A dino gets into Nedry's Jeep and kills him. Nedry is the one who set up the power systems to fail so he could steal the dino embryos. Two points here. We had thought he was going to play a bigger part, but his story turns out to be just a setup for other action. Second, the killing is handled very discreetly, as is all the violence in the film. For commercial reasons, the makers wanted a PG-13 rating, but as filmmakers in the golden age of movie censorship in the thirties through the fifties knew, sometimes *suggesting* violence is more powerful than showing it. We are 74 minutes into the film.

Grant rescues Tim as the van slides down the tree. Why is this not a particularly compelling suspense scene? There will be a "falling trailer" scene in *The Lost World* that is much better conceived, written, and directed. Grant and the kids climb another tree and see one of the herbivore dinos, which they treat like a pet. Even the dino knows Grant will bond with the kids.

Watch Richard Attenborough, who plays Hammond, both act and read lines as he describes the flea circus he ran as a young man, in a scene as close as we get in this film to a character scene. In the control center, Arnold, a technician, has a long string of techno-babble about a plan to shut down the system. Unlike Jeff Goldblum, who gives his techno-babble twists and turns, Samuel L. Jackson, playing Arnold, just barrels through it as quickly as possible. The system has shut down, but for everything to then come back on-line, they have to go hit the circuit-breakers in a shack outside. Of course, if they were in the basement, it would be way too easy. Arnold goes off to do the job. Grant and the kids come to the electric fence. They realize the electricity is off and they start to climb over the fence just as Sattler, who found only Arnold's arm in the shed, is turning on the power. This is a nice suspense scene, cutting back and forth, as opposed to a pure action sequence. Change the rhythm of your different scenes.

Grant and the kids get back to the main building and find Sattler, who has somehow lost the pink blouse she has been wearing for most of the film. Where did it go? That was the one major continuity gaff I noticed. Go look at the goofs section on this film on IMDb. The missing blouse is not even mentioned along with *all* the others. Why did people not notice more of these? Because the story grabs us, and if the story grabs us, continuity goofs *may* not bother us. Do not let your screenwriting career depend on this, but if you catch us up in the story and the characters, we may not sweat the small stuff.

Two velociraptors come after the kids, who hide in the kitchen and outwit them. After the big outdoor scenes, this is a nice change of pace: interior, smaller dinos, the kids on their own. How do the kids beat those velociraptors? If the humans can just get the system going…but the late Arnold has already ready told us it is impossible to override Nedry's efforts. So Lex sits down at the computer, has it all figured out in a minute, and bolts the doors. Yes, she had been established earlier in a line of dialogue as a computer geek, but still, doesn't this strike you as just a little bit of sucking up to the tween audience?

The survivors get on a rescue helicopter and fly away. At the two-hour mark, the credits begin.

As much as Spielberg loves actors, he has throughout most of his career been less interested in character, and when the character material is not in the script, as here, the film is weakened. On the other hand, Spielberg and his crew spent a lot of time on the "performances" that were essential to make this film work: the dinosaurs. As a writer as well as a director, you have to develop a sense of what the heart of your material is. The heart of *Jurassic Park* is the dinosaurs. Get them right and the movie pretty much works. Which it did, making a very large pile of money. But the demands of the sequels are a little different.

> **THE LOST WORLD: JURASSIC PARK** (1997. Based on the novel *The Lost World* by Michael Crichton. Screenplay by David Koepp. 129 minutes)

A title tells us the island we see is Isla Sorna, eighty-seven miles from Isla Nublar. Not eighty-six or eighty-eight, but eighty-seven. If you are telling a tall tale, try to be as precise as possible so people will believe it (e.g., the opening titles of *Psycho* [1960]). And we know this island is safe because Isla Nublar was where the park was in the first film, right? Guess again. This first scene is in bright sunlight, and while suggestive (for now we think the little girl is dead), it does not have the obvious suspense and horror of the opening scene in the first film. Why not? Because the audience already knows what kind of film this is going to be, so all they need is a little reminder, not a big one. We are 4½ minutes into the film.

Ian Malcolm's role in this film has changed. He is no longer the smart-mouthed comedy relief, but the action hero, and he has been given a lot more character. Malcolm meets Hammond's nephew, Peter Ludlow, a new character. Ludlow runs Hammond's company, and we can pretty much tell from his attitude that he is not one of the good guys. Malcolm and Hammond now have the bane of all sequels: the explanation of what happened since the first film, and the setup for the new one. Listen to what all this ten-minute-dialogue scene sets up, particularly how Koepp introduces the paleontologist, her character, and her relationship with Malcolm. Her character is more fully drawn in this one scene than Sattler's was in all of the first film. Koepp juggles a lot of balls well in this scene (Hammond also mentions that the girl in the opening will recover), and Attenborough and Goldblum are good at reading the lines. But if you are including a scene this long in your sequel, it had better be to a movie that audiences loved as much as they did *Jurassic Park*.

In the warehouse we meet the people going on the expedition. Van Owen, for example, establishes himself quickly as the equivalent to Malcolm in the first film: wise-ass comic relief. Listen to how few lines it takes. Malcolm's daughter Kelly takes the place in this film of Tim and Lex, but she is not a particularly interesting character, and her contribution to the action is limited (and from the line about her gymnastics, you can guess what it will involve). She is black, but almost nothing is made about it. I suppose it may be a triumph for racial equality that she is allowed to be one of the blandest characters in the film, but Koepp could have done more with her.

At 19 minutes in we get to the island. Malcolm, Clark (the technician), and Van Owen start out to track down Dr. Sarah Harding, the paleontologist. They see dinosaurs at about the same point we did in the first film. They find Harding's backpack, which is a mess. Van Owen jumps up on a log to take pictures of the dinosaurs, and there is Harding doing the same. We get reactions from all to the dinos, which leads to a good line from Malcolm, "'Ooh, ahh,' that's how this all starts, then later there is running and screaming."

Harding is surprised to see Malcolm (and why did she not respond when they called her name? She was not that far away). As in the first film, techno-babble establishes her character. The guys were concerned that the condition of her backpack meant she had been attacked, but she says it is just her lucky backpack and that's why it's a mess. Surely if Malcolm and Harding had been together for several years, he would already have known that. Harding and Malcolm's disagreements are much more detailed and varied than those between Grant and Sattler. We are also going to see Harding do more than Sattler got to do in the first film. It will be well into the film before she actually screams. A triumph for feminism.

At 33 minutes Ludlow's boat lands on the island with large crates of equipment. Roland Tembo, this film's Great White Hunter (and a bit livelier than Muldoon in the first film), is given a nice introduction, better than his introductory scene in a Deleted Scene (included on the DVD). Here we learn about him in the middle of the action.

Ludlow's Jeeps and motorcycles chase dinosaurs, who astonished us in the first film simply because we had never seen anything like them. We assume we will see the same thing here, and we accept as natural what four years before was revolutionary. One difficulty in sequels is going beyond what was done in the previous film or films, and that is true of the script as well as the special effects.

Our guys look on the hunt with dismay, even Van Owen. Being an action junkie cameraman, wouldn't he have thrown in with the hunters? Tembo finds tracks of a T-Rex (we know what they look like from the first film; you can take advantage of what the audience knows or thinks it knows in a sequel) and goes off to hunt it. Dieter Stark, played by Peter Stormare in his Gaear Grimsrud mode, finds a small dino and kills it, an effective if brutal way to establish him as a bad guy. I am not sure that with Stormare in the role you have to make that effort to establish him as a baddie, since the casting does the work for you. If Stormare were playing a *good* guy, you'd have to establish his goodness. That is the sort of screenwriting "polishing" that goes on as the film gets close to and into production: adjusting the script to take into consideration the actors you have hired.

Malcolm says the bad guys are going to take the dinos to San Diego. How does he know? Van Owen says Hammond told him that Ludlow might show up and that he sent a backup plan: "Me." When did he become an action hero? The bad guys' camp is attacked by dinos, which Van Owen has let out of their cages. That's the backup plan, to unlock the cages?

Van Owen and Harding take a baby T-Rex that Van Owen rescued back to their trailer, where Harding sets the baby's leg fracture in a cast. This leads to what Koepp, Spielberg, and Michael Kahn (the film's editor) turn into one of the greatest action/suspense scenes ever made. Look at how they use the two trailers, the cliff, the rope, the winch, the cracking glass, the backpack (you thought it was just for character purposes, didn't you?), the car with the winch, Clark, the rain, and the mud. And look at *when* Koepp brings each one of those to bear in the scene. This is one of the most beautifully structured action sequences I know, unlike many scenes that are merely chases, fights, etc. Compare it to the clunky simplicity of the "falling van in a tree" sequence in the first film. Here is the advantage of doing a sequel: getting a chance to do better, or even do right, what you did in the first film. I have the sneaking suspicion that this is why Spielberg did this film. His direction of the first film was one of the worst directing jobs he has ever done. Here he improves on his direction and corrects his mistakes from the first film. There is more characterization in this script than in the first one, and Spielberg has given the acting a greater consistency than the first one had.

The trailer sequence starts a little before the one-hour mark and goes until a little after it. By the end of it, the trailers are at the bottom of the cliff, Clark is dead, and our guys have finally made contact with the bad guys. Ludlow says the only problem getting to the communications center to call for help will be velociraptors, and we get an unneeded explanation of velociraptors. Always a question for the screenwriter in sequels: how much do you have to explain, and/or how much can you, hopefully, assume the audience will remember? Maybe my memory is going, or maybe, unlike younger moviegoers, I see most movies only once, but I have found it hard to get back into a lot of sequels. The filmmakers often assume that the audience has seen the original many times, which the most devoted fans have. But what if your audience has not?

Dieter wanders off to take a pee in the woods and is chased and killed by dinos. This is one of those action sequences I referred to earlier, with a very simple structure. Yes, Dieter does seem to get away a couple of times, but what more could you do with this sequence? And would you want to at this point in the picture? Tembo realizes Dieter is missing, goes to look for him, comes back to say he only found some remains, "parts they didn't like," a line that is creepier than anything we saw in the actual Dieter sequence.

At camp at night, we get a big puddle of water vibrating, which is not as inventive as the glass of water in the first film. More "running and screaming." Harding and Kelly get away, although we may have thought for a minute that the T-Rex ate them. But Harding is one of the stars and Spielberg generally does not kill children, especially in a PG-13 film.

As the T-Rex chases people, we get a shot from behind them as they are looking back at the dino. File this away for future reference. We also get an inventive bit where the T-Rex stomps on a guy, and as he brings his leg up, we see the guy stuck to his foot like a piece of chewing gum. After a couple of steps, the guy falls off into a puddle. Typical of sequels: variations on a theme. There are a number of these in the second half of this film, as if, having tossed off the great trailer sequence, everybody decided to relax and have some fun. We will eventually see the problems with this. We are 84 minutes into the film.

Harding, Malcolm, and Kelly get to the operations center, where they are attacked by velociraptors. This velociraptor scene is not as suspenseful as the "kids in the kitchen" scene in the first film, because it is diffuse: the creatures attack different people in different places. Kelly shows her gymnastic skill, but the payoff is not worth the setup effort earlier. You have to figure out the balance between your setups and your payoffs.

At 98 minutes the rescue helicopters arrive. Tembo refuses to go back to San Diego with Ludlow and his T-Rex. Tembo tells Ludlow he has seen enough of death. This is one of the strangest exits I have ever seen in a movie. I suppose it is because we have not gotten to know him that well and don't understand why he would be so upset. I suspect the writers may have had a more complex idea of this character, judging from some stray lines, but he may have been too complex to fit into this film. From their helicopter, Malcolm, Kelly, Harding, and Van Owen see the T-Rex in a cage. We see the helicopter flying through the night. We start to stand up, because the movie is obviously over, with the T-Rex being saved for the next sequel.

The movie continues on for another *twenty minutes*. We are in San Diego, several of our characters have disappeared, and the ship smashes into the pier. The T-Rex escapes and crashes through the "Welcome to the United States of America" sign by customs and immigration. Did the projectionist get the reels from a comedy mixed up with this film? The T-Rex is rampaging in the streets. In the street we see, from the back, a group of four Japanese businessmen who are running away, looking back and screaming.

Are you familiar with the term "jumping the shark"? It refers to an episode of the television series *Happy Days* (1974–1984) in which Fonzie jumps over a shark on his motorcycle. The term is used on the website www.jumptheshark.com as "a defining moment when you know that your favorite television show has reached its peak. That instant that you know from now on...it's all downhill." The "Japanese businessmen" shot, at 113 minutes into *The Lost World*, is the "jump the shark" moment for the *Jurassic Park* films: the moment when they stop being completely serious. Why? Because the shot looks like something out of a *Godzilla* movie (and not the crummy 1998 American remake). The

Godzilla films, for all their grazing on social issues, were camp from the beginning, in a way that the *Jurassic Park* movies were not, until this moment. We will shortly see the implications of this for the third film in the series, although given the results, I am not sure the term "downhill" is necessarily appropriate here.

The T-Rex is captured, put back on the ship, and sent back to his island (even after he eats Ludlow), and we end with a whole collection of dinos on the island.

Okay, so it jumps the shark, but I still think it is a better movie than the first one. The storyline is stronger and the scenes are more inventive. The writing, direction, and acting of the characters is more consistent than in the first film. And the trailer sequence clinches the deal.

But if they have jumped the shark, what can they possibly do for a third film?

JURASSIC PARK III (2001. Based on characters created by Michael Crichton. Screenplay by Peter Buchman, Alexander Payne, and Jim Taylor. 92 minutes)

Look at those credits for a minute. No novel by Crichton this time, just "characters," and, as we will see, that does not turn out to be entirely true. No David Koepp either, but three new writers. If you follow low-budget indie films, you might recognize the names Alexander Payne and Jim Taylor. They wrote and Payne directed *Citizen Ruth* (1996), *Election* (1999), and after *Jurassic Park III*, *About Schmidt* (2002) and *Sideways* (2004). As you may suspect, the tone of *Jurassic Park III* is going to be closer to that last twenty minutes of *The Lost World* than to the other parts of the earlier films. And Spielberg is only the executive producer this time, not the director. The director is Joe Johnston, whose directorial resume includes the family comedies *Honey, I Shrunk the Kids* (1989) and *Jumanji* (1995). And note the running time: it is half an hour shorter than either of the first two films. So we can expect a quicker and funnier movie than the two previous ones, which was probably the only way to go after the end of *The Lost World*. This is certainly a less pretentious film, which is why I think it is the most purely entertaining of the three.

We get a typical *JP* opening: two people parasailing over Isla Sorna go down behind a hill. Guess how many minutes we are into the film? Check the first two films.

Dr. Alan Grant is back. Obviously he got over his fear of kids, married Sattler, and settled down, since he is talking to a child. He also seems to have lightened up. Grant had a couple of jokes in the first film, but here he seems almost comic. I have no idea of the collaborative process on this film, but it would not surprise me if Sam Neill talked to the writers and producers and said this was how he had finally figured out how to play Grant. Except we now learn that Sattler is married to Mark, who works for the State Department, and who Grant calls a "great guy." Aren't they civilized about all this? Grant says he is working on raptors and has figured out that they do communicate, and Sattler says this proves their theories. A nice scene: two people who had a romance remain friends and still have intellectual interests in common. So much for Laura Dern's cameo. When he leaves, she says he can call her any time he needs help. Surely by now you can recognize a setup line when you hear it.

Grant speaks to a large group about his research. Listen to how the writers cover what happened since the last film and set up this one. Better than Koepp did in *The Lost World*. One person asks Grant if he would want to go to Isla Sorna. He smiles and says, "No force on earth or heaven could get me on that island." Grant is serious, but Neill knows that a line like that in a picture like this only guarantees he will go, especially since we are only 10 minutes into the film.

We see Nash, Cooper, and Mr. Udesky firing guns and talking about ammunition. All very macho, although Mr. Udesky is played by Michael Jeter, who is certainly less macho than the other two. Who are these guys?

At Grant's dig in Montana, Brennan, Grant's new assistant, shows Grant a machine that takes measurements of bones by computer and then carves a model, in this case of a raptor's "resonating chamber." When blown, it makes the sound of a raptor. There is a much smaller amount of techno-babble in this film. At the third film in the series, we pretty much know what we need to know and are ready for action.

Paul Kirby, obviously one of Crichton's dangerous entrepreneur/businessman types, interrupts them. Look at the details that establish his character. He says that for their anniversary, he and his wife want to fly over Isla Sorna to see the dinosaurs. Kirby is played by William H. Macy, Jerry Lundegaard of *Fargo*, so we may be a little suspicious, but Macy nails the off-the-wall quality the very rich often have.

We are on the plane, with Grant taking Brennan along because he does not want to be stuck with the Kirbys alone. Brennan has brought his lucky backpack, the strap of which once saved him. (Is he Sarah Harding's brother?) Cooper, who is now much more well-dressed than when we first met him, is in the back of the plane. Brennan asks how he knows the Kirbys, and Cooper, dark glasses on, replies, "From church." That line is much more Payne and Taylor than Crichton. They fly over the island and Grant points out the herds of dinos, at about the same amount time into the film that we first saw dinos in the first two films. Cooper knocks Grant out.

When Grant wakes up, he finds the plane has landed at an airstrip on the island. Amanda is on the runway with a large bullhorn, calling for "Ben." Grant tells Kirby that it's a bad idea to make that much noise. Kirby yells this at Amanda, who yells back, through the bullhorn, "What?" We know the rich can be crazy, but still… There are the sounds of stomping, which we recognize from the first two films. Udesky and Nash run back to the plane, get it started. The plane crashes in the jungle. Into a tree. The plane crash is a good solid action scene, if not quite up to the level of the plane crash in *Cast Away* (2000). The plane sliding down the tree is better than the van–tree scene in the first film, but not as good as the trailer scene in the second one. Johnston has a nice shot of Kirby running out, seeing a dino, turning on a dime, and running back in. Not only is there comedy in the lines, but also in the sight gags, in the manner of the last twenty minutes of *The Lost World*. Everybody in this film is making the same movie.

The survivors (Nash and Cooper are dead) begin to sort out what is really going on. Kirby explains that their son, Erik, was parasailing with a "friend" named Ben, apparently Amanda's boyfriend, since Kirby and Amanda have been divorced for several years. They got no help from the Costa Rican government or the Embassy. Grant asked why they wanted him on the search, and Kirby says because he had been on the island before. As Brennan and Grant explain, Grant was not on *this* island, but on Isla Nublar. Ben and Erik have been missing for eight weeks, so Grant does not hold out much hope that either survived. They all head for the coast. We are half an hour into the film.

Kirby and Amanda change clothes facing away from each other, complimenting each other, again a nice couple scene. Brennan and Grant see Kirby, who has claimed to have had many adventures, very awkwardly putting on a backpack, and they confront him. Kirby admits that his business is just a paint and tile store in a mall. And Udesky is not really a mercenary, but a booking agent. What the writers and Johnston are doing is adding a new color to the *Jurassic Park* films. The filmmakers here cannot go back to the original horror/sci-fi approach. There is still enough of that left to satisfy the fans of the originals, but the filmmakers are working with the shift in tone from the second film and developing it. In the first two films, both based on Crichton's books, everybody is pretty much exactly who they are established to be when we first see them, or in Sarah Harding's case, hear about them. The filmmakers here figure they can play with the characters and the tone, as long as they give the audience the requisite thrills. They manage the balance nicely. The question is, could they have been this playful in the first film? I think they could have, since variety of character and tone can always perk up a genre film, as we saw with *Fargo* and *Bound*.

Kirby finds their son's video camera, and we see that at least Erik survived the fall onto the island. The parasail is found, but with Ben's rotting corpse attached to it. The survivors run through a stampede, a more technically complex but less interesting version of a scene in the first film.

Grant is surrounded by raptors. He is rescued by...Erik. We are now a little more than halfway through the film. Erik has read both of Grant's books, thinks Ian Malcolm's book is too "preachy" and "chaotic." He thinks Malcolm was high, and Grant replies, "That's two things we have in common." Like some of the gags in *The Lost World*, here are some riffs on the films to amuse die-hard fans. The audience I saw the film in a theater with appreciated most of them.

The survivors get to yet another deserted building, where Brennan asks for his lucky backpack back. Grant looks in the bag and discovers...dino eggs. Brennan had taken them to fund research, and Grant, although he disapproves of Brennan's action, decides to keep the eggs, since they may be useful to get off the island. To get to a boat to get to the coast, they have to cross a bridge, which Grant realizes is part of a giant...bird cage. For flying dinosaurs, who attack the people. Our guys, except for Brennan, escape. The bridge sequence is one of the better action scenes in the film. Why? It is different from the others. It is not in a building or in the jungle, which we have seen a lot of in the films. It takes place in a fog.

In the morning the people float past grazing dinos, in a scene reminiscent of the first viewing of the dinos in the first film. At night the people get off the boat and find a pile of T-Rex dung. They dig through it to try to find Kirby's phone, which was established earlier as being inside one of the T-Rexes. A T-Rex comes across them and just gives them a "Who are these crazy animals digging in my poop?" look and ambles off. Give even your monsters good reactions to play. They find the phone and, when back on the river, they realize there is only power for one call. Whom do they call? You remember the setup, right? So Laura Dern gets to work a second day. Grant calls, but he gets Charlie, her three-year-old. Grant tells him to get his mommy. Charlie wanders off, sees mom outside, then gets distracted by Barney on television. Cute, but also suspenseful, because a T-Rex has attacked the boat. When Sattler finally gets the phone, she hears dino noises and realizes immediately what's up. On the river the survivors escape from the T-Rex. We are about 80 minutes into the film.

At the shore they are surrounded by velociraptors. Grant has all the people kneel down and gets the two eggs from Brennan's backpack. He lays them out on the ground, then discovers Brennan's model of the raptor's resonating chamber. Did you guess that model was a setup? Why not? He blows it and two raptors each pick up an egg and go away. Music has charms to soothe the savage beast? Well, maybe, but it's a stretch, even with the lighter tone of this film.

The army and the navy arrive, in force. Or did you forget that Sattler's husband was with the State Department? They, including Brennan, who survived, take off in helicopters, and as they fly away, Grant and the others notice that the flying dinos are flying alongside. Grant allows that they are looking for a whole new nesting area. He smiles—like this is a *good* thing? Maybe he has an idea what the next film in the series should be. Even though this film cost more and grossed less than the first two, it made enough to at least get people thinking about another one. As of this writing (mid-2007), plans are in the works for #4. Where can they go from here?

10

SOME *LAWRENCE* WANNABES

L*AWRENCE OF ARABIA* was not only a great movie and a huge hit, it was a very influential film. Many historical epics since have been affected by it, some directly, some indirectly. Here are a few recent films, along with what they learned and/or failed to learn from *Lawrence*. They are in order of release.

> **TROY** (2004. Inspired by Homer's *The Iliad*. Screenplay by David Benioff. 163 minutes)

Notice the credits say the script was "inspired by" rather than "adapted from." David Benioff wondered why there had not been a big-screen version of the story of the Trojan War since the fifties. Benioff told David Goldsmith, "I proposed a ruthless adaptation" in a five-minute pitch to Jeff Robinov, the President of Production at Warner Brothers, who said simply, "Are you ready to start writing?" The film went into production eighteen months later.

Benioff realized the adaptation would have to be ruthless because *The Iliad* has more than a few dramatic problems. It begins in the tenth year of the Trojan War and ends before the fall of Troy. It is mostly about how the great warrior Achilles refuses to come out of his tent and fight because Agamemnon, the leader of the Greek army, has taken Briseis, a woman captive Achilles had seized. Achilles spends most of *The Iliad* sulking in his tent, like a $25-million-a-picture star staying in his trailer because he doesn't get his perks. Achilles might be very much a hero for our age, but not until late in the story is he a very active one.

The Iliad also gives us no background on the events leading up to the war, and does not show the Greeks' scheme to infiltrate Troy with a huge wooden horse. The Trojan Horse does not appear in either of Homer's two epic poems, *The Iliad* and *The Odyssey*, but later in the Roman poet Virgil's *The Aeneid*, which tells of the Trojan survivors of the war. The problem for Benioff, or anybody telling the story of the Trojan War knows, is that contemporary audiences, if they know of the war at all, know about the Trojan Horse. Stopping the story where Homer does, without the Horse, would have audiences throwing things at the screen. I have read some reviews and comments on IMDb complaining about Benioff not following "the facts" of the story, but there *are* no facts to the story. The tales of the Trojan War are highly mythologized versions of what was, even when Homer was writing, a very distant historical event. And there are many, many versions of the stories, which means that Benioff's ruthlessness would still be in keeping with the traditions of storytelling about the War.

Another change that was trickier for Benioff to deal with was that in *The Iliad*, the gods and goddesses play a very active role, such as rescuing Paris in his duel with Menelaus. Benioff decided that while the characters often talk of the gods, we would not see them. He was undoubtedly thinking of the 1981 film *Clash of the Titans*, which kept cutting away to actors like Laurence Olivier and Ursula Andress wandering around in the clouds portraying the gods. It looked silly to audiences in 1981 and it would look silly to audiences in 2004. Since the Greek gods are not a part of contemporary audiences' lives, Benioff worked hard to drop them from the story. Read at least a CliffsNotes® version of *The Iliad*, then watch the movie, and you will have a great appreciation for the work Benioff did.

Benioff has said his most specific inspiration in writing the script was *Spartacus* (1960) rather than *Lawrence*. He was dealing with the same problems that Dalton Trumbo had on *Spartacus* and Wilson and Bolt had on *Lawrence*: how do you make the culture of the past alive for contemporary audiences? In some ways Benioff had it harder, because audiences, even contemporary ahistorical ones, probably know, or think they know, more about the Trojan War than audiences in the early sixties thought they knew about Spartacus and Lawrence.

The film begins with titles telling us it is 3,200 years ago, and explaining the political situation in Greece. It is not clear here who the narrator is, but when he returns at the end of the movie, it appears that it was Odysseus. Why do you think Benioff handles it that way?

Two minutes into the film two armies are facing off on a plain; this is not a small movie. The Greeks are led by Agamemnon and the Thessalonians are led by Triopas. Agamemnon suggests that they settle the battle "the old way": our best fighter against yours. Triopas agrees and calls forth his man, who behaves like something out of the World Wrestling Federation, which is one way to connect with contemporary audiences. Agamemnon calls for Achilles. Who is not there, a foreshadowing of what is to come. A Boy is sent to his tent, where he finds Achilles nude with two women. Achilles puts on his armor, goes out, and kills the Thessalonian warrior with one blow.

One note that Benioff got from the studio was that Achilles was too arrogant. Benioff told writer David S. Cohen, "He's not likeable. You're not going to have a pet-the-dog scene with Achilles. It is something I had to resist." Achilles is the best, fiercest warrior, and he knows it. The problem with the film comes in casting Brad Pitt as Achilles. Fierceness is not really in his normal range, especially when he is going up against actors like Brian Cox (Agamemnon) and Brendan Gleeson (Menelaus) who can do fierce with one hand tied behind their backs. (For a really fierce Achilles, look at Stanley Baker in the 1956 film *Helen of Troy*; it is one of the few things that film gets right.) There seem to be two Brad Pitts. One is a terrific character actor, as seen in *Twelve Monkeys* (1995). The other is the movie star, who seems bland, as in *The Mexican* (2001). Unfortunately for *Troy*, the movie star showed up.

Next we meet the second hero of the film, Hector. He is part of a peacekeeping group gone to Sparta to sign a treaty with Menelaus. Benioff picks up the trip at the final banquet. Menelaus is something of a pig, making out with the dancing girls while his much younger wife Helen looks on. And makes eyes at Hector's brother Paris. Well, we know what is going to happen with them, but Benioff is way ahead of us. Paris and Helen sneak off, and in a couple of quick lines of dialogue we learn their romance has been going on for a couple of nights. Ah, Paris and Helen, the great lovers.

And impossible characters to write. Paris is, in the legends, an irresponsible cad and a coward to boot. Helen is even worse. Well, not actually in Homer, who is somewhat sympathetic to her plight, but in later works. William Shakespeare, who was no slouch at writing romantic heroines (Cleopatra in *Antony and*, Juliet in *Romeo and*), knew enough to avoid Helen as a major character. In his one Trojan War play, *Troilus and Cressida*, Helen has a very minor supporting role. And Christopher Marlowe just makes her a walk-on in *The Tragical History of Doctor Faustus*, so that Faustus can get off the great line about hers being the "face that launched a thousand ships." The problem dramatically is that Helen is inert: everybody adores her (why, other than her good looks?), but she is acted upon rather than taking action. Will was one smart playwright: Cleopatra and Juliet *do* stuff.

So what can Benioff do with the characters? Not much, since he pretty much sticks to the idea of them as the great lovers, but it only means that Orlando Bloom (Paris) gets to look stricken, first with love and then with remorse at what he has caused. Neither Benioff nor Bloom give their Paris any texture. Diane Kruger (Helen) can be fun to watch, as in *National Treasure* (2004), but here she does not have enough screen presence to make up for the fact that her face alone would launch three hundred, maybe four hundred ships, tops. She may simply have been intimated by the role, but Benioff doesn't help, giving her nothing to do and no reactions to play. How could you write Paris and Helen?

By 14 minutes into the picture, Paris has secreted Helen aboard his ship. Hector, the smart one, wants to take her back, but decides not to. Menelaus goes to Agamemnon to get him to make war on Troy to get Helen back. Agamemnon has been looking for a fight with Troy, and we see he is determined to build an empire. Agamemnon sends the wily (as Homer always refers to him) Odysseus to talk Achilles into joining the war. When he arrives, Achilles is practicing dueling with his cousin and protégé, Patroclus, so the scene introduces both of the other men. Achilles's interest in glory is re-enforced by Odysseus appealing to his love of glory, which also establishes how clever Odysseus is. Odysseus mentions that Agamemnon is putting together a fleet of a thousand ships, which wittily leads us to believe that somebody, somewhere, will use Marlowe's line about Helen. Benioff doesn't. Good for him. Sometimes you just have to give up the obvious.

Helen arrives in Troy with Paris. We have no idea why she is so immediately welcomed by Troy and Paris's father, Priam. We meet Hector's cousin Briseis, who is going to work as a maiden in the Temple of Apollo. The "real" Briseis was captured by Achilles on a raid on the way to Troy, but Benioff is packing events and characters tighter than Homer.

At 34 minutes into the film, the Greeks ships are spotted off Troy. Achilles lands first and his men destroy the Temple of Apollo. Hector mounts a counterattack. He and Achilles face off for the first time, but Achilles does not kill him because "It's too early in the day for killing princes." Or too early in the film; Hector is not Marion Crane, after all. Agamemnon takes Briseis shortly before the one-hour mark. We have seen Achilles in action twice, so we are probably ready to let him sulk in his tent for a little while, especially since there are other action scenes to take up the slack.

Paris challenges Menelaus to a duel. Menelaus thoroughly beats him, and Paris crawls in the dust to Hector, who then kills Menelaus. Huh? In Homer and in other ancient writings, Menelaus survives to the end of the war, gets Helen back, and takes her back to Sparta. In one of the best scenes in *The Odyssey*, the question of Helen's behavior comes up after she's back home, and she says that the gods drove her crazy. That's her story and she's sticking to it, and Menelaus is buying it because he truly, deeply loves her. Okay, that's Homer, and Benioff is rightly being ruthless, but one day I would like to see that scene as a film about Helen. Killing Menelaus at this point in the film ups the pressure on everybody. Besides, nobody but those of us who read the classics will complain. See the advantage of telling a story your audiences do not know as well as they think they do?

We next have a big battle scene outside the walls of Troy, and as usual with these kinds of scenes today, there is an over-reliance on CGI effects. The closer scenes of a few men fighting mean more to us than the long shots of thousands, because there are characters we know involved. The Greeks are driven back. Agamemnon's advisors convince him that they need Achilles and he agrees to give back Briseis. She in turn pulls a knife on Achilles, but he seduces her. In *The Iliad*, Briseis is just an object passed around by the Greeks, and this is how Achilles thinks of her. Benioff has tried to develop a romance between Briseis and Achilles, but the characters are not drawn carefully enough for it to work.

The Trojans attack the Greek camp the next morning. Notice how Benioff has given us a variety of action scenes: the Paris–Menelaus duel, the army battle before the walls of Troy, and now an early morning attack on the Greek camp. The Greeks think Achilles has come out to lead them and are horrified when Hector kills him. Only it is not Achilles, it is his cousin Patroclus, who had dressed in Achilles's armor. Achilles seems much more upset at this than his sulking about Briseis, which is true to Homer. And it serves Benioff well, since Odysseus says, "I don't think anyone is going home now." At the funeral pyre for Patroclus, Agamemnon says, "That boy has just saved this war for us."

Achilles goes to the gates of Troy and calls Hector out to fight. Hector asks before the duel that if he dies that he be given proper burial rites. The duel starts shortly before the two-hour mark and is more exciting than the larger battle scenes because there is so much more at stake for these two characters. Achilles kills Hector, then lashes his body to his chariot and drags him around the walls of Troy. That night Priam comes to Achilles's tent to ask for Hector's body so it can be given a proper funeral. This is one of the most dramatic and moving scenes in *The Iliad*, and Benioff handles it well. The problem is Brad Pitt. Either Benioff has not given him the reactions or he does not do them, but he is blown off the screen by...ah, yes, Peter O'Toole, Lawrence his own self, as Priam. O'Toole knows how to quietly hold the screen in a way that Pitt does not. Benioff has certainly given O'Toole enough to work with.

Odysseus is, as usual, thinking. He sees one of the men whittling a small wooden horse. His eyes light up. No dialogue. We do not need it. We know what he is thinking because we know the legend. We see Hector's funeral pyre, which is where *The Iliad* ends, at 2 hours, 15 minutes into the film. As I have pointed out, that by itself is not going to be satisfying to an audience that knows the Trojan War primarily from the Horse. So the Trojans come down to the beach to find…the wooden Horse. They take it into Troy and the battle for Troy begins.

Now what at this point do we need to see to be satisfied we have seen a complete film? Here is what Benioff gives us. Andromache, Hector's widow, goes out the escape passage, taking Helen with her at Paris's insistence. Paris takes up the bow and arrow, and it turns out that he may have a bit of the warrior in him after all. Agamemnon kills Priam and then finds Briseis. Who kills Agamemnon. Wait a minute! It's one thing to kill Menelaus, but quite another to kill Agamemnon. After all, if he dies at Troy, he does not get to go home to his wife Clytemnestra, who then kills him, setting off bloodshed in the house of Atreus, giving us the story for the first great Greek tragedy, *The Oresteia*. In other words, if Agamemnon dies at Troy, there is no western drama: no Greek tragedy, no Shakespeare, no *Cats*, and probably no movies. Okay, no review of *Troy* that I saw made this point, because if you are into the film by that point, Briseis killing Agamemnon makes perfect sense. He took her away from Achilles, gave her to the troops for their amusement, and was an all-around swine. The issue is not, does it work with its literary precedents, but does it work as part of your script?

Achilles finds Briseis, whom he has been looking for during the siege, and he is shot in the heel with an arrow from Paris. Now, the whole mythology of his heel being Achilles's vulnerable part has not been dealt with at all in the film, and it is too late to bring it up. If you know about it, you understand. If you do not, it doesn't make any difference, because Paris shoots several other arrows into Achilles. Briseis is upset, but Achilles says to her, "You gave me peace in a time of war." The problem is that we have not *seen* that in their relationship.

The film ends with Achilles's funeral pyre and the narration mentioned above.

Troy only (only?) grossed $133 million in the United States and Canada, but grossed $364 million in the foreign market, for a total of $497 million. Why was it bigger overseas? Probably because there is a greater interest in historical films in other countries, since the same pattern holds true for some other historical films. But since pictures the size of *Troy* are being made by companies that are now international conglomerates, the companies, such as Warner Brothers with *Troy*, are willing to invest in them.

How does *Troy* stack up to *Lawrence of Arabia*? It is not as good, of course, but it has an epic sweep, some interesting characters, and a real sense of how to structure an action film. Now if they had just had Russell Crowe as Achilles...

Sources
My favorite general source for information about the classical world is *The New Century Classical Handbook* (Catherine B. Avery, Ed., Appleton-Century-Crofts, 1962). Yes, I am sure there are more modern ones, but I have been using it since 1962, and I love the way the writers give you all the different versions of the legend. For an interesting look at the "real" Helen, see the 2005 PBS documentary *Helen of Troy*, in which British historian Bettany Hughes gives you all the possible variations on Helen. There are two articles on David Benioff and the writing of *Troy* that have been referred to and quoted from. The best is David S. Cohen's "Script to Screen: *Troy*," *Scr(i)pt*, May/June 2004; almost as good is David E. Goldsmith's "*Troy*," *Creative Screenwriting*, May/June 2004. The box office take on *Troy* is from "2004 Top 125 Worldwide," *Variety (W)*, January 17–23, 2005.

KING ARTHUR (2004. Screenplay by David Franzoni. 126 minutes)

David S. Cohen thought Benioff was writing *Troy* as though he were writing about the real events that inspired the myths. There is not so much a feeling of that in *Troy* as there is in David Franzoni's screenplay for *King Arthur*. Years before, Franzoni had come across research suggesting that the prototype for King Arthur had been a Roman who was part of the Roman occupation of England during the Dark Ages. He then made the creative jump to his concept for *King Arthur*: King Arthur and his Knights as *The Wild Bunch*. After all, Franzoni had been the original writer on *Gladiator*, and that film and *Braveheart* had shown the commercial possibilities of a grungier look at the past than we have been used to in historical films. The advantage/disadvantage Franzoni had was that there have been far more films about Arthur than about Spartacus, Lawrence, and Helen of Troy. The advantage was that Franzoni could play with the audience's knowledge (as Benioff does with the line about a thousand ships), which he does beautifully. The disadvantage is that the Arthurian purists would attack him, which they did, even before the film was released.

The first title card indicates that the King Arthur of the fifteenth-century legends was based on someone who lived a thousand years before, and that "recently discovered archeological evidence sheds true light on his identity…," which tells us we are not going to be in the fantasy world of *Camelot* (1967). Lancelot takes up the narration (interesting in view of Lancelot being killed near the end of the film; *King Arthur* as *Sunset Blvd.* [1950]?), beginning with, "By three hundred AD, the Roman Empire extended from Arabia to Britain," which both calls *Lawrence* to mind and helps set up the Sarmatians, warriors from the Asian steppes that the Romans brought to Britain as cavalry.

In his research, Franzoni found that there were elements of the Sarmatians' mythologies that seemed to have been taken over when British mythmakers turned Arthur into a Celt. As Franzoni told writer Kate McCallum, "For instance, the Sarmatians had a holy cup that was a source of great quests which likely became the Christian/Medieval Arthurian Grail. Also, the Sarmatians worshipped swords stabbed into the earth, had a Lady of the Lake, used round tables and so forth." Look at which of those Franzoni uses and how he uses them.

Ah, now the crucial question: do we the audience care whether Arthur was a Sarmatian or not? No, we do not. The Sarmatian Arthur is a flying saucer. For purposes of a film, we will believe in both of them, whether we do in "real life" or not. Franzoni had more historical detail in the earlier drafts of the script, but it was condensed to just what he *needed* to tell the story in an entertaining way. For example, in reading the Roman poet Ovid's descriptions of the Sarmatians, Franzoni came across a description of a battle between the Sarmatians and the Roman legions on a frozen lake. What a great idea for a battle. Sergei Eisenstein thought so too, and did the first great battle on a frozen lake in *Alexander Nevsky* (1938), which I assumed until I read the interview with Franzoni was the inspiration for the battle here. Just as Wilson and Bolt turn the attack on Aba el Lissan into the attack on Aqaba, Franzoni turns the battle on the ice into the first major battle between Arthur and the Saxons.

Look at the ways Franzoni has fun with what we think we know about the Arthurian legends. Merlin is referred to, before we meet him, in a line about how some people think he is a wizard. But since Franzoni is dealing with the "reality," we do not get any magic tricks. We all know about the affair between Lancelot and Guinevere, but here we see that Lancelot flirts with every female he comes across. On the other hand, I have real mixed feelings about Franzoni's take on Guinevere. She has traditionally been a love object, without much to do but look gorgeous and be loved by Arthur and Lancelot. Franzoni turns her into Xena, Warrior Princess. Not your father's Guinevere, maybe too much so, but as played by Keira Knightley, a lot of fun.

If Franzoni has turned Lancelot into an all-purpose flirt and Guinevere into a warrior, what is his take on Arthur? He is mostly sullen, which Clive Owen can do well, but Franzoni and Owen's Arthur does not really show the leadership that Arthur, even in the fourth century, should have. Now if they had just had Russell Crowe...

Source
Kate McCallum's interview with David Franzoni, "The Great Idea: *King Arthur*," is in *Scr(i)pt*, July/August 2004.

> **ALEXANDER** (2004. Written by Oliver Stone, Christopher Kyle, and Laeta Kalogridis. 175 minutes)

Remember the opening of *Lawrence*? "He was the most extraordinary man I ever knew" to "some minor function on my staff in Cairo."

Now listen to the opening of *Alexander*. The elder Ptolemy tells us Alexander was a great man. And he tells us again. And again. This is a terrible setup for the character, and even worse for the actor: who can live up to that introduction? Colin Farrell can't. I know, I know...if they'd just had Russell Crowe.

We then get Alexander as a young man and see the difficulties he has dealing with his father, Philip of Macedonia, and his mother, Olympias (of God knows where; you try identifying Angelina Jolie's accent). Then we suddenly jump ahead several years: Philip has been killed and Alexander has taken over. How did that happen? We have no idea. Much later in the picture, after we have accepted that we will not be getting the story of Philip's death, suddenly we get a flashback that shows us. It spends more time than it needs telling us what we already know.

The writers seem to want to try to deal with Alexander's bisexuality, if not homosexuality. There are a number of scenes with Alexander and the love of his life, Hephaistion, but the scenes dance around the issue. You will remember that David Benioff in *Troy* avoided the problem altogether by introducing Achilles in bed with two, count 'em, *two* naked women, which then hangs over the scenes with Patroclus so we do not get suspicious (unless we already are). Late in the picture the writers pair up Alexander with the woman Roxane. Their love scenes are more explicit than the scenes with Hephaistion, but in the film her emotions never seem to be consistent. The casting of Rosario Dawson, who bears a striking resemblance to Angelina Jolie, raises all kinds of Oedipal questions the script never deals with.

The first big battle scene is the defeat of the Persians at Gaugamela, and like the big battle scenes in *Troy*, it is overloaded with thousands of CGI troops, and we do not know what is at stake. The other battle scene, in India, is more compelling because it puts Alexander up against elephants, something we have not seen before.

Part of the problem with the script was also a problem in Robert Rossen's 1956 film *Alexander the Great*: Alexander led an epic life, but not a very dramatic one; he conquered the world, then he died. How can you make that interesting on film?

KINGDOM OF HEAVEN (2005. Written by William Monahan. 145 minutes)

William Monahan admits that *Lawrence of Arabia* was an influence on him in this film. You can see it in the overall story, and you can see it in individual scenes. You can also see in the mistakes Monahan makes that he did not learn well enough from *Lawrence*.

The story is set at the end of the twelfth century, between the second and third Crusades, so like *Lawrence*, the film is dealing with the clash of western and middle eastern cultures. The Wilson and Bolt screenplay follows Lawrence from a rather clumsy misfit into a leader, and then to the psychic exhaustion that leadership brings. Monahan's leading character is Balian, a young French blacksmith who goes to the Holy Land. Nice idea for a character, but he is not particularly well drawn. We are introduced to him in France, where he is going through a crisis of faith because of his wife's suicide. He lights out for the territories, as Mark Twain would put it. Godfrey, a knight on his way back to the Crusades, shows up out of nowhere, announces he is Balian's father, and asks Balian to join him.

The first problem is that while Balian is established as a blacksmith, we do not really believe it. Partly this is the casting of Orlando Bloom, unfortunately in his Paris mode, who does not look like he would lift any of a blacksmith's tools (I know, I know...but could Russell Crowe?). But in Monahan's writing throughout the film, we get nothing that specifically tells us about his smithing. If you are going to pick an occupation for your main character, get some mileage out of it, as Hayes did with Jeff's photography in *Rear Window*.

Once Balian and Godfrey are on the road, we get a little bit of Godfrey training Balian to be a knight, but not nearly enough. Godfrey gets killed too soon. We do not get from the scenes that he has taught Balian enough to turn into the fighter he becomes. Nor do we get a sense that he has taught him anything about leadership. In *Lawrence* we see Lawrence develop his own leadership skills, but there is nothing equivalent here.

When Balian gets to Jerusalem, we see him sitting at Golgotha staring out into space, a scene that recalls Lawrence coming up with the idea of attacking Aqaba by land. We know Lawrence is thinking about what to do, but we have no idea what Balian is thinking. The Lawrence scene works dramatically; the scene here is just a nice-looking shot.

Balian is introduced into the political intrigues of the Crusader politics, which Monahan handles reasonably well, with some interesting characters, such as King Baldwin, his advisor Tiberias, and the bad guys Guy de Lusignan and Reynald (Brendan Gleeson, Menelaus from *Troy*), as well as Queen Sibylla, a rather nicely drawn seductress (I think that's in the script, although it may just be Eva Green's eyeliner). So does Balian become immediately involved in the politics? No, he goes out and becomes…a farmer. Where does that come from? He was not a farmer in France. He has expressed no desire to become a farmer, but there he is. This takes us out of what we thought was the story, and Balian is not an interesting enough character to hold our interest in all of this. Unlike Lawrence, who by this point in his film was leading the trek to Aqaba, Balian is tending to irrigation ditches. Not the same thing.

The politics and Queen Sibylla eventually catch up with him and Balian begins to show some leadership skills, although we have no idea where they came from. He eventually keeps the Christians in Jerusalem from being massacred by the Muslim leader Saladin by surrendering the city. Smart move, given that they are outnumbered, but it makes for a rather bland ending.

A word here on the portrayal of the Muslim characters. Even before the film was completed, there were articles condemning it for being too anti-Muslim, too pro-Muslim, not anti-Muslim enough. I think Monahan, like Bolt in his revisions of Wilson's screenplay, has drawn the Muslim (and non-Muslim, for that matter) characters very well, which undoubtedly offended the anti-Muslims. Monahan also gives the best line to Saladin. When Balian turns over the city of Jerusalem to Saladin, he asks him what Jerusalem means to him. Saladin replies, "Nothing," then, seeing Balian's surprised reaction, adds, "and everything." The late Robert Bolt would be proud.

Sources
Peter N. Chumo II wrote about the development of the script, with comments by Monahan, in "Coming Soon: *Kingdom of Heaven*," *Creative Screenwriting*, May/June 2005. Islamic scholar Hamid Dabashi gave input on the script and film and wrote about the experience in "Warriors of Faith," *Sight &*

Sound, May 2005. Dabashi deals with the criticism of the script and film in a very perceptive and nuanced way.

A note on period dialogue: go back to the films in this chapter and listen to the dialogue in them. You will notice that none of them are obviously "historical," i.e., filled with obscure expressions of their periods. Back in the heyday of Cecil B. De Mille's historical spectacles, De Mille insisted on very arch, very artificial "period" dialogue, but then occasionally let the actors get away with current slang. The dialogue in those films does not hold up well, to put it politely, as in Queen Berengaria's famous line to Richard in *The Crusades* (1935): "Ya gotta save Christianity, Richard, ya gotta!" One improvement in modern screenwriting is the tendency to tone down period excesses.

The current trend is to write the dialogue in a reasonably literate way, but also so that actors can get their mouths around it. That is true of the scripts discussed in this chapter. There is an effort to avoid dialogue that calls attention to itself, which would take modern audiences out of the story. You want dialogue that gives us people's *attitudes* of the time, rather than specific linguistic twists. That does not mean that you will not include a line or two that gives a sense of the period, such as Benioff's having his characters refer to the gods, but don't overdo it.

11

SOMETHING'S GOTTA GIVE

> **SOMETHING'S GOTTA GIVE** (2003. Screenplay by Nancy Meyers. 128 minutes)

SOMETHING'S GOTTA GIVE is an entertaining adult romantic comedy that is not quite as good as *Bull Durham*. And like *Collateral*, it goes wrong in the last half hour.

It is also a star vehicle for Jack Nicholson and Diane Keaton, and the film needs them more than they need the film. They give a first-class demonstration of how much both talent *and* stardom can help a picture. So before you watch it for the first time, think about what Nicholson and Keaton mean to you as stars. O.K, then try to watch it a second time, imagining a couple of unknown, middle-aged actors. See? So among other things, you can learn from this film how to write for stars. Meyers, by the way, wrote it with them in mind, but they did not commit to it until they read the script. You write great roles for stars, they do your movie.

Meyers begins the script with shots of young women in New York, which gets expanded in the film into the title sequence. Then we hear Harry's voiceover about the satisfactions of the Younger Woman, who in the punch line he says he has been dating for over forty years. In the script Meyers brings Harry on camera with this description: "What is it about him? Could be his eyes, the turn of his mouth—something about this guy is just so damn appealing. Maybe it's just the way he wears the Young Slinky Girl on his arm. He's confident, cool, enviable" (page 1; numbers by themselves will be the page numbers of the screenplay; minutes into the film will have "minutes" after them). Yes, that description is certainly Jack Nicholson. But think about it. If Nicholson had turned it down, Meyers could have gone to Redford, Beatty, Pacino,

Hoffman, De Niro, etc. Like Hayes's description of Jeff in *Rear Window*, this is a great star description.

And this entrance does not appear in the film. In the script, the voiceover continues as we see and hear Harry imagining himself with an older woman, but the film cuts (Meyers actually writes [2] the overused and redundant phrase "SMASH CUT," which I always think looks silly; it's just a cut) to Harry in a car with Marin, his thirtyish, gorgeous girlfriend. And that is the last voiceover we ever hear from Harry. Why drop the voiceover? Used later, it would take us out of the story completely, especially when we get into the extended double scenes with Harry and Erica. Those scenes require a balance that giving one character a voiceover would throw off. So why not just have his comments as part of Harry's conversation in the car with Marin? We could get what we need of Harry's attitude anyway, both in the scene with Marin and later. They probably didn't have time to go back and rewrite and reshoot the car scene.

Marin seems like a smart girl, and is very aware of Harry's reputation for dating younger women. While Meyers is more sympathetic to Erica, Marin's mother, she doesn't do it at Marin's expense. Which in turn keeps us from seeing Harry as a mere predator of younger women. Rather like the Epsteins and Howard Koch turning Bogart into a romantic hero in *Casablanca* (1942) by having the beautiful Ingrid Bergman be in love with him. The characters your lead likes, or who like your lead, can help us understand your main character. Meyers however plays the American Puritan card by letting us know they have not yet had sex. If this were a French film… But Meyers figured, and she may have been right, that American audiences would find it too creepy if Harry were to have sex with both the mother and the daughter. On the other hand, Benjamin did in *The Graduate*…but that was, like, the sixties, man.

At Erica's beach house, before they can make love, Harry is in the kitchen in his boxer shorts as Erica and her sister Zoe come into the house. We are on page 8 of the script, but only 6 minutes into the film because of the cuts. It becomes clear when Marin comes in that she assumed her mother would not be here for the weekend. Notice how late in the action that is nailed down. And here is Erica's reaction: "No, no, I should've told you we were coming. Obviously. Yes. Well. Here we are." Now, there are many actresses who could get a lot out of that, but doesn't it sound like Diane Keaton?

Zoe thinks they can all survive the weekend together. Zoe is described in the script as "the loose one. Smart and unafraid" (8), and Frances McDormand, Marge Gunderson her own self, runs with that. It's not a great part, but it still gives her some nice moments, and some others that she makes into nice moments. Even if you are writing for stars, you will want to give them interesting supporting characters to play off. Meyers does not have as many as she might, but McDormand and Amanda Peet as Marin are not just collecting unemployment benefits.

While shopping, Erica and Harry have their first extended dialogue. We learn that Harry owns a record company that releases hip hop records. Why this detail, since we never see or hear any of the records the company releases? It establishes Harry as not just a geezer. And it gives Erica something to react to. It has been established that she is a successful playwright, so she objects to the language in rap. Harry insists some people see it as poetry, but Erica replies, "Yeah, but come on, how many words can you rhyme with 'bitch'?"

At dinner, Zoe (why her and not Erica?) realizes she had read an article about Harry in a magazine about his avoiding marriage. Zoe, who teaches women's studies at Columbia, does an aria on how older men are celebrated for not marrying, while her sister stays home "night after night after night" because guys her age want younger women. The speech is nearly a full page and you can see why Meyers, who also directed the film, hired McDormand. A lot of actresses would make it angry, but McDormand plays it like she is thinking out loud, as intellectuals do. What could be a dead spot turns into an amusing moment. And notice how much later in the scene Erica objects to the "night after night after night," saying, "one 'night after night' would have been enough." Marin joins the conversation in the kitchen and sticks up for Harry and his *ten* companies, to which Erica replies, "What does that mean he owns like ten companies? He can't commit, that's what that means." Why isn't Zoe given that line? Because it's a writer's line and not an intellectual's line. Keep your characters separate.

Top of page 23, 17 minutes into the film: Harry has a heart attack while "fooling around" with Marin. At the hospital he is treated by Julian, a doctor in his mid-thirties. Julian asks Harry if he has taken Viagra. Harry says no, but when Julian warns him about the dangers of Viagra with the medicine in the IV drip, Harry pulls the drip out. In the film the scene stops there, but in the script (26–27) we get Harry's apology to Julian ("Sorry, had an audience") and Julian's reply ("It was a great save"), as well as Marin's reaction afterward to Erica, "This is a nightmare. I go out with a man who's so old, he takes Viagra." Harry and Julian's lines are not crucial, and Marin's seems out of keeping with her character.

Julian, it turns out, is a big fan of Erica's, and is obviously interested in her. He becomes Harry's competition for her, but his character is not as well developed as the four characters we have followed so far. Harry wanders around in a hospital gown that shows his ass, a use of nudity that sets up a later scene and provides a great line for Zoe: "That was one great ass for a guy that age." Alas, the line was cut from the film. Thirty-six hours later Harry's assistant Leo shows up with Harry's two gorgeous female assistants. Leo has more scenes in the script than he does in the film, but Jon Favreau, who plays him, suffers the same fate Chris O'Donnell did in *Kinsey*: cut scenes.

Harry faints in the parking lot and Julian says he either has to go back to the hospital or stay somewhere in the area for a few days. Would a doctor really make such an offer? Okay, if he doesn't here, there is no movie. Erica mouths "Forget it" in the script, "No" in the film, and we cut to Erica's house. Neither in the script nor the film is there any discussion. Why not? We know he is going there, so why delay the inevitable? We want to see Erica try to nurse Harry, and not just because these are our two stars, but because we see they are slightly attracted to—as well as irritated by—each other. As Harry settles in the guest bedroom, Erica is in the kitchen talking to Dave, complaining about— wait a minute, who is Dave? We haven't seen him before, but he seems right at home. Look at how long it is in the scene before Marin comes in and says, "Dad!" We accept Dave before then because a) Erica accepts him, b) there is enough going on in the scene for us to be involved without having to worry about him, and c) we have faith by now that Meyers will let us know. What do you have to write in the first pages of your script that will get us to have that kind of confidence in you?

Harry and Erica are now alone in the house. We are 40 pages into the script and 30 minutes into the film. And Meyers cuts two pages of scenes from the script that establish that Harry and Erica are getting along and that Harry and Erica have the same prescription in their glasses. Okay, we do not need to see them getting along, since it will be more fun when they are not. But the business with the glasses? If you jump ahead to the end of the film, they return each other's glasses, which they ended up with. Isn't it essential that it be established they have the same prescription? Not really. We come to realize it as they do, which makes it more subtle and charming at the end. Which is *really* when you need subtlety and charm in a romantic comedy.

On the other hand, Meyers has Erica working on her play, and in the film, but not the script, we see she is writing lines of dialogue that Harry, Zoe, and the others have said, which tells us the play is the story we are watching. This gives it away too early. The script is better than the film on this point.

Then we get the scene that everybody who saw the trailer has been waiting for: Erica is nude on the way to the bathroom when she is seen by Harry, who is trying to find the kitchen. Their separate reactions are in the script, but they are elaborated on in the film. Well, you want actors like Nicholson and Keaton to bring their A game to a scene like this. On the other hand, their reactions do seem a bit excessive for two sophisticated adults, but comedy is the art of excess. And audiences loved it.

The next day Erica is dressed so no skin is showing *anywhere*. She does not want to talk about last night. Harry talks about it with Julian, who comes to the house to check him out, but we do not quite know what Julian's reaction is. Harry asks when he will be able to have sex again, and Julian tells him that when he can climb a flight of stairs, he can have sex. Cut to—sometimes you just have to go for the obvious joke because the audience will not forgive you if you don't—Harry looking up the stairway from the beach to the house. And trying it. Julian meanwhile asks Erica to dinner.

Harry asks Erica to go for a walk on the beach, 38 minutes in. Richard Roeper, of *Ebert &*, had a line in his review that was used in the ads: "...just the two of them walking along the beach having a conversation is thrilling cinema in its own way." He is referring to this scene, and he is right. Why? Character. They are at ease with each other in a way they have not been before. Sometimes you need to loosen the tension you have built up, for rhythmic reasons if nothing else. Both have looked up the other on the Internet. Why did we not see them do that? Because it is more interesting to hear them talk about what they learned.

Both Harry and Julian are impressed by Erica, who is now not in the turtlenecks we have seen her in most, or in the overdressed fashion she was earlier that day, but in a killer little black dress, ready for her date with Julian. Later, Harry wanders around the house, unable to get any of his girlfriends on the phone. Read this line out loud to yourself, then listen to Nicholson: "Everybody's out but old Har...Old old old old Har..." That is why he gets several million dollars a movie and you don't. At dinner Julian admits he is falling for Erica. Julian here, as in the rest of the film, seems as much a plot contrivance as a character. Aside from the fact, not a minor one I suppose, that he is perfectly willing to be with a woman twenty years older than he is, there is nothing distinguishing about him.

After the date, Erica and Harry meet in the kitchen, in their pajamas, for food. He has rightly assumed that she did not actually eat anything at dinner, since "women never eat on dates." Listen to how their dialogue in the kitchen suggests that they are beginning to appreciate each other. What details does Meyers use in this scene? This is interrupted by Marin, bringing food. Marin sees how Harry looks at Erica.

The stage direction (68) reads, "At first she's shocked. He likes my mother??? Then a flash of jealousy. He likes my mother!?! Then pure joy—realizing how absolutely perfect it is." In the film we only get part of the first reaction. Why drop the others? Some of the details are in the "How Do You Show This?" category, such as "realizing how absolutely perfect it is." Was Amanda Peet not up to delivering those changing reactions? There is nothing in her work here or elsewhere that suggests she could not do it. It might have suddenly made her too interesting a character for the film, although Meyers has not run away from her character. In the following scene, Marin encourages Erica to get together with Harry. Her reactions may have been cut because it was felt the next scene carried that information, making earlier reactions unnecessary. I still would have liked to have seen those reactions, since, as you should know by now, reaction shots are the lifeblood of cinema.

Marin goes out to the beach to break up with Harry. We only see them, but do not hear them. Marin returns, tells Erica she has broken up with…and then realizes Harry has in fact broken up with her, saying, "He's a genius." Harry and Erica talk on their cell phones, with Harry claiming that Marin broke up with him. A word here on the uses of technology. This is a dialogue-heavy film, but look at how Meyers has spread it around. Meyers plays the scenes all over the house and out on the beach. And she breaks up the face-to-face dialogue scenes with instant messaging, cell phone conversations, and discussions between people not in the same room. This is not quite on the order of Hayes writing *Rear Window* for one set, but it's close. And she handles it without being obvious about it, as opposed to some computer-driven films, which are just photographs of people typing.

Harry and Erica are now alone again, and when the power fails, they light candles and kiss. And since he seems to have an erection without Viagra (is this the new sign of true love in American films?), they have sex. Harry does raise the question of birth control, to which Erica replies, "Menopause," and she insists on taking his blood pressure first, but the question of sexually transmitted diseases is never brought up. If Meyers could get some good jokes about menopause and blood pressure in, surely she could have come up with something for STDs.

We are now halfway through the film, a little further along in the script. The sex is not shown explicitly, but we do get several minutes of their reactions to the experience. This, after all, is a turn in the story, and Meyers takes the time to deal with it. And they are funny and even touching scenes. A scene of Marin calling and talking to her mother about her having had sex with Harry (77–78) has been cut from the film, which is too bad, because it's funny. Sometimes you have to give up the good stuff.

You can tell this film was written and directed by a woman: there is a lot of discussion of food, a lot of eating, and a lot of scenes in the kitchen. Erica and Harry are eating and she mentions a bistro in Paris she likes. We have been hearing her play French music all along, and in particular we have heard "La Vie en Rose." The bistro will show up in the film; "La Vie en Rose" will show up later in the script, but be dropped from the film.

When she gets up in the morning, Erica "walks away with the achy walk of a woman who hasn't had sex in many a year but has more than made up for it in the last twelve hours" (82). I love Keaton, especially in this film, but that is one bit of action that is only clear in the film if you know what the script says. Harry tells Julian he can do the stairs, "several times, actually." Now imagine that line without the context of the film. Not much of a line, is it? Given what we know about the stairs, sex, and what has gone on with Harry and Erica, it is funny. Context is all.

To celebrate being allowed to go home, in the script (85–86), Harry takes Erica to a club, where he does a karaoke version of "La Vie en Rose." I suspect this may have been like the "dinner with subtitles" scene in *Kinsey*: too much of a showstopping scene to have survived into the film.

Marin is upset that her dad is marrying a woman only two years older than she is. She needs Erica to come into town, which she does, leading to a scene in which Marin goes into detail about her being upset, more than Erica is, about her dad's new marriage. It's an odd scene, played a little too straight. The comic idea is a good one—daughter more upset than mom about dad's remarriage—but Meyers has not pushed it far enough. I would guess it could get a little too creepy, sneaking into Electra-complex territory, but sometimes you just have to be courageous. Meyers isn't here. Ninety-two pages into the script, 80 minutes into the film, Marin and Erica have dinner with Dave and Kristen, Dave's fiancée. This also could be a better scene than it is, but we get almost nothing about Kristen. Meyers perhaps guessed it didn't work well, since the second half of the scene was cut from the film.

Erica sees Harry with a beautiful young girl at the restaurant. She leaves as he sees her. They are both in the street, talking to each other on their cell phones, until he catches up with her. They agree it is over, and at the top of page 99, 86 minutes into the film, she gets into a cab and rides off. The movie is over. Fade Out. Roll credits.

Ah, not so fast. Meyers has *thirty-six minutes* of scenes left to show you. What more do we need to see? They had an affair, it didn't work out, end of story. Well, this is a comedy, so presumably we want the two stars to get together, especially since they seem to be able to at least begin to adjust to each other. Okay, but why take thirty-six minutes to do that?

Here is *some* of what happens in the script and film. We get a long montage of Erica crying and writing. In the script Harry is sitting with Leo (remember poor Jon Favreau?), eating bowls of pasta, watching *I Love Lucy*. If a man had written this script, what would they be eating and watching? The scene is not as sharp as it might be, and it has been cut from the film. Erica and Julian kiss, but there is no indication that they go to bed. He thinks her new play is the best thing she has ever done. He is sincere, which proves Annie Savoy's theory that a man will listen to, or read, anything if he thinks it is foreplay.

A young blond actress talks to somebody about her audition for a play about a young woman dating an older guy who has a heart attack... In the script (109), we do not learn until the end of her monologue that she is talking to Harry. In the film (104 minutes in), Meyers cuts to Harry in the middle. Why? It is awfully late in the picture to bring in a brand new character and give her a thirty-second monologue. And the quicker we get to Harry, the more we get of Nicholson's reactions (yes, that is plural, and that's why he gets millions...) to her. In writing, directing, acting, ice hockey, whatever, go with your strengths.

At the play's rehearsals, Meyers having Erica write lines from "life" works against the film. In *The Producers* (1968), Mel Brooks deliberately does not give us any of the show *Springtime for Hitler* until we get the title number and its full impact on opening night. In the script (113–114) Harry sits in Central Park on a bench next to a woman he had dated forty years before who has gone on to a great life: a doctorate in marine biology, author of nine books, a happy marriage, kids, and grandkids. The scene was dropped from the film. She is way too interesting a character to have for only one scene late in the picture, with no other connection to the story. There is also a tricky political question. If the movie is critical of Harry's behavior, and it is, certainly more so than it is of Erica's, then doesn't this woman redeem him by suggesting that having a Harry in their lives can help women achieve great things? There is nothing else in the picture (other than Erica completing her play) that suggests Meyers believes this.

Six months later, Erica's play is a success, and Harry finds out from Marin that Erica is in Paris. Guess where in Paris he finds her? Julian is in Paris too, which Marin didn't mention, silly girl. Meyers is getting into "If somebody says one smart thing, the entire movie will collapse" territory, often a flaw in romantic comedies as well as horror movies.

Julian has been out shopping for a ring-sized box, which he puts on the table. Now wait a minute. Julian has had at least six months to make his move. How slow is this guy? Harry thinks they are happy and exchanges Erica's glasses for his, a moment that could have been touching, but is in so crowded a scene that it does not have the full impact it should. Sometimes you just have to clear the decks for action to give the scene its proper focus. Harry lets them ride off in the cab outside the restaurant.

He walks to a bridge, where who shows up but Erica, who tells him that Julian realized that she still loves Harry. Is Julian a prince, or what? If Annie Savoy is a fantasy figure for men, Julian is one for women. Or maybe he's just afraid of commitment? It has been six months, after all.

At 122 minutes, the credits (finally) roll.

Now go back, read my description of the last half hour, watch the film, and figure out how to rewrite the last third of the movie. I told you my suggestions on *Collateral*. This one is up to you.

Sources

The screenplay I referred to was the one provided "For Your Consideration." It appears to be an undated shooting script, with revised pages from March through July 2003.

Fred Topel's interview with Nancy Meyers, in which she discusses the film, appears in the October 2003 issue of *Screenwriter's Monthly*. It is reprinted in Patrick McGilligan's *Backstory 4* (University of California Press, 2006), along with interviews with several other writers.

12
THREE SLICES OF *AMERICAN PIE*

AMERICAN PIE (1999. Screenplay by Adam Herz. 95 minutes)

ADAM Herz based *American Pie* on his youth in the eighties in East Grand Rapids, Michigan, and on the films of those years. You might think this would be the genteel films of John Hughes, such as *Sixteen Candles* (1984) and *The Breakfast Club* (1985), but *American Pie* is more in the tradition of Bob Clark's *Porky's* (1982). Though Herz shows some of Hughes's sensitivity, he is, like Clark, more honest in depicting the sexual urges of male American teenagers. Both Clark and Herz are able to get outside of the testosterone-driven male and make the female characters more than just sex objects. There is a sweetness in their films that is also part of highly successful raunchy comedies, such as *There's Something About Mary* (1998), *Wedding Crashers*, *The 40-Year-Old Virgin* (both 2005), and *Knocked Up* (2007). If you are determined to write raunch, you should study all these films.

In *American Pie*, the raunch begins with sexual moans on the soundtrack under the Universal logo. The picture opens with Jim trying to watch a porn movie scrambled on cable. Why not a videotape? Because a scrambled image makes us think more about what we are seeing, and provokes a greater variety of reactions. Jim's Mom enters, suspicious of the sounds, especially when a line of dialogue is distinctly heard. Jim's Dad then enters, assumes it is just bad reception and grabs the remote, which pulls the pillow off Jim's lap, revealing the tube sock he is wearing to cover his erection. Sex and embarrassment. We are only 1 minute, 41 seconds into the film, and the main character, the tone, and the subject matter have all been neatly established.

Jim and Oz drive to school discussing how hot Ariel, the Little Mermaid, is. Compare the brevity of this scene to the car returning from the airport in *Y Tu Mamá También*. Herz is about laughs, a little less about character and culture, and virtually nothing about politics. As Kevin, Jim, and Oz pass by members of the band in the hallways, one of them, Michelle, suggests they all play backward to confuse the conductor. What seems like a throwaway moment to give us some texture of high school is really a setup of Michelle.

Vicky talks to Jessica, a very knowing but not completely cynical friend, about maybe having sex with Kevin. Stifler reminds Jim, Kevin, Oz, and Paul about the party at his house. Stifler is loud and crude, mentions that the four have not had sex, and says he will put them in the "'no fucking' section" of the house. At a fast food restaurant, Jim tells his three friends he is thinking about talking to Nadia, a Czech exchange student. The friends give him a hard time about not even knowing what third base feels like. He asks what third base feels like, and Oz holds up two fingers and says it's like "warm apple pie." Obviously a setup.

We are at just under 6½ minutes into the film, and look at the number of characters and situations Herz has established. In an ensemble piece, you are not going to have much time to spend with each character, as we saw in *Love Actually*. Herz gives no more than one characteristic to each person in addition to their search to get laid. Look at how Herz spreads out the Oz, Kevin, and Paul scenes to vary the rhythm of the film, and so he will always have something to cut to.

At Stifler's party we meet Sherman, who is even geekier than our four. Sherman is bragging about how he is going to score tonight, which is depressing for our guys and creates sympathy for them. Jim tries to talk to Nadia but geeks it and walks away. Oz thinks he is going to score with a college girl, but she tells him what he's doing wrong and how he should try to have a conversation with a girl. This sets up his motivation for the rest of the film, but it also shows how Herz is portraying the women characters as mostly smarter than the men. In the bedroom, Vicky is giving Kevin head, and he comes into a nearby glass of beer. They are interrupted by Stifler and a girl who want to use the room. Do we follow Vicky and Kevin out? With a beer glass full of sperm in the room? Not a chance. Herz and the directors take their time to get to the obvious because they realize the laughs are in the variety of reactions Stifler has when he drinks from the glass, both immediately and later.

Vicky tells Jessica she doesn't know if she has ever had an orgasm and has never masturbated. Jessica asks, "You've never double-clicked your mouse?" Notice that the girls are talking as much about sex as the guys, and Herz gives us girls with a variety of attitudes, something a lot of writers of horny teenager movies do not do.

The girl with Stifler comes out of the room with his vomit on her dress. We did not have to see the vomiting. The audience can put two and two together. Two other guys, Justin and John, are looking at large photographs of Stifler's Mom, and say she is a "MILF: A Mother I Would Love to Fuck." This in a left-handed way sets up the later scene with her. The party scene has taken ten minutes.

The next morning our guys are upset that it seems Sherman has scored before they did, and they make a pact to lose their virginity by graduation, three weeks away. So what used to be called in playwriting the Main Dramatic Question has been raised: are our four guys going to have sex? They agree in the next scene that it will have to be consensual sex (so we don't have to worry about any rape scenes) and it cannot be with hookers (eliminating the potential hooker scene that Bob Clark has already handled delightfully in *Porky's*). We are 17 minutes into the film.

In the montage of our guys preparing to have sex, look at the details that Herz uses, particularly the ones that will come back into play later in the film.

Stifler drags Kevin and Jim to see that Oz is now…singing in the choir. With an eye on Heather, the cutest girl in the choir. Oz tells the guys that since none of the girls in the choir know him, he can try what the college girl has told him: listening and talking to girls. Stifler replies, "I don't know, man, that sounds like a lot of work." This makes the others seem sensitive in comparison to Stifler, which helps us like them better. And we get to laugh at his line as well.

As Dad comes in to Jim's bedroom, Jim puts the condom in his drawer. Dad has brought some nudie magazines to "inform" Jim. Notice the ones Herz has selected, and Jim's reactions to them. Reactions double the laughs. It helps to have Eugene Levy playing Dad, and Jason Biggs as Jim. Dad puts the magazines in the drawer, sees the condom, and says, "Well, it's better than a tube sock." Context makes it funny, like Nicholson's "Several times, actually."

Paul tells Kevin to agree to anything he hears about Paul, setting up Paul's story. After Paul leaves, a girl comes up to Kevin and asks if it is true that Paul is well-equipped. Surprised, Kevin agrees he is. Kevin calls his brother for advice about orgasms, and his brother guides him to a "secret manual," supposedly from Amsterdam, that is hidden in the school library. It is less a book than a collection of clippings, handwritten notes, etc. In other words, a school legend.

At 31 minutes into the film, Jim comes home and finds his Mom has left a freshly baked apple pie for him. If we had not had Oz's description of third base, Jim would seem weird, not just funny. Look at Jim's reactions to the pie. Needless to say, he is interrupted by…who would you send in? It could have been Mom, but Dad is the parental unit Herz is focusing on. We do not see them cleaning up the mess, but we do see them at the table with the remains of the pie in its tin. Cleaning it up might make a good slapstick scene, but we don't need to spend that time, and Herz gives Dad a great, deadpan line: "Well, we'll just tell your mother we ate it all."

After lacrosse practice (kudos to Herz for not making it football; a little freshness never hurt anybody's script), Oz asks Heather to the Prom, but after she walks away Stifler starts behaving like, well, Stifler. Heather sees this and assumes Oz is just a dumb jock laughing at her as well.

Kevin is trying to give Vicky head, reading in the manual as he goes. He is managing to do it when her father comes upstairs to call her down to dinner. He has his hand on the door when she yells, "I'm coming!" He turns away. Well, we have had Jim's parents interrupt him at the wrong time. Here is a different way to handle a similar situation.

Jim's Dad wants to talk to him about masturbation. He admits he did it, but "Of course, I never did it with baked goods." Look at how Eugene Levy underplays that line; he knows it is a great line and needs no spin. Listen to the rest of the discussion. And watch the reactions.

Nadia approaches Jim and asks if he can help her with history. She has ballet practice and will come by his house and change her clothes there, if that is okay with him. Finally, something is going to go right for Jim. The guys think Jim ought to set up his webcam so they can see what goes on in his room with Nadia.

At 43 minutes, Nadia shows up at Jim's room. He leaves her there to change and goes to a friend's house, where they watch on a computer. Nadia finds the magazines in Jim's drawer. Did you forget about them? Herz hasn't. She begins to masturbate to them. Kevin and Paul convince Jim that this is his chance to score with Nadia. What we (and not them) are just now (why now, why not earlier?) learning is that the webcam connection ended up being to the whole school's directory. So we now not only have our guys watching, but a lot of other people we have never met. Reactions, reactions, reactions. Most of the reactions are what you would expect; what different reactions could you write? Nadia wants Jim to strip for her, which he does, dancing badly to music. When she gets him into bed, he ejaculates prematurely. Twice. At school the next day, everybody is laughing at Jim. Jim tells his friends that Nadia's sponsor saw the video and she has been sent home. We are 55 minutes into the film. Why have we gotten rid of Nadia?

Why is she an exchange student? For the same reason that Ingrid Bergman was cast in *Casablanca*. In the stage play, her character was American. This is one reason the play was not produced on Broadway: what American woman would commit adultery to get the letters of transit? Hal Wallis, the producer, made her European, because everybody knows that European women either have looser morals than American women, or are just more sophisticated about sex. Herz is doing the same thing with Nadia. And if Nadia stays, then we have to deal with the difference in sexual sophistication between her and Jim, and that is a bit beyond where the film is willing to go. (For an amusing documentary look at a similar situation, see Keva Rosenfeld's brilliant *All American High* [1987]. It follows a Finnish exchange student through senior year at an American high school. She says American teens talk about sex more, but Finnish teens do it earlier.)

In class, Jim sits next to Michelle, who starts talking relentlessly about what happened "one time, at band camp." Apparently not knowing about the webcast, she is one of the few people in school not laughing at him. So he asks her to the Prom. She says yes, and he almost immediately regrets asking her when she starts another band camp story. How depressing to lose Nadia and end up with Michelle.

Jessica admits to one of our guys that she started all the rumors about Paul. Her favorite, which we have not heard yet, is that he slept with an older woman. In the locker room, Oz starts singing and Stifler half-jokingly accuses him of being gay. This is the only example of homophobia in the film, unlike the second and third films. I suppose in films aimed at the American male fourteen to twenty-five demographic, it is not surprising that homosexual panic becomes a source of humor, but it is usually very badly handled. Here it is brief and relatively benign.

At the lacrosse game, the coach (written as a cliché) gives a pep talk about the importance of the game, which only pushes Oz to realize the importance of choir, which he goes to sing in. He and Heather kiss.

Vicky and Jessica have another discussion about sex. We do not usually get this kind of sexually frank discussion in teen comedies, or even in American films, the most notable exception being *Fast Times at Ridgemont High* (1982). Herz gets away with it because he is doing it in the form of a teen comedy, and he is writing these discussions for characters we like. A lot.

We get a montage of our guys preparing for the Prom, including Dad giving Jim instructions to be very careful "pinning on the corsage," complete with winks and rhythmic backslapping. For once Jim is not embarrassed by his Dad.

At 71 minutes, we are at the Prom. Our four guys get together for a status check. Kevin is definitely going to get laid, Oz maybe, Paul no way, and Jim is just upset at all the pressure, again something you do not see with male characters in most teen comedies. Jessica asks Paul to dance, but tells him there is no way she is going to have sex with him. Why not put those two together? He's a virgin and she would destroy him. Vicky talks to Sherman's girl, who says that all she and Sherman do is have long talks. Vicky enlightens her. At the band break, Sherman's girl takes the microphone, calls Sherman a liar, says he has never had sex, and oh, yes, when he gets nervous, he wets his pants. Now the question here is, do you cut immediately to his wet pants, or do you cut to his face first?

By 78 minutes, we are at Stifler's house by the lake. Michelle is trying to get Jim to tell her some guy stories. Paul, the geekiest one of the group, wanders into the pool room, where he finds...Stifler's Mom. With her, Paul is actually...cool. Michelle is finishing her story about a game of spin-the-bottle where she had to kiss a trombonist for a long time. At 84 minutes into the film, Michelle turns to Jim and says, "And this one time, at band camp, I stuck a flute in my pussy."

That is one of the greatest payoff lines in the history of movies. Let's take a minute here to figure out why it works. Look at how Herz has set up Michelle. She is comedy relief, a nerd, and we have no reason until this line to think she could possibly have a sex life. She is cute, but not gorgeous, and in the natural hierarchy of American films, gorgeous girls have sex and cute ones do not, especially if they are as goofy as Michelle. It also helps of course that Alyson Hannigan gives a perfectly pitched performance. Well, perfectly pitched for *this* film.

Now, with that line, where can you go? First you have Jim's reaction, which is a standard spit-take. Michelle asks if they are going to have sex soon. They find a room (Stifler's little brother's room; how do we know?) and Michelle gives Jim two condoms. She says they will desensitize him so he will not come too soon. Yes, she had seen the webcast, and that is why she agreed to go to the Prom with him: she figured he was a sure thing. They have sex and she calls him her "bitch."

In the pool room, Stifler's Mom asks Paul, "Are you trying to seduce me?" Stifler's Mom takes his hand and says, "You're dead." Wait a minute. I just said that *Jessica* would have destroyed him, so wouldn't Mom be even worse? No, and you can tell why by listening to the soundtrack in this scene. Yes, it is "Mrs. Robinson," from *The Graduate*. Herz and the filmmakers are letting the earlier film do most of their work for them. Mom is given very little characterization of her own here, and the sex is played for the laughs we remember from *The Graduate*. Because of that film, this film does not have to deal with the implications of this scene.

The next morning, at 87 minutes, Vicky tells Kevin that next year they will be at different schools, and implies their relationship will not be able to continue. It is clear to us and to her, if not yet to him, that this was a good-bye fuck. I think it was intended to be a touching scene, but neither the writing nor the performances are up to it. Jim wakes up in the bed, saying, "She's gone! Oh my God, she used me. I was used. I was used! Cool!" Look how Jason Biggs's reactions change in the course of the line. He is as good at reading this line as Nicholson is with the "old old old" line in *Something's Gotta Give*. This scene is also a great way to get rid of Michelle, since she is a one-joke character, and the joke is over. Yeah, well…

Stifler comes into the pool room. We do *not* see what he sees, since the young male makers of the film probably thought it would gross out other young men to see a young man actually intertwined with a woman who is, eww, fortyish. Some older viewers might not have been so squeamish. Stifler's reactions are about what you would expect, including his fainting. Can you think of more interesting reactions?

Our four guys are together in their fast food restaurant. Paul is singing the praises of older women. The guys agree this is the end of high school and this part of their life. We see Jim at home setting up his webcam to talk to Nadia back in the Czech Republic. He starts to dance as he did when he was stripping. Dad stands at the door, looks, then starts dancing himself in the hallway.

The credits roll, on the 96-minute Unrated version on DVD, at 91 minutes in. The theatrical version runs 95 minutes. The DVD box says that in the Unrated version you see more of Nadia, more of the pie, and more of the sex manual. The Unrated version is a marketing ploy, which appears to have worked (just try to find the theatrical version on DVD), but it adds nothing substantial to the film. While you may think the gross-out gags are the heart of this script, look at all the gross-out comedies that do not work. Herz is perceptive enough about his own script to know that the heart of it is the characters and the story. As always.

AMERICAN PIE 2 (2001. Story by David H. Steinberg and Adam Herz. Based on characters created by Adam Herz. Screenplay by Adam Herz. 108 minutes)

It is now one year later. Why? Adam Herz remembered that the first time his "old gang" from high school got together was the following summer. I guess nobody went home from college for Christmas vacation.

No moans on the soundtrack, just rock music. We are on a college campus with people going home for the summer. How do we know? Look at the details in the opening shot. In a voiceover a girl tells Jim they will just be having "friendly good-bye sex," and Jim points out they never had hello sex. They start, and Jim's Dad walks in on Jim and the girl. Everybody is flustered, including the girl's parents when they arrive. How do her parents know to go there if it's Jim's room? The question did not even occur to me until the third time I watched the scene, which means Herz was doing his job getting me involved in the situation. On the other hand, the scene is virtually identical to the opening scene of *American Pie*. As with many sequels, this comes close to being a remake of the first film.

On another (?) campus, Stifler—who let him into college?—and Oz have a conversation similar to the "hard work" conversation in the first film. Oz picks up Heather, who is going to have a summer abroad. Why? Herz may have had trouble figuring out what to do with her and Oz. We will see his solution later.

Paul comes into the guys' fast food place speaking Japanese, since he is dating a Japanese girl. He has dated other girls, but none can compare to Stifler's Mom. The implication is that he has not seen Stifler's Mom for the past year. What, they don't have phones in Great Falls, Michigan?

Well, following the pattern of *American Pie*, it is time for a party at Stifler's, and we see the same kind of action as in the first film. Our guys talk about how they are now college guys and decide they have a chance with the girls who are a grade younger, but two of the girls have seen Jim on the Internet. Paul says, "It's exactly like old times." Jim sees Jessica and Vicky and thinks Vicky has gotten hot, although she looks no different to me than she did in the first film. Kevin talks to her and agrees to just be friends. Paul goes into Stifler's Mom's room, sees pictures of her, smells her perfume, and sees a book on tantra. Stifler finds him there and wants to throw him out. Why would Stifler even let him into the house in the first place? The dialogue establishes that they had a fight a year ago, but they have sort of made up. Justin and John, of the "MILF" conversation, admire Paul for having had Stifler's Mom. Instead of the sperm in the beer, we have John peeing over a railing and hitting Stifler, who thinks it is champagne a girl is pouring on him. Does he have no sense of smell? The joke is mildly amusing, but not quite up to the beer glass sperm. The cops break up the party. We are 19½ minutes into the film, a little longer than the end of the party in the first film.

Kevin calls his brother to tell him that the cops have shut down Stifler's house permanently as a party site, and they have no place to go. The brother tells him that he and his friends rented a beach cottage as a place to party all summer. Nadia is on the phone to Jim from…New York. She is in the country for the summer and will be in Michigan at the end of the summer. Jim tells Oz and Paul that Nadia is coming and he knows she will be disappointed that he cannot make love any better. At 22 minutes, Kevin tells them the plan for the summer beach house. Paul notes that while having the house may allow Jim to get practice before Nadia returns and Oz to have a place for when Heather returns, they cannot afford it. Kevin says he has added one more person to the group.

Yep, it is Stifler. Stifler does provide a laugh or two, but he is an obnoxious character, and the least interesting of the group. Like Michelle, he is a one-joke character, and he cannot really sustain a major role. Herz is making the same mistake Bob Gale did in the screenplay for *Back to the Future Part II* (1989), which turns Biff, the least interesting character in the first film, into a major character. I suspect that Stifler can be fun to write, or at least fun to talk about in story conferences, but he wears out his welcome very quickly. In *American Pie 2*, his enlarged presence reduces the charm the first film had.

The guys arrive at the house, a veritable mansion. Look at the details Herz gives each guy in the montage of their moving in. Why *this* detail for *this* character? To help pay for the cottage, our guys get a job painting a house. Jim complains about how bad he is at sex, but only one person knows for sure how bad. Oz asks where she is. We cut to Tall Oaks Band Camp. Now, band camp was a great running gag, with a great payoff in the first film, but actually going there is a disappointment. There is virtually nothing Herz can do that will live up to what we have imagined goes on there, as you can see by studying the scenes. Jim sneaks into the camp and finds Michelle, who has reverted to being just as goofy as she was in the first part of the first film. But we know now that she is not really like that, so why write her as though she is? Jim says he left three phone messages for her (so there *are* phones in Michigan), but she didn't call him back. She says he "sucked" at sex and agrees to give him pointers.

A beach house party seems to have attracted mostly guys, including Sherman, or "the Sherminator," as he calls himself. Jessica tells Sherman to stop the "Sherminator" routine, since he will never get a girl with it. Stifler asks Jessica how many girls she has had. It is a homophobic question, but an interesting one. We have never seen Jessica with a guy, and she and Vicky do seem close…

At the painting job, the guys just now notice that there are two beautiful young women living in the house. How come they just now noticed? Lazy screenwriting. Stifler sees them with their heads together talking and becomes convinced, being Stifler, that they are lesbians. Paul actually calls Stifler homophobic and says women can hold hands without being gay. Herz is trying to have it both ways here, getting laughs from Stifler's obsessions with lesbians and criticizing it at the same time. He is a little too obviously playing to the young male demographic in the audience.

Oz and Heather are on the phone trying to have phone sex, but are interrupted by Stifler. This could have been a good running gag, but Herz handles it in a lackluster way. Look at the scenes and figure out how could you better develop the idea.

At the painting job, Stifler finds a dildo in the house, which convinces him that the two women *are* lesbians, which proves he knows very little about lesbians (and women). At 46 minutes in, the women discover Stifler, Jim, and Paul. The women realize that the guys think they are gay, and they agree to kiss, fondle, etc. each other, *if* the guys will do it as well…to each other. The humor comes from how desperate Stifler and the others are to see the girls do "lesbian" things. The scene plays on the homosexual panic of the guys, which it does in some funny ways, especially since we like seeing Stifler hoisted on his own petard. Because of that target demographic audience, the film never goes all the way with it, an even bigger problem for the third film. The scene gives the guys interesting reactions to play, but the two women are very generic characters. In the *American Pie* tradition, they are smarter than the guys, but that's about it. To Herz's credit, he leaves the question of whether they are actually gay up in the air until the end of the film. Kevin, outside the house, is trying to talk to the guys on their walkie-talkies. Since this scene is the equivalent of the Nadia–Jim Internet scene in the first film (and notice how much more we know about Nadia than we do the two girls here, and how much more is at stake in that scene), the conversations are overheard by a variety of people. Who would you have overhear these conversations? The entire scene runs ten minutes.

At the beach house, Stifler shows up with a box of porn tapes and lubricating jelly. Stifler's Mom calls to say she will be there at the end of the summer (What sort of life does she lead? Why is she never home? Where is Stifler's dad?), which Paul finds exciting. Jim gets lessons from Michelle, who is becoming a little less goofy than she was in the first film and the beginning of this one. Herz and the others have probably begun to realize that as the one-joke character in the first film, she cannot sustain as a major character in the second film. So they make her everyday behavior a little more "normal," which is not consistent with what we know of her.

Interesting footnote: on the DVD of *American Pie 2* are the casting tapes from the first film. Hannigan's performance on the tape is much less goofy than she was in the film. Given the setup for the payoff line, you can understand why the performance developed the way it did in the film, but it puts limitations on her character in this second film, which Herz and everybody else has tried to finesse by changing rather than developing her character. The character change is more damaging here than Malcolm's from *Jurassic Park* to *The Lost World* was, because in the latter film Koepp just established Malcolm as changed and moved on. Herz, however, seems to waffle back and forth throughout both this and the third film.

The "teaching" scenes with Michelle are funny, and more in keeping with the tone of the first film. Listen to the details Herz gives to Michelle in this scene; you will never think of pre-heating an oven in the same way again. At the beach house, Kevin has his brother's book on his summer fling, but we get even less of that than we do of the "secrets" book in the first film. Like many things, it seems like a holdover from the first film that has not been developed as well as it could be. What would you do with those books? Jim breaks a lamp, fixes it with glue, then inadvertently uses the glue instead of the lube while watching a porn tape. He ends up with one hand glued to his penis and the other to the porn tape. Dad is at the hospital, and we get the worst Dad scene in all the films. Dad is a sweetie, and nowhere else is he as nasty as he is in this scene, telling off a woman in a wheelchair. We are 76 minutes into the film.

The doctor tells Jim the damage to his penis will clear up in eight to nine days, but Nadia is due in seven, so the doctor gives him some cream that should speed up the recovery. We then get a nice scene with Jim's Dad, and we are relieved to see he is back in character. Stifler's little brother shows up at the beach house for the "pussy." Where *are* the parents of these two? When Nadia shows up early, Michelle tells Jim that she will pretend to be his girlfriend, so Nadia will be willing to wait to have sex, and then Jim and Michelle will break up when he is healed. They "break up," with Michelle accusing Jim of just being too sexy. When did Nadia get stupid enough to believe this? Michelle stomps out and sits in the car, where we can see she is actually sad over the "breakup." This is known in acting terms as a "privileged moment," when we see something about the character that nobody else sees, and Hannigan handles it well, even if it is not consistent with what we know about Michelle.

At 84 minutes, the party begins. Vicky is there with a gorgeous guy, which upsets Kevin. He admits to the guys, referring to the final scene of the first film, that he did not take the "next step" to dating other girls. Like the resolution of the Kevin–Vicky story in the first film, this should be more emotional—yes, even in a comedy—than it is. The Kevin–Vicky story has simply never been as compelling as it needed to be to hold its own with the other storylines. Paul says he is still obsessing over a woman he cannot have a future with. Stifler sees his little brother using Stifler's move and sends him out on cop watch, complete with walkie-talkie. Guess whom he ends up talking to? Amber and Danielle, the two women from the painting job. Jim and Nadia go to a lighthouse, but Jim realizes that it is Michelle he wants to be with. Nadia sends him off to his band geek, saying someday she will find hers.

Nadia is talking to Sherman, who uses his "Sherminator" line, which she finds…charming. She knows she has found her geek. The Sherminator? Are we ready for that? It comes out of left field, and is more bizarre than funny, if only because it goes against everything we know about Nadia, Sherman, and Jessica's intelligence in telling him to stop using the line. Stifler and Jessica watch in amazement as Sherman and Nadia go upstairs, then look at each other. Jessica says, "Forget it," and Stifler replies, "Like you have a chance." Well, why not get these two together? And why not get somebody for Jessica, male or female? What does Herz think is wrong with her, anyway?

Little brother shows up with Amber and Danielle, and Stifler tells him they are lesbians. One replies, "We never said that." Ah, but what if they are and end up with Jessica? Sorry. Just looking for a way to get beyond the limitations Herz accepts. Kevin tells Vicky he would rather have her as a friend than not in his life at all. Are we supposed to believe him?

In the morning Oz and Heather—who actually showed up some time ago but who cares?—are in bed. Jim and Michelle are in bed. Stifler is in bed with Amber and Danielle. Okay, where is Paul? And Jessica?

The guys are packing up the truck, and expressing their regret that Paul did not score. Why didn't he? Is he saving his sexual energy? A black car pulls up. It is…Stifler's Mom. Paul goes over, talks to her, asks her name. Jeanine. He says he is moving on and not going to be obsessed with one woman. She says, "You want to get into the car?" He does. On another beach, we see the car rocking and hear the car alarm going off. This is what Paul was saving his sexual energy for. Jeanine says, "Call me 'Stifler's Mom.'" At 103 minutes the credits begin.

The script, and the film, fall into a lot of traps sequels often do. It repeats more of the first film than it needs to. It focuses on the wrong character, in this case Stifler, while under-serving the other characters. It ends up having to change Michelle's character mid-film to make everything work out in story terms. It goes off on tangents (The Sherminator and Nadia!?!) that betray the characters and tone of both the previous film and this one. Still, there was enough of the *American Pie* kind of humor for the film to work, at least in a modest way.

AMERICAN WEDDING (2003. Based on characters created by Adam Herz. Screenplay by Adam Herz. 96 minutes)

We find Jim and Michelle having dinner in a fancy restaurant. It is now three years later. How do we know? Jim prepares to propose to Michelle, but Jim's Dad calls to say Jim left the ring at home and Dad is bringing it to the restaurant. Michelle crawls under the table to give Jim head. Why? Dad arrives, but when Jim stands up, his pants are down. Michelle comes out from under the table, Jim proposes, she accepts. They hug, his pants drop, revealing his erection.

We may have chuckled a little bit, but we haven't laughed yet. Partly because this is more of the same with Jim, Dad, and especially Michelle. The proposal, which does set up the story, comes as something of a surprise. It also takes the film series out of just being about sex and makes it about a social event: a wedding. The problem will become that Herz really does not have enough new insights into weddings to go beyond every other movie about weddings. The raunch of the first film was refreshing because only *Porky's* had really gone there before.

Jim, Michelle, Paul, and Kevin talk at a bar. No Oz. And later, no Jessica. Why have these characters been dropped? This would not be a problem if there were interesting new characters, but there are not.

Jim's parents have a party to congratulate the couple. Michelle's parents, Harold and Mary, arrive. They have somehow, in the three years that Jim and Michelle have been going together, not met Jim. Why is that? Not a clue. And we are unfortunately not given much in the way of characterization for them. Mary likes chocolate, which will pay off later in a gross gag, but Harold has no distinguishing characteristics. Harold and Mary have brought their dogs. Jim and Michelle have smartly agreed not to invite Stifler to either the party or the wedding, but he shows up, driving a school bus. What school system would be crazy enough to hire Stifler to drive a school bus? No explanation. He crashes the party and ends up with the dogs, the cake, and Jim in a set of positions that look obscene when Harold and Mary come into the dining room. Here is a chance to establish some sort of character for Michelle's parents with some—yes—reactions, but no such luck.

Jim, Michelle, and her parents talk. The parents are not happy about the marriage, but aside from the episode with Stifler, we are not sure why. The implication is that Jim will have to prove himself worthy of Michelle. The parents seem remarkably uninformed about their daughter. Stifler meanwhile immediately begins to plan the bachelor party. He is obviously not going to go away. The thinking here, I am sure, is that Stifler breaking up a staid affair like a wedding will be funny. It worked with the Marx Brothers and the opera in *A Night at the Opera* (1935), but Stifler is no Groucho. Stifler is a one-note character being asked to be more. Herz struggles mightily to do more with him in this film, but the character resists, as we will see.

Michelle, for all her, ahem, free-spirited ways, wants a very traditional wedding. And congratulations to Herz: there is not a single "wearing white" joke in the entire film. Not even a good one, as in *Bull Durham*. Jim is upset that Michelle wants him to dance with her at the wedding. Jim is not a dancer. Kevin, who has been reduced from a major character in the first film to a sidekick here, says the wedding is doable, and Paul says he will find out what kind of dress Michelle wants.

Jim learns that Stifler thinks he is coming to the wedding, so Jim confronts him at football practice (whatever happened to lacrosse?), where Stifler is...an assistant coach. What kind of high school is this? Surely they know what Stifler is like, since he went there. Stifler makes a speech to the football players denouncing Jim, saying he has looked out for Jim's sex life through high school. And still Stifler is not fired. He does know how to dance, and offers to teach Jim if Jim will let him come to the wedding and plan the bachelor party. Okay, where did Stifler learn to dance? And why? This may be an attempt to enlarge Stifler's character, but it seems to come out of left field.

Paul has found a store in Chicago that sells the kind of dress Michelle wants. We do not see him learn this because he is hardly even a secondary character in this film. Stifler overhears Paul and invites himself to go to Chicago with them. At 20 minutes in, we are in Chicago. Structurally this is either too early or too late for a side trip. You could start with them in Chicago (but why would they be there in the beginning?) or have them go later (when there is more at stake), but here it seems an interruption in the story. Paul has Stifler stay in the car while they go into the department store because these are Paul's people. Stifler: "They're gay." Paul: "No, they have style and culture." Stifler: "They're gay." Yes, this is typical Stifler, but it is also a setup. The clerk at the store tells them the dressmaker usually hangs out in bars after work. The boys end up in a bar and Stifler hits on a woman who is obviously a guy. Another girl brings a "friend" to meet Stifler: Bear, a large gay man. This evolves into a dance contest between Bear and Stifler, and they end up with some mutual respect for each other. Is Stifler going soft, or at least more sensitive? Well, you could maybe take it that way, but then he is not Stifler. When they are leaving, Stifler says to his friends, "I told you that guy wanted to fuck me." In other words, he changes, he's the same, he changes, he's the same, etc. This will continue through the movie and give us whiplash trying to figure out what Stifler believes. Can you figure out how to make the sensitization of Stifler work? That is, without offending all those young men with homosexual panic who are the major audience for the *American Pie* films?

One of the men at the gay bar turns out to be the dress designer (and why didn't the clerk mention that "Leslie" was a man?) and he agrees to do the dress. Bear gives the boys his card, saying he manages a couple of girls they might want for the bachelor party. At 28 minutes, we are back in Great Falls, where Jim tells Michelle that Leslie will do her dress.

Michelle and Paul (Why Paul? Why not Jim?) pick up Michelle's sister Cadence at the airport. A new character, with lots of possibilities. What is Michelle's sister like? If she is exactly like Michelle, we have already been there. What have we not seen among the female characters in the films so far? What will give you the most interesting character to play off the characters we already have? Alas, she is just a very conventionally cute young woman. She does seem torn between studying and not studying, and she has just broken up with her boyfriend and suggests to Michelle that she wants to get rowdy. But we get very little sense of what "rowdy" means to her. She does not seem as "wild" as Michelle. Paul, however, is immediately in love. Stifler sees Cadence and is also immediately in love.

Paul and Cadence have lunch and Stifler shows up, dressed as a preppy. Why would it occur to Stifler to dress like a preppy? He is pretending to be nice, but it is not clear if he is just doing it to impress Cadence, or if it is part of a program to learn how to behave well at the wedding. You could get laughs either way, but the lack of precision here keeps Herz from getting as much out of it as he could. Stifler meets Mary, and they gush over chocolate. The question of who is going to hold Michelle's grandmother's ring until the wedding comes up. Stifler suggests Mary get to know the three potential best men (Jim has not yet decided who it will be; why not?) before she decides who will carry the ring. Michelle and Jim are astonished to find Stifler helping her mom select flowers. Behind Mary's back he is making gross-out faces. Michelle is upset he is there, and thinks he is just trying to "bone" Cadence. Jim says that for "all the 'fuck's and 'shit's and 'blow me's [Stifler] is a very sensitive person." On what evidence? And if he is, he's not Stifler. After all, nobody accused Groucho of being sensitive.

When Paul learns that Cadence is getting tired of intellectual stuff, he starts behaving like Stifler, which she likes. Jim and his Dad have a conversation about Nadia. Jim asks Dad, "Would you have passed up sex with Nadia?" Dad insists he is a married man. But if you weren't? Well, I am too old. But if you weren't? The rhythm here, in case you do not recognize it, is the lead-up to the final line of *Some Like It Hot* (1959). But if you were the right age? "Why, did she say something?" Now, "Why, did she say something?" is not a *joke*, and neither is *Some Like It Hot*'s "Well, nobody's perfect," but it is the perfect line for the situation and the character. Stifler's character is constantly changing within the film, but Dad's character is well-established and precisely defined. Again, it also helps to have Eugene Levy reading the line. It may not surprise you to learn that this was the only line I laughed at in this movie. Usually I am an easy laugh.

We are approximately halfway through the film and we get a big set-piece scene: the bachelor party arranged by Stifler. He, Paul, and Kevin set up the party at Jim's house when they think nobody will be home. Bear arrives with the two strippers (hookers? We can't tell for sure), Brandi the French maid and Krystal the cop. The party is starting without Jim, but Paul, covering himself in chocolate, discovers a turkey cooking in the oven. Jim, who has been trying to get Michelle's parents to have a serious talk, has arranged to have dinner for them. Hijinks ensue when they show up, so Paul, Kevin, Stifler, Bear, and the girls hide, pop in and out of doors, try to explain what they are doing there, etc. It could have been a classic scene, or at least funnier than it is. To make that kind of farce work, you need to be very precise, which the script simply is not. Stifler is still waffling back and forth between characterizations, and Herz has not provided anybody with interesting reactions. Harold seems to get a bit of pleasure when Krystal hits him with a whip, but that comes out of nowhere and goes nowhere. While the first film created some interesting—in terms of the particular story—female characters, Herz has simply plugged in standard-issue strippers for Brandi and Krystal. What could you do with the characters of two strippers in that situation? For one solution, look at Cherry Forever in *Porky's*.

At the end of the scene, Jim takes the blame for the events, but Mary says that if he puts as much effort into the marriage as he has into the dinner, then she will give her blessing. Since Stifler also accepts some of the blame, she gives him grandmother's ring to hold. We are 53 minutes into the film.

Everyone drives north to the large resort hotel where the wedding will take place. Dad is seen with his mother, who is in a wheelchair. Stifler realizes he has put the ring into the doggie treats he is feeding Harold and Mary's dogs. So instead of going beyond a kiss with Candace, his attention, much to Cadence's irritation, is focused on waiting for the dogs to poop. Which they do, and he finds the one with the ring. He places it in a doily. Harold and Mary see the doily, not having seen what went into it. Mary assumes it is chocolate and wants a taste, but Stifler has to eat it before she does. Herz is trying to get as much out of the buildup as he can, but with all the talk, it certainly occurred to me that *somebody* ought to be able to smell it, being fairly fresh and fragrant. If you are doing comedy, go as fast as you can so logical people like me do not question it.

At 64 minutes Jim's Grandma meets Michelle for the first time and gets upset that she is not Jewish. Where did that come from? It seems to be played for comedy, but it takes us out of the comedy of the rest of the film. And then it is pretty much dropped from the film, as though, having brought it up, Herz didn't know what to do with it. If you cannot figure out how to use some great inspiration, drop it; it probably was not that great an inspiration in the first place. Cadence apologizes to Stifler for freaking him out with the kiss, and they agree to meet in the linen closet at midnight. Stifler steals some champagne, but in the process turns off the electricity in the greenhouse, causing all the wedding flowers to wilt (in one night?). Jim asks Stifler to leave, and he does. If the film and Stifler's character had been working until this point, we might shed a cardboard tear for Stifler, but it has not and we do not. He finds a flower shop, wakes the owner, gets the boys on his football team to help make up some new flowers, and delivers them all in his school bus. So that's why he drives a school bus. But the lacrosse team could have done the flowers just as well.

Cadence tells Stifler he's an asshole and asks if he brought the flowers to have sex with her or help the wedding. Stifler replies, "Both," then wonders with Paul whether he is going soft. Paul reminds him that he, Paul, has had sex with Stifler's mom, "Twice." Whoa, where did that come from? We have not seen or heard from Stifler's Mom since the end of the second film, nor, apparently, has Paul. Cadence comes to tell Stifler she is ready to have sex with him in the linen closet. Michelle asks Jim's Dad for help in writing her vows, which eventually evolves into a sweet scene, in which he suggests she not include in the vows that Jim shaved his balls for her. Meanwhile Kevin asks two groomsmen, Justin and John (remember them?), to take care of Grandma. Stifler runs to the linen closet. Kevin finds the groomsmen and asks what happened to Grandma. They say they have safely stashed her. Stifler is in the closet without light. And Cadence is talking to somebody…outside the hotel. Kevin and Paul open the closet door. Stifler freaks, Grandma slaps his face and says, "Focus."

At 83 minutes in, the wedding starts. Kevin is kidding Stifler about Grandma and Stifler replies, "Pussy's pussy," which seems to contradict his reaction in the closet. Dad says to Kevin, "Look at the smile on my mother's face. Do you know how long she's been waiting for a day like this?" And what about her objection to Michelle? Grandma doesn't say anything more about it. When Michelle asks Jim what happened, he tells her Stifler "talked" to her. Surely Michelle of all people can take the truth. But is this the solution to the problem of racism in the world: have Stifler have sex with all the racists so they will forget about it? I somehow don't think that is very practical. Michelle says in her vows that love is "not just a feeling, but something you do. It's a dress, a visit to band camp, a special haircut." She may be civilized after all.

At 86 minutes the reception begins. Jim and Michelle dance, and she is delighted he has learned how. Harold and Mary are emotional, but we are not sure at what. Is it just that their daughter is married? Or, since it comes after the dance, do they know the meaning of the dance? There is no indication they do. Stifler and Cadence dance. And in the greenhouse overlooking the reception, Paul finds…Stifler's Mom. Where has she been the last three years? They agree they are both over each other, but she mentions she had a two-room suite at the hotel, and off they go.

On the dance floor, Michelle says she is still a "nympho" and Jim is still a "perv," but they are "normal." Now that is an interesting idea for Herz to bring out at this point, or rather it would be if he had prepared for it. Unlike Ron Shelton (*Bull Durham*) and Bill Condon (*Kinsey*), but unfortunately like most male American screenwriters, Herz has trouble writing a sexually active woman as someone…normal. See Jessica for the most obvious example. Jim has always been a more or less normal person, but Michelle has had something of a split personality: cute and nerdy, but highly sexed. Maybe Herz simply could not figure out how to bring those two elements together, since his original concept was that she was a one-joke character. This is a problem with both Michelle and Stifler in this film, and is often a problem in trying to develop shallowly conceived characters in sequels (and televisions series that spin off supporting characters into their own series).

After Michelle and Jim's conversation, the film fades out. It's over, isn't it? Yes, it is, but Herz has added a scene that has Justin and John trying to spy on Paul and Stifler's Mom in the bathtub. It is not much of a scene, doesn't tell us anything we do not already know, and is certainly not worth coming back out of what appeared to be a final fadeout for.

The film simply does not work, for all the reasons suggested here. It is not as fresh as the first film, and it gets away from the emphasis on sex of the first two films. It gets into the social event of the wedding, without having anything fresh to say about it. It tries to develop two of the characters, Michelle and Stifler, that resist development. It drops several of the interesting characters from the first two films (Nadia and Jessica) or reduces their roles drastically (Kevin). It also probably made its money back. Why? Because we wanted to see what happened to those characters, particularly Jim and, however limited, Michelle. But like most sequels and series, there was a law of diminishing returns, both artistically and financially.

In 2005 Universal released another sort-of-sequel direct to DVD, called *American Pie Presents Band Camp*. Having read all of the above about the first three movies, you will understand that even before I heard the plot of the fourth film—Stifler's younger brother being sent to band camp—I avoided seeing it. In 2006 there was another direct-to-DVD sequel, *American Pie 5: The Naked Mile*. Bullets apparently cannot kill it.

Sources
Adam Herz's background comes from the biographical entry on him on IMDb. His comments on the development of *American Pie 2* are from the documentary *The Baking of American Pie 2*, which appears on the DVD of *American Pie 2*. The cast audition tapes for *American Pie* also appear on the DVD of *American Pie 2*, as do some interesting outtakes, particularly some Jim and Michelle scenes.

13

SHORT TAKES ON SOME NOT-QUITE-SO-GOOD SCREENPLAYS

THE films are in chronological order of release.

> **SPEED** (1994. Screenplay by Graham Yost. 116 minutes)

The basic idea is, of course, preposterous. If a bomb on a Santa Monica Big Blue Bus was set to go off if the bus went under fifty miles per hour, the movie would be over in ten minutes. Graham Yost, however, has told the story in inventive ways. The script and film are considerably different from the brief description actress Halle Berry gave in a 1995 interview, "One of the script versions they sent me, the bus never got out of Dodger Stadium, it just kept driving around and around the parking lot!"

Structurally, the script could conceivably fit into Syd Field's paradigm. It is 107 pages long (although there are also many partial pages scattered throughout). The first major plot point, which Field says should come about pages 25–27, is the explosion of the first bus, which tells us that Fisk (Payne in the film), the bomber, is at work again. This comes on page 24. Plot point two should come, according to Field, between pages 85 and 90, and if you consider the second plot point to be Fisk on the phone demanding the money after the bus explodes into the jet at the Los Angeles International Airport (LAX), it arrives on pages 91–92. Close enough.

On the other hand, *Speed*, in both the reading and the watching, does not feel like a script strapped to the Field rack. There is simply too much going on at any given time and handled in too many inventive ways to feel mechanical. The first act of the script could be considered to be the bombing of the elevator, ending with the party with Jack Traven and the cops. The first act lasts 22 pages (27 minutes in the film, which includes the terrific credit sequence, not described in the script). For all the explosions, falling elevators, and gunfire, the first act is more a suspense sequence than an action sequence (and the action is fairly slow speed).

The first act is reminiscent of the long opening of *Raiders of the Lost Ark* (1981), but it also sets up the main storyline, although in a stylistically different way. The elevator sequence is an interior sequence, with the action in vertical lines (the elevator cables, Jack being lowered head-first to the elevator), unlike the main section of the film, where the action is exterior and horizontal. Make your action scenes different, yadda, yadda…

The second act of the script, the bus with the bomb rigged on it, begins on page 23 and ends on page 91. The emphasis in this section is on action as well as suspense. Yost is very inventive in virtually every aspect of this segment. The bus is eventually driven not by its regular driver but by a (gifted) amateur. The bus stays on the freeway from pages 28 to 44A, then gets off onto city streets, where it has to deal with cross traffic and, in one of Yost's more inventive touches, that old cinematic standby, the baby carriage. Since audiences have seen the baby carriage in jeopardy from *Potemkin* (1925) to *The French Connection* (1971), we assume it is in jeopardy here. Yes and no. Look at Yost's payoff.

The bus then gets back on the freeway from pages 51 to 65, but this turns out to be even more dangerous for them. Fisk sets off a bomb when Helen, one of the passengers, tries to get off the bus, killing her and reminding the audience that lives can be lost: *Speed* has one of the lowest body counts of any recent big-budget American thriller. Then of course the freeway turns out not to be completed, and the bus must jump the break. After that, there is nothing else that can be done on the freeway, so Yost brings the bus into LAX where it can blow up in an appropriately flamboyant fashion. After all, Yost has been promising us an explosion since this act began, and the explosion has to top the one at the beginning of the sequence.

Act three, from pages 91 to 107, takes us inside again, but this time we are horizontal, and going, if anything, faster than we were on the freeway. The focus now closes in on Jack, Annie, and Fisk, with the other police disappearing after the threesome get on the subway. The film ends with not another explosion, but a flashy crash and, by having the subway train come up in front of the Chinese Theatre in Hollywood, a reminder that it is just a movie.

Speed being an action picture, and a contemporary one, there is not a lot of characterization, and as is true with many American films, there is less in the film than there was in the script. In the party in the bar after Jack and Harry receive medals, there are several bits of information about Jack that did not make it into the film. Annie is also diminished from the script to the film. When I first saw *Speed*, I assumed that since nobody talked about what sort of work Annie did, there was going to be a payoff where we discover she is a cop or a defense attorney or something interesting. There is no such payoff, and the reason is that her occupation is dealt with in a scene early in the script, not in the film, and then never mentioned again.

Characterization is also limited for the other people on the bus. We are a long way from *Stagecoach* (1939), where all the passengers are given detailed stories, or even from the *Airport* movies (1970ff). At least there is an accurate racial cross section, typical of busses in the Los Angeles area, but nothing much is made of it. In the film we never learn why Ray, the Hispanic, was worried about the cop on the bus, and why he had the gun. In the script (70) he explains to one of the other passengers that he stole the gun from his cousin for protection. That's too textured a scene for this movie.

There are no guest stars on this bus. There is only speed.

Sources

The script under consideration for this essay is the revised draft of August 31, 1993, with eight sets of revisions dated between September 3 and December 1, 1993. The Halle Berry interview is in the April 1995 issue of *Movieline*. A longer, more detailed version of these comments appeared as "*Speed*: Speed, Only Speed," in *Creative Screenwriting*, winter 1995.

> **DEEP IMPACT** (1998. Screenplay by Bruce Joel Rubin, Michael Tolkin, and, uncredited, John Wells. 120 minutes)

Deep Impact was originally conceived as an unofficial remake of the 1951 science fiction film *When Worlds Collide*. In the earlier film two heavenly objects, one a roving planet, the other a comet, are coming toward Earth. The comet will hit and destroy earth, but the planet will pass by first, causing tidal waves and assorted other trouble. A Noah's Ark of a rocket is built to fly to the new planet. It is a clunky script, and the film is remembered today for a single striking shot of New York City being flooded. I once heard George Pal, the legendary producer of the film, say that one effect cost $1.98. He was only slightly exaggerating.

The first screenwriter hired for *Deep Impact* was Bruce Joel Rubin, who remembered seeing the first film and standing around on a street corner as a kid for four hours afterward talking to his friend about it. The first director attached to the project was Steven Spielberg. As mentioned before, one of Spielberg's weaknesses as a director has been a lack of interest in character, and his idea for the film was to do it all in the form of television coverage. As Rubin said years later, "I think it was a really interesting *idea*." We will see later why it probably would not have worked on film. Rubin wanted to cover a lot of different characters in the film, but Spielberg picked and chose the storylines he was interested in. Rubin eventually left the project and was replaced by Michael Tolkin, and there was additional work on the script by John Wells, the showrunner of the television series *ER* (1994ff). By then Spielberg had left the project, and he was replaced by Mimi Leder, a longtime director on *ER*.

Leder's work for television and film shows a much greater interest in character than Spielberg's, and Wells wrote to that strength. What the final script of *Deep Impact* does is take the story and its characters seriously, something unexpected in a big-budget science fiction movie. Look at the gallery of characters the various writers have come up with, and more important, the scenes they provide for them. Look at the scenes between Jenny, the television reporter (the remains of the original idea of doing the story through media coverage), and her divorced mother and father.

The problem with the script is structural. The first half follows Jenny as she uncovers the information about the Wolf-Biederman comet approaching Earth. Astronauts are sent up to try to destroy the comet. Their attempt is the biggest suspense and action scene in the film, but it comes less than halfway through. They only succeed in blowing the comet into two parts, so now the film has to essentially start all over again, with an enormous amount of mid-picture exposition. Jenny gives a lot of exposition in the form of her television newscasts, and here you can begin to see why Spielberg's idea of doing the film only as media reporting would not have worked. For all the different events reported on, they are just that: reported on. We stay outside of them while we hear about them and watch them from an emotional distance. The idea might have worked in a low-budget art film, but not in a film intended to be a big crowd-pleaser. On the other hand, Spielberg made the scene of a lot of people reacting to the coverage of the Olympic massacre work in *Munich* (2005), but a) that is only a scene, and b) it works because it is based on—wait for it—reactions.

One half of the comet is destroyed, but the other half lands in the Atlantic Ocean, causing tidal waves. Yes, there are shots of New York City being flooded, in tribute to *When Worlds Collide*, but the tidal wave shot that sticks in the mind from this film is one of Jenny and her father facing the wave alone on a deserted beach. In other words, a character scene.

The first preview screenings of *Deep Impact* did not go well, and there was additional cutting and reshooting, but it was assumed that the picture would not do well. Paramount thought *Deep Impact* might pull in $20 million the first weekend, $30 million tops. It grossed over $40 million the first weekend. Sometimes, character does count.

Sources
The history of the writing of *Deep Impact* is from "Two Hours to Make a Deep Impact: An interview with Bruce Joel Rubin," in *Creative Screenwriting*, July/August 1998. The previews and the industry attitude about *Deep Impact* are from Peter Bart's *The Gross* (St. Martin's Press, 1999).

> **ARMAGEDDON** (1998. Story by Robert Roy Pool and Jonathan Hensleigh. Adaptation by Tony Gilroy and Shane Salerno. Screenplay by Jonathan Hensleigh and J.J. Abrams. 150 minutes)

There is this asteroid heading directly toward Earth and—wait a minute, didn't we just see this picture two months ago? Wasn't it called *Deep Impact*? Well, yes and no.

Deep Impact took the story and its characters seriously. What *Armageddon* does is take a whole different tone with similar material. While *Deep Impact* is relatively restrained, restraint is not a word anybody connected with *Armageddon* has ever heard. Instead of the slow character scenes, here we get fast scenes with cartoon-shallow characters. Structurally *Armageddon* is better, since the destruction of the asteroid is the big action scene at the end. Instead of exposition and techno-babble, we get action: oil-driller (huh? I told you this was a cartoon) Harry Stamper rounding up a crew of "roughnecks," getting trained by NASA, and rocketing off into space. And, in keeping with the tone of the whole enterprise, a lot of wise-ass dialogue. Critics hated the film.

And it was a big success, grossing $201 million to *Deep Impact*'s $140 million. Would it have been as big a hit if it had come out before *Deep Impact*? Maybe. *Deep Impact* might not have been as big a hit as it was if it came out after *Armageddon*, since it would have been hard to take *Deep Impact* as seriously after the comic excesses of *Armageddon*. The point for screenwriters is that you can handle the same idea in two completely different ways and have them each work in their own way. And it helps if your serious version comes out first.

Sources

Peter Bart's *The Gross* (see above) discusses *Armageddon* as well as *Deep Impact*. The total grosses are from "The Top 250 of 1998," *Weekly Variety*, January 11–17, 1999.

> **SHREK** (2001. Based on the book by William Steig. Screenplay by Ted Elliott, Terry Rossio, Joe Stillman, and Roger S.H. Schulman. 90 minutes)

Nice story: Shrek, an ogre, tries to get Farquaad, the ruler of the kingdom, to stop putting all the magical characters into Shrek's swamp. Farquaad agrees, if Shrek will bring him Princess Fiona, since Farquaad needs to marry a princess to secure his position. Shrek finds Fiona, they fall in love, and in a really anti-Hollywood twist, she turns out to be an ogre herself. Okay, a cute ogre, but still…

Nice characters. Nice dialogue. A few nice in-jokes with the magical characters.

And, since this is a production of DreamWorks, which is run by Jeffery Katzenberg, who was kicked out of Disney by its then-boss Michael Eisner, there is a little satire of Disney.

Well, some satire of Disney.

Oh, all right, a lot of satire of Disney.

A *whole* lot of satire of Disney.

A POUNDING, HONKING, OVERBEARING SATIRE OF DISNEY.

Did I mention there is satire of Disney in the film?

Sometimes screenplays get bent out of shape by the egos of the stars. Sometimes they get bent out of shape by the egos of the directors. Here is a nice script bent out of shape by the ego of the studio head. So what you should do as the writer is write the best script you can, and if the other egos involved want to bend it out of shape, they probably will. You now understand why writers become producers and directors: to try to protect their material.

Two other things: all the Disney satire did not kill the picture, which was a big hit. Probably for the same reason that in Catholic countries, pornography usually portrays priests and nuns. Disney is our religion, and there was a certain joy in being sacrilegious about it.

Second thing: sanity prevailed with *Shrek 2* (2004) and *Shrek the Third* (2007). There was no more satire of Disney, and the satire of Beverly Hills was relatively restrained in the former, and while the satire of high school was obvious in the later, the satire of Disney was subtle. Well, relatively subtle. Even people with huge egos can learn to control themselves.

Source
For a discussion on the development of the characters in *Shrek*, see the interview with Ted Elliott and Terry Rossio in *Creative Screenwriting*, May/June 2001.

> **PEARL HARBOR** (2001. Screenplay by Randall Wallace. 183 minutes)

Pearl Harbor is a guilty pleasure for me. I grew up in the forties and beyond, watching World War II movies, and *Pearl Harbor* includes elements from almost every World War II movie ever made. There's the hotshot pilot Rafe, usually played in the forties by Tyrone Power. Rafe flies for the R.A.F., just like Power did in *A Yank in the R.A.F.* (1941). He has a quiet friend and romantic rival, Danny, the part played earlier by Dana Andrews opposite Power in *Crash Dive* (1943). There is the object of their affection, Evelyn, played earlier by Betty Grable, or Anne Baxter, or pick your forties female lead. There is the pre-attack life in Pearl Harbor, seen in *From Here to Eternity* (1953) and *In Harm's Way* (1965). There is the spectacle of the attack from *Tora! Tora! Tora!* (1970). There are the nurses from *So Proudly We Hail* (1943) and *Cry 'Havoc'* (1943). There is even the sneaky Japanese spy from a hundred or so "B" pictures. And finally there is the Doolittle raid on Tokyo from *Thirty Seconds over Tokyo* (1944). *Pearl Harbor* is one-stop shopping for all your World War II film needs.

Needless to say, most of those earlier films handle the material much better. The special effects in *Pearl Harbor* are state of the art, but they go on and on and on. The film is, to use an old line from the *New Yorker*, inhumanly overproduced. However, enough of what Randall Wallace attempted in the script survives to hold the film together. Wallace was interested in how America turned from isolationist in the thirties to involvement with the rest of the world. Look at how those elements are present in the film and support the structure.

The producer of *Pearl Harbor* was Jerry Bruckheimer, noted for his critically condemned large-scale action films. But if you look carefully at his films, you'll notice that the scripts have interesting ideas for stories, even if they are overproduced. It is not therefore surprising that Bruckheimer has been one of the few film producers to have extensive success in television, where story and script are more of a necessity because of limited budgets and lack of special effects. If, like me, you like stories and characters, you may prefer Bruckheimer's television work (the *CSI* franchises [2000ff], etc.) to his films.

Sources:
David Konow's "The Last Epic" in *Creative Screenwriting*, May/June 2001, includes quotes from Wallace talking about his intentions with the script. An interesting discussion of the differences between *From Here to Eternity*, *Tora! Tora! Tora!*, and *Pearl Harbor*, and what those differences tell us about changes in Hollywood, appears in the fourth edition of David A. Cook's *A History of Narrative Film* (Norton, 2004).

SLEEPOVER (2004. Screenplay by Elisa Bell. 89 minutes)

Producer Chuck Weinstock called writer Elisa Bell with what the late screenwriting teacher Marvin Borowsky used to call a "producer's idea." That's an idea that is so vague and general, or else such an obvious ripoff of some other film, that you should approach it with extreme caution. His idea: young girls moving from middle school to high school have a sleepover. It certainly appealed to Bell, since she had had sleepovers when she was that age. If a producer comes up with a "producer's idea" and you think you can make something out of it, why not?

Bell realized the girls could not stay in the house all night. Why not? John Michael Hayes, *Rear Window*, enough said. Bell happened to overhear some kids who were obviously on a scavenger hunt. So what could be the stakes for a scavenger hunt that would get the girls out of the house? A promise by the socially prominent girls of the school that they could have the best lunch spot on campus if they did everything on the list. The list includes getting into a nightclub, where they discover one of their teachers, and getting the underpants of one of the boys our main girl Julie likes. Okay, now wait a minute.

These are girls not yet in high school, but they are going into a club and flirting with a teacher? And winding up in a boy's bathroom while trying to get his underpants? Yes, these could certainly be wish-fulfillment fantasies for tween girls, but they are also on the border-line of being just plain creepy.

Bell and the director manage to handle those scenes reasonably well. The picture stuck me as cute, and not as creepy as the plot summary might indicate. The picture opened to decent business the first week-end, but then it dropped off 72 percent the second weekend. Ouch. Obviously both mothers and tween daughters who saw it found it creepy enough to give it bad word of mouth. What happened? The little red dress.

Alexa Vega, whom we saw as a kid playing Carmen in the *Spy Kids* movies (2001ff), plays Julie. We saw her as a kid, but here she is begin-ning to grow up. The little red dress she wears through most of the film is one of her mother's dresses cut down to fit. It fits in some interesting ways. The dress is not overtly sexy, but it does emphasize her budding sensuality. Teen comedies handle sex, but, like most American films, have trouble with sensuality. The film was rated PG for "thematic ele-ments involving…some sensuality," so the ratings board got it. Unfor-tunately the film's almost inadvertent emphasis on tween sensuality unnerved both mothers and daughters.

Sometimes you can write a nice little script and the smallest detail of the production can cause trouble. As my wife said, little red dresses have been known to cause lots of problems. Sometimes you *have* to sweat the small stuff.

Source
Elisa Bell's "*Sleepover: How I Turned My Adolescence into Research*," in *Scr(i)pt*, July/August 2004, goes into more detail on the creation of the script. The box office results are from IMDb.

THE INCREDIBLES (2004. Screenplay by Brad Bird. 115 minutes)

The GAPs are back, in this case with Brad Bird. This film gets off to a great start, showing how superheroes were put out of work because of all the problems superhero behavior would cause if it happened in a real world. Look at how Bird uses what we know and what we assume about the behavior of superheroes and how the world reacts to them, and then tweaks both of those ideas. The next section is equally great, as the family tries to deal with involuntary retirement. Here Bird uses what we think about our daily lives and plays that off against what the superheroes think about it. And look at the characters' reactions to the experience.

Then the superheroes have to get back into action. Since they are all out of shape, they have to get new costumes, which allows Bird to bring in a great character, the costume designer Edna "E" Mode. She is a combination of movie costume designer legend Edith Head, actor Linda Hunt, and who knows what else. The timing of her entrance is perfect, and Bird gets as much out of her as he can.

Then the problems begin. The Incredibles are back on the job, which gives them actions to do, but we begin to lose the attitudes and reactions that made the first half of the film so fresh. The action begins to seem conventional. The look of the film, which has been equally fresh, begins to look like a collection of animated variations on Ken Adam's designs for the James Bond movies (the archvillain's lair, the group of islands from *The Man with the Golden Gun* [1974]), with shots that reference other action films (the cars in traffic that pop up in the background from *Independence Day* [1996]). Did Bird run out of imagination halfway through the film?

> **THE UPSIDE OF ANGER** (2005. Screenplay by Mike Binder. 118 minutes)

Terry Wolfmeyer's husband runs off, she assumes, with a young Swedish woman. Terry has to deal with her four daughters in their teens and twenties, and she develops a romantic relationship with a former big league baseball player, Danny, who is now a radio talk show host. Binder has written great characters in Terry and Danny, and Joan Allen and Kevin Costner knock them out of the park. The four daughters are almost as good. The film is about real people and real relationships. What's not to like?

The little red dress of this screenplay: where does Terry's money come from? We, and Terry, think her husband has run off, so presumably he is not sending her any money. We find out later that—spoiler alert—he did not run off, but died in a fall in the woods beyond their backyard, which explains why no money is coming from him, and why Binder does not have Terry chase him down. Terry does not appear to have a job. And she spends a lot on booze. And she has a big, beautiful house. And four daughters in various colleges, schools, conservatories, etc. So as much as we are trying to concentrate on the Terry–Danny romance, we keep wondering, how can she afford this? All it would have taken is a line on the order of "Well, at least we have money from Mother's estate" to put our minds at ease. What does the audience *have* to know to keep them in the story? And how simply can you let them know it?

> ***JUNEBUG*** (2005. Written by Angus MacLachlan. 107 minutes)

Madeleine is an art dealer in Chicago who meets and marries George. She is worldly and sophisticated, he is from a small town in the South. When she learns of a potential artist for her gallery that lives near his hometown, they go back. She has not met his family before, and the film is about her dealing with the interesting gallery of characters in the family. MacLachlan has written great parts in Madeleine and the family members, and we get a non-clichéd look at small-town southern life.

The problem is that he has not written a part for George. He is a blank, and often he is simply not there while Madeleine deals with what is after all *his* family. We get no conversations between Madeleine and George discussing what his family is going to be like before they see them, what they *are* like once they get there, or what they *were* like after they leave. George appears to be the star of the family, but we have no idea why. One family member says to him late in the film that he has always been there for them. He has?! We have seen no evidence of it in the film.

If you are going to write a character piece, you have to make sure the characters are properly balanced.

The Bad

14

TITANIC

> **TITANIC** (1997. Screenplay by James Cameron. 194 minutes)

EVER since the *Titanic* sank on April 15, 1912, there have been movies about it. In 1943 the Nazis made *Titanic* as propaganda about the excesses of British capitalism. Joseph Goebbels, the Minister of Propaganda, banned it because he thought Germans undergoing Allied bombing might panic as the passengers did. Goebbels had already had the film's director killed, but for treasonous statements rather than creative differences; some producers are tougher than others.

The two best films about the *Titanic* were the 1958 British film *A Night to Remember*, with a screenplay by Eric Ambler based on the 1955 bestselling non-fiction book by Walter Lord, and the 1953 *Titanic*. That script, by Charles Brackett, Richard L. Breen, and Walter Reisch, tells the story of the fictional, upper-class Richard and Julia Sturges and their children returning to America. The story foreshadows James Cameron's script for the 1997 film. The 1953 script is so dramatically powerful (look at the scene at the dining table between Richard and Julia), it won the Academy Award for Best Story and Screenplay. And it only runs 98 minutes, half the length of Cameron's film. Longer is not better.

After some faux 1912 newsreels of the *Titanic* and the main credits over the ocean, we see Brock Lovett, the expedition leader, inside a deep-sea-diving device. He says that coming on the wreckage of the *Titanic* "gets me every time," which tells us this is not his first trip. When he starts to get poetic, Bodine, a hairy assistant out of a Michael Crichton film (see the hairy assistants in *Twister* [1996], for example), says, "You are so full of shit, boss." An odd way to begin a film attempting to be a great, nostalgic, romantic epic. Perhaps Cameron is suggesting differences between the romantic past and the more cynical present, but that is not carried through the film.

Through Brock's video camera we see a lot of the wreckage. A whole lot. Longer is not better. The explorer's mechanical claws eventually find a safe, and someone says, "Payday." Now, are Brock and his crew scientific researchers or just looters? The film never really clarifies this. At any given point, they seem to be one or the other. In Cameron's first draft there are scenes with Brock's "money guy" that make it clear he is after the loot. At nearly 9 minutes in, on the surface research vessel, a lab assistant shows Brock a sketch they have found in a file in the safe. It is a rather mediocre sketch of a nude woman wearing a necklace. A necklace Brock has a photo of. And the sketch is dated April 14, 1912, the night the *Titanic* went down.

In an airy little house, Old Rose (that's how she is identified in the credits, folks) perks up when she hears a discussion on television about the *Titanic*, and when Brock shows the drawing, she says, "I'll be god-damned." In spite of her name in the credits, she is not senile and she still has a feisty spirit, unlike most elderly people in American films.

Old Rose asks Brock on the phone if he has found the "Heart of the Ocean." She says she is the woman in the picture. Why is this not the heart-stopping moment it should be? Old Rose and Lizzy, her grand-daughter, arrive on the vessel, and Rose sees the drawing. Lizzy is not sure the woman in the picture is Old Rose (how would you react to a picture like that of your grandmother?), but Old Rose assures her she was "quite a dish." Brock shows Old Rose some artifacts he brought up. We do not get as much of her reaction as we should. This should have been like the scene in *The Grapes of Wrath* where Ma is throwing out knickknacks. We do not know exactly *what* each one means to Ma, but we can tell from her reaction that it means *something*. Brock asks Old Rose if she is "ready to go back to *Titanic*."

A word here on language. From the beginning Brock has referred to it simply as "*Titanic*," rather than "the *Titanic*." Okay, researchers de-velop their own phraseology, but just "*Titanic*," without the article, does not fall easily on the ears, especially since no point is made of why he uses that construction. My guess is that Cameron found that research-ers spoke of it this way and he decided to put it into the film. But he has everybody refer to it that way, except the TV interviewer earlier in the film. I once asked Gloria Stuart, who played Old Rose, about it, and she had no idea. She's a pro, and that's what was in the script, so she read it. I have the suspicion, given what we know about Cameron's ego (cf., using the "king of the world" line from the film when he won one of his Oscars), that it came down to this being a JAMES CAMERON film from a JAMES CAMERON screenplay, directed by JAMES CAMERON, and the actors were damn well going to use the language that JAMES CAMERON wanted them to. Where is Goebbels when you need him?

Brock and Bodine show Old Rose a computer simulation of the *Titanic* hitting the iceberg and sinking. This is a rather clever preview of coming attractions, since we know the full version we will get in the film will be more detailed. We get the technicalities now so we will only have to worry about the characters then. As Old Rose begins to tell her story, we see a full-color shot of the *Titanic* being loaded at Southampton. It is now 21 minutes in. Go through that first twenty-one minutes and figure out what you could cut to get us into the story quicker.

Young Rose (hereinafter just Rose), her mother Ruth, and her fiancé Cal Hockley arrive at the pier. Rose is unimpressed with the ship, but Ruth says, "So this is the ship they say is unsinkable," to which Cal replies, "It *is* unsinkable." Now, isn't this a little obvious? Yes, it does establish Ruth and Cal as wrong-headed, but what would be some subtler ways to do it? And this is not the last time Cameron will have characters emphasize their own stupidity by talking about how unsinkable the ship is. Look at the ways Brackett, Breen, Reisch, and Ambler handled the same kind of material.

Rose and the others board while we see some of the lower class passengers checked for fleas. Cameron is trying to make the class distinctions a theme, but they are handled in only the most obvious ways. As Rose boards the ship, we hear Old Rose talking about how the *Titanic* was a "ship of dreams" for most people, but a "slave ship" to her, that she was being taken back to America "in chains." We see nothing of that in her reactions to Ruth and Cal in this scene. As he often does, Cameron has Old Rose's voiceover give us details that we should get hints of visually but do not. Balance between voiceovers and visuals is fundamental to screenwriting. Listen to *Y Tu Mamá También* again.

On the pier Jack and his friend Fabrizio play cards, and Jack says, "When you got nothing, you got nothing to lose." Which tells us, well, what? That he is a gambling man? Yes, but anything else? He wins two tickets in steerage on the *Titanic*. At 27 minutes into the film, the ship sails. This is obviously designed for the special effects team to show off their skills. And we get a lot of the art direction of the ship as a waiter shows Cal his private promenade deck. Rose unpacks the paintings she has bought in Europe. They are Picassos, but since this is before Picasso became famous, we are supposed to admire her adventurous taste in art. Guess what Cal's reaction is to them? Referring to Picasso, he says, "He won't amount to a thing, trust me. At least they were cheap."

At a stop at Cherbourg, we see Molly Brown get on board, but in one of the least interesting entrances for a character ever. She is identified in an Old Rose voiceover, including the knowledge that she would become known as "The Unsinkable Molly Brown" for surviving the sinking. Do we need to see her get on at Cherbourg? No. Cameron could introduce her better by using her first scene on the ship as her entrance.

Out to sea, Captain Smith gives the orders to open her up. Smith is a potentially interesting character, but not in this script. Look at how the same character is dealt with in the 1953 *Titanic* and in *A Night to Remember*. As the ship picks up speed, Jack and Fabrizio go to the bow and stand with their arms out, and Jack says, "I'm the king of the world!" the line that would come back to bite James Cameron in the ass. And a line that is not in the first draft of the screenplay.

At what appears to be the number one table in the dining room, we meet Bruce Ismay, of the White Star Lines (owner of the *Titanic*), and Thomas Andrews, who designed the ship. Ismay, throughout the film, is given only one note to play: pride in the ship and the desire to show it off. Andrews has a slightly more varied palette: he is proud of his work, but very aware of the limitations of the ship. Also at the table are Rose, Ruth, Cal, and Molly Brown. When Cal stops Rose from smoking (because it is not socially proper), Molly Brown asks him if he is going to cut her meat for her. See what I meant about that being a better entrance for her? Molly asks Ismay if he thought up the name "Titanic," and he says he did, that he wanted a name to convey size, strength, and stability. Again, obvious foreshadowing. Rose wonders what Dr. Freud would say about this obsession with size. Cal insists to Molly that he will have to start minding what Rose reads. Is Cal getting a little one-note for you?

Jack sees Rose on the upper deck and is struck by her beauty. She notices him, but that is all. It is 37 minutes into the film. Over a shot of the glamorous first-class passengers, we hear Old Rose tell us that she saw what her life would be like: parties, chatter, etc. We see none of this in Rose's reactions to the people. Rose runs to the stern, climbs the rail, and is about to jump, but when she slips, Jack grabs her. Rose tells Cal that she was leaning over the rail and slipped and Jack rescued her. He goes along with that, although Lovejoy, Cal's valet, notes to Jack that he obviously had time to untie his shoes before he grabbed her. Cal asks Jack to join them for dinner the following night.

In the stateroom, Cal tells Rose that he knows she has been "melancholy," so he gives her a present: the Heart of the Ocean diamond necklace. We get a repeat of exposition about it. Rose seems impressed by the necklace, at least as this point. Cal asks her to "open up her heart" to him, but we cannot tell what her reaction is. What would her reaction be?

On the promenade deck the next day, Jack tells Rose about himself. She thanks him for his discretion, like the proper young lady she is. She explains to him what we have already heard from Old Rose's voiceover about the "inertia" in her life. He asks, "Do you love him?" Now, she has just talked about her deeper feelings, but she gets upset with this question and thinks it is "rude." Jack pushes the question and she starts to walk away, then out of nowhere her mood changes as she grabs his sketchpad, asking what he is always carrying around. Is this woman bipolar? She seems to be at least three different characters in this scene: the spoiled society girl, the sensitive young woman, and a pleasant companion. You might be able to tie all those together in a scene, but Cameron doesn't. And then she says the sketches are "rather good," but if her taste runs to modern art, why would she like these medio-cre realist sketches? Has she changed characters again, and now likes Jack? She is impressed he has been to Paris, and notices the nudes in his sketchbook. Jack says, "That's the good thing about Paris. Lots of girls willing to take their clothes off." And she *doesn't* get up and leave in a huff. She thinks he was in love with one of the models, but he assures her he was only in love with her hands (hands of course being a big visual theme in the film). Rose says she sees people, and he replies, "I see you." Rose says, "And?" "You wouldn't have jumped." Well, how does he know this? There is nothing we have seen in her behavior to suggest she wouldn't have if he had not been there.

Ruth explains to a countess that Rose does not need to go to college, since she already has a fiancé. I admire Cameron's late-twentieth-century feminism, but does he have to beat his characters over the head for not agreeing with him? Ismay tells Captain Smith that he wants to impress newspapers with the ship's speed: "The maiden voyage of *Titanic* [sic] must make headlines." Okay, the picture runs 194 minutes, we are less than an hour into it, and now I am going to stop quoting Cameron's lines condemning characters for not knowing what we know. Just don't do it, folks.

Back on deck with Jack and Rose. She likes that he can go off on his own. He suggests they will go west where she can learn to ride western style—wait a minute. They will go west? When did they decide they were going to be together? Maybe he is just pulling her leg. He teaches her to spit, which she does not seem to mind.

Jack of course looks gorgeous in Molly's son's tuxedo, but also a lit-tle awkward at the grand staircase. He observes people and picks up details of behavior. Molly tells him to pretend he has money. Cameron has an interesting idea of making Molly Brown Jack's patron saint, but aside from a few bits of advice and the tux, he has not developed it. What could you do with Molly Brown? This dinner scene could have been wonderful, but Cameron hits only its most obvious notes.

Jack takes Rose to a "real party" down in steerage. Needless to say, the passengers there are earthy, friendly, play more energetic music, and dance up a storm. In other words, they behave exactly like the lower classes tend to in movies, which are aimed at a large audience, including the lower classes. To beat the point to death, Cameron cuts back to the rich at brandy and cigars. Yawn.

Cal is beating *his* dead horse about how Rose must behave. He upsets a table. At least that is a movement forward in our understanding of his character (he may be violent as well as thoughtless), although 70 minutes in is a long time to wait for it. Ruth tells Rose that she must marry Cal to pay their family's debts. Ruth is afraid of poverty, but this is so late in the picture and so clumsily written that it does not make us sympathetic to Ruth at all. Cameron is sneaking into Edith Wharton territory, but without her elegance.

In the wheelhouse, a radioman gives Captain Smith a message warning of icebergs. On deck, Rose mentions to Andrews that she has only counted enough lifeboats for half the passengers, and Andrews says he was overruled on putting a second row of lifeboats in. I mentioned some of the previous features about the *Titanic*, but did not mention the many documentaries, all of which gave us knowledge Cameron could play with, as he does with Bodine's animation, but here as elsewhere he is rather leaden about it.

Jack steals a coat to sneak up to the First Class decks, where Rose tells him that she is engaged and loves Cal. When did that happen? We have seen no evidence of it, and the way the scene is written, we cannot tell if she truly believes it or has talked herself into it. At a dining room table, Rose sees a little girl unfolding her napkin. Rose finds Jack on the bow and says she has changed her mind. Huh? What was it about the little girl and the napkin that changed her mind? We have no idea. What could Rose see that would tell us she is changing her mind? Jack takes her up to the bow, has her stand on the bow, hold her hands out, and close her eyes. She feels like she is flying. Into the sunset. Of April 14th.

Old Rose turns from a monitor and says that was the last time the ship saw sunlight. Brock, in case we are really slow, says, "Only six hours left." Is this really what you want to say to an audience less than halfway through a film that runs 3 hours and 14 minutes (or as the studio executives who were worried about an over-three-hour film called it, 2 hours and 74 minutes)?

In Rose's stateroom, Jack is impressed by her Monet. Now, wait a minute, isn't this rather generic "good art"? Picasso and the Cubists are very different from Monet and the Impressionists. I suppose we are to think she has rather catholic tastes. She takes the necklace out of the safe, calling it "hideous." Well, it is no Monet water lily, but it's not that bad. Ah, she means hideous because the hideous Cal has given it to her. Right, she hates the necklace. Hold that thought.

She tells Jack she wants him to make a sketch of her "like one of your French girls." Okay, Jack has been very quick-witted throughout the film, but this goes right past him. She adds, "Wearing this." "All right." "Wearing *only* this." *Now* he gets it. Could we have a little consistency of character here, folks? As Rose poses, Old Rose tells us that her heart was pounding, that it was the most erotic moment of her life. But we do not see that on Rose's face. Why? Two hundred million dollars, that's why. That is the supposed cost of the film, which means it would have to make a lot of money just to break even. Which means you do not want an R rating, because it limits the number of theaters you can play in, and it restricts your younger audience to coming with their, eww, parents. The rating code in this case let the film get away with a PG-13 for the brief shots of Rose's breasts, as long as there was nothing sexual *visually*. We will see the reverse of this in the later love scene.

Rose puts the drawing and note she's written into the safe with the necklace. Lovejoy sees Jack and Rose leaving her stateroom. He chases them up and down the hall, elevator, and stairs. This is written, as are later scenes, so the director can show off his sets. Rose and Jack wind up in a car in the cargo hold. They make love, but now we get no nudity, just a hand on a steamy back window. Protecting the $200 million again.

Cal finds the drawing and note in his safe. The note says, "Darling, now you can keep us both locked up in your safe." Parse this one with me, folks. She is leaving, so she has the drawing made to give the guy something to keep, even though she thinks he has trapped her. But she has had the drawing made with the necklace on her. But she is *leaving* the actual necklace. Okay, love fries the brains, but still…

On deck, Rose tells Jack she is getting off the boat with him when they get to New York. Two lookouts in the crow's nest look down on them. Which means Cameron is coming pretty close to suggesting that Jack and Rose making out was the cause of the collision, which is historical revisionism of the worst sort. But the lookouts do see the iceberg and call down the alarm. At 100 minutes into the film, the *Titanic* hits the iceberg. By 100 minutes in the 1953 version, the ship had already sunk and the audience was out of the theater.

Members of the crew below decks drown, passengers in third-class panic, and the first-class passengers assume nothing is wrong. Cal and the Master at Arms find the necklace Lovejoy has planted in Jack's coat. Rose is not sure he didn't take the necklace. Some supportive lover she is. Jack is handcuffed to a pipe in the Master at Arms's office. Andrews, with blueprints of the ship, explains to the captain and Ismay why the ship will sink. Everybody just looks stricken, with no variation in their reactions. Captain Smith does say, "You may get your headlines, Mr. Ismay," a rather obvious payoff to the earlier line.

Cal gives Rose a hard time, even slapping her, the cad. At least Cameron did not give him a moustache to twirl. Captain Smith tells the radioman to send the distress signal and to say they are going down by the bow. This is a very flat, literal scene, with no texture. Think how you could make that scene more interesting. Andrews reminds Rose of their previous discussion about the lack of lifeboats. This is one of the few scenes in the script with any subtlety.

The steerage passengers are blocked by a gate from coming up on deck. The water is up to the porthole in the Master at Arms's office. On deck Rose, finally, tears into her mother and Cal. Rose says he is "an unimaginable bastard." Uh, Rose, he has been that for the first 117 minutes of the film, and if you didn't know it, you are even stupider than I think you are. Why are you just now getting around to saying it?

Ruth and Molly (remember her? I told you she could have been used more in the script) try to get Rose into the lifeboat. Cal tries to keep her from going to Jack as his whore. She replies, "I would rather be his whore than your wife." These characters might say these things, but they are a little too "on the nose." To break away from Cal, she spits on him. At least this is something we saw her learn.

Rose starts running to find Jack. From minute 118 to minute 127, she is running up and down watery hallways, finding Jack, trying to find the key, getting an ax to smash the handcuffs, escaping with Jack. That is nine minutes of watery hallway running. And then some more with Jack. They end up in steerage and cannot get through the gates. Didn't we just see a scene with people at the gates? They eventually break through. Cal puts the necklace in his own coat pocket. Cal makes a "deal" with one of the boat officers, giving him money to assure him a place on the lifeboats. Then Lovejoy tells Cal he has seen Rose going toward the bow. Now, what does Cal do? Nearly everything we have seen or heard from him or about him says he gets in the lifeboat. But he doesn't. He goes to look for Rose. Why? It appears at this point in the film that Cal actually *is* in love with her. There have been a few hints ("open your heart") that he might love her, but much more evidence that he simply wants to own her. To have him suddenly be in love changes everything we know about him, without any preparation.

Rose does not want to go in the boat without Jack, but Cal insists. Cal gives her his coat. Yeah, the one with the necklace in it. Yeah, love fries… She gets into the lifeboat, and as it lowers we have longing looks between her and Jack. Then she jumps back on board the ship. Love really fries, etc. Jack and Rose run around the ship. Cal explains to Lovejoy that he gave his coat to Rose, with the necklace in it, the implication being that he just now realized it. Jack and Rose find themselves behind a, yeah, you guessed it, a locked gate. They open it, but do we need *three* gate scenes in the picture? At least the three train raids in *Lawrence* are *different*.

Cal finds a stray child, pretends it is his, and gets aboard a lifeboat. Captain Smith wanders into the wheelhouse, looking lost. If his character had been better served by the script earlier, this might be a moving moment, but it is not. The band stops playing, begins to break up, then the violinist starts again, and the other players return: a simple, moving scene in among the special effects. The music continues over a montage of various characters, some of whom we know, some of whom we do not.

The bow begins to go down and Jack and Rose go to the stern. They climb up on the rail as they watch people lose their grip and fall. The ship breaks in half, the bow pulls the stern straight up, then down into the water. The shots are much more impressive than Bodine's animation. Just before the stern hits, Jack and Rose jump into the water. We are 164 minutes in, and we have half an hour left. All right, only 23 minutes until credits start.

Rose crawls up on a large piece of wood. Jack cannot get on it without tipping it over, so he stays in the water. Jack is freezing, but tells her never to let go. But when she wakes up, he is dead, so she pries his fingers off. She promised him she would never let go. Well, she was also not sure he didn't take the necklace. On the rescue ship *Carpathia*, she avoids Cal. Rose gives her name as Rose Dawson (Jack's last name) to a ship's officer. Old Rose says Jack saved her "in every way that a person can be saved."

Brock talks to Lizzy. He is fingering a cigar and says, "I will savor this when I've found the diamond." So he is a scavenger. How could you write this so he is more? He says for three years he has thought about the *Titanic*, "but I never let it in." The implication is that hearing Old Rose's story, he has let it in emotionally, but we do not see that in his reaction.

Old Rose goes to the stern of the ship and climbs up on the rail. She has the necklace (we have seen Rose discover it in Cal's coat pocket). She smiles. Why is this woman smiling? She thought the necklace was hideous, remember? And then Cal used it to frame Jack. Why would she have kept it? Okay, the diamond may have been too hot to hock, but there are ways… She drops the necklace into the ocean. Why? If it is the only thing she has to remind her of Jack, I would think she would want to hang on to it. Or, since it has been eighty-four years, why hasn't she dropped it into the ocean before? Maybe she gave up on ships. But how could she know that eventually she would be able to get back to the spot where Jack's remains are underwater? I know, I know, this is supposed to be a great romantic moment, and love does fry…, but still…

Old Rose goes back to bed, and we see pictures of her life, including one of Rose on a horse, western-style. The sunken *Titanic* becomes the old *Titanic*, as the camera glides through the doors to the grand staircase. At the top of the stairs is Jack, dressed very steerage. He holds out his hand and Rose takes it. We are at 187 minutes and the credits begin.

Okay, as filmed it is a bad script, for all the reasons suggested above. But the first-draft screenplay was only three-quarters as bad. Let us look at how the script turned into the film. The production, as befits the $200 million that was spent, is lavish. Not without reason did the film win most of the "pretty" Oscars (art and set direction, costumes, cinematography), but the production was deeply flawed. Many of the special effects were bad, especially the water effects. I spent two years on board a ship in the Navy, and I stood on the bow of a ship, looking down as it cuts through the water, and it doesn't look like it does in the movie. I suspect the water effects were done by a computer geek who had never been to sea. See now the downside of CGI as opposed to the real world?

Then there is the question of length. Longer is not better. It occurred to me as I watched the film the first time that if you were to take out all the shots that were virtual duplicates of the previous shot, you could take out half an hour of the picture with nothing serious lost. And if you took out another fifteen minutes, you would have a running time of about two and a half hours, which the script might support. Guess what, folks? The first-draft screenplay is 153 pages, which at a minute a page would have been…just over two and a half hours. In that script, the flashback begins on page 16. Remember the running through the watery hallways? In the script it takes four pages, about half what it runs in the film. And when the stern begins to go up, Cameron is obviously in love with the shots of the stunt people falling down the length of the ship. By my rough count, he has twenty-one of those shots. There is only about half a page of that in the script. I was astonished that the film not only was nominated for but won the Oscar for Best Film Editing.

Because Cameron the director is loading up the special effects and art direction shots, he ends up leaving out scenes from the first draft that helped it make more sense than the film. In the first draft, at the end, Lizzy and Brock discover Old Rose about to drop the necklace, and we get a dialogue scene that (sort of) explains why she kept the necklace.

With the characterizations so feeble in the script, good actors like Frances Fisher (Ruth), Billy Zane (Cal), and Bernard Hill (Captain Smith) cannot really give the performances they are capable of. Victor Garber does a little better with Andrews, and Gloria Stuart puts all her sixty-plus years of experience as a screen actress at the service of a sly performance of Old Rose.

The worst performance is Kate Winslet's as Rose. Winslet is one of the great actors of her generation, and in virtually every other film she is superb. Here she is defeated by a badly conceived role. In the first draft the character is a little more coherent. The promenade scene, where she seems to be three different people, makes more sense in the script. In the revised version of the scene, it has begun to make less sense. By the version that appears in the film, it is a mess. If you are going to "develop" a scene, do so in a way that makes it better, not worse. Winslet is often adequate in a given shot, and she certainly has her charming moments, but nothing comes together as a character.

So *Titanic* has a bad script, bad water, bad performances, bad CGI, and goes on way longer than it needs to. It was nominated for fourteen Academy Awards, but not, it should be noted, Best Original Screenplay. It won eleven, including Best Picture.

And it brought in $2 billion (yes, that's billion with a *b*) at the box office worldwide, making it the highest grossing movie of all time, a record it still holds.

How?

Two words:

Leonardo DiCaprio.

Before *Titanic*, DiCaprio was a great actor and a rising star. After, he was a star. He made the picture, and the picture made him. Purely as a performance, his acting in *Titanic* was adequate, given the limitations of the script. With a one-dimensional character, there is very little conventional acting you can do, as we have seen from some of the other performances. What DiCaprio gives is a great *movie star* performance. He holds the screen so that when he is on it you cannot not watch him. DiCaprio picks up on Jack's enthusiasm and focuses it on, well, everything. Look at him look at the passengers as he draws them. Look at the enthusiasm with which he teaches Rose to spit. Look at the

360-degree turn he does when Ruth and Molly find him teaching Rose to spit. DiCaprio is always doing something to draw your eye. And doing it with Jack's enthusiasm. Unlike Sam Neill in *Jurassic Park*, he realized he was going to have to do a lot to hold the screen with one of the most attractive women in film, Winslet, and with the production values, special effects, and action sequences. And in all the fourteen nominations, DiCaprio was not nominated, even though Winslet was.

As many have pointed out, one audience demographic that made *Titanic* a hit was tween and teen girls. You can see the advantage of keeping the rating a PG-13. The next time somebody complains about the short attention span of kids today, by the way, remind them who turned out to see all 2 hours and 74 minutes of *Titanic* many, many times. DiCaprio's performance helped with this demographic because he was so lively and adorable. And unthreatening. The mediocre performance from Winslet may have helped attract this demographic as well, since if she had been more compelling, the young female market may have been turned off by having to "share" Leo! Leo! Leo! with her.

Sometimes you get lucky with a bad script, and the film and/or its star delivers enough of what the potential audience for the film wants. But you cannot count on it.

DiCaprio's star power didn't help his next film, *The Beach* (2000). Or *Gangs of New York* (2002).

Sources
Information about the 1943 German film and its director is from David Stewart Hull's *Film in the Third Reich* (Touchstone, 1969). Material on the other *Titanic* films comes from IMDb. Material on the Academy Awards comes from Robert Osborne's *70 Years of the Oscar: The Official History of the Academy Awards* (Abbeville Press, 1999).

The first draft of the screenplay, dated May 7, 1996, is in the Herrick Library. It was also published as *Titanic* (Harper, 1998), but with the script page numbers replaced by book page numbers. The book includes notes on what was cut or changed. If you can find a copy of the book, it is fascinating to read as you watch the movie. There are even more scenes than I have written about here that are better in the first draft than in the film. We all know directors often screw up the work of writers, but it is relatively unusual for a director shooting his own script to mess it up. I suspect that Cameron got into the director mode and began to lose focus, something that often happens under the crushing weight of a large-budget production. There is a Revised Working Copy dated March 17, 1998, at the Herrick Library, which includes revisions for the promenade deck scene.

15

ANCHORMAN: THE LEGEND OF RON BURGUNDY

> **ANCHORMAN: THE LEGEND OF RON BURGUNDY**
> (2004. Screenplay by Will Ferrell & Adam McKay.
> 94 minutes)

A few readers of early drafts of this book got upset about this chapter, saying comedy is "subjective," and so how can I put a comedy in the Bad section, since so many people laughed at it? Oddly, none of those readers objected to my comments about the *American Pie* films, two of which were not good. As you may have gathered from at least some of what I have written, I do have a sense of humor. I did not find *Anchorman* funny; others did. But the problems with it are not just that I didn't laugh at the jokes, but that the screenplay was badly done in almost every other way. I don't object to movies that are stupidly funny. I do object if they are more stupid than funny.

Take the opening title: "The following is based on actual events. Only the names, locations and events have been changed." As one reader wrote, "That's a joke—a stupid one, but it's a stupid film." My problem with the line is not just that it's stupid, but that it makes no sense in the context of the film. The story is not based on actual events any more than any other fiction film. There are occasionally nods to the possibility that it might have been a mock documentary, or mockumentary, like *This Is Spinal Tap* (1984), but they are not developed.

The narrator, and we have no idea at first who he is, sets the scene, telling us that this is about local television news in the seventies. But notice the emphasis is just as much on Ron Burgundy being a man as being a news anchor, which is a major theme in the film. This is one of two reasons why the film is set in the seventies. The other is to get a few laughs out of the seventies clothes.

The narrator sounds a bit like the narrator of another film about television news, *Network* (1976). A problem for contemporary screenwriters is that so many subjects have been dealt with before, and often very well. Remember *Pearl Harbor*? If you are writing about television news, you are going up against not only great films and television shows, but also peoples' memories of those films and shows, a major problem for *Anchorman*.

Ron prepares to go on the air by doing vocal exercises. Some of them look silly, but the vocal exercises actors and TV performers do tend to look foolish, so we do not really know how silly he is. We then get a parody of a title sequence for local news, with the anchorman, sportscaster, weatherman, and reporter walking toward the camera. Yes, we have all seen those walks, but just referencing something does not make it a parody, as several critics pointed out about *Date Movie* (2006).

We get shots of people in San Diego reacting positively to the news show and to Ron, including guys in a biker bar. We do not know why they love him. He seems to be a caricature of a pompous, self-involved local anchorman, but Ted Baxter in the *Mary Tyler Moore* show (1970–1977) set that bar very high. Look at episodes of that show to see how it should be done. The station manager Ed comes in after the show and tells everyone that they are again number one in the ratings. We are 5 minutes into the film. As an aside to Grant, his assistant, Ed says to try to keep them from partying too much.

Guess where we are next? At the party, the narrator introduces us to the members of Ron's news team. Each of them talks directly to the camera, as though they were being interviewed for a documentary, but this approach is never used again. First up is field reporter Brian Fantana, the name is likely a reference to investigative reporter Frank Fontana on *Murphy Brown* (1988–1998). He is sitting on a couch with a beautiful young woman and talking to the camera about his nicknames for his penis and his testicles, adding, "You ladies play your cards right, you just might get to meet the whole gang." Except he is not talking to the woman. And the woman has no reaction to what he is saying. What could her reaction be?

Next is the sports guy, Champ Kind, who talks to the camera about his on-the-air catchphrase. I am not going to tell you what it is, but see if you even remember it the only two other times in the film it is used. Brick Tamland, the weather guy, admits that people like him because he is polite, and that a doctor will later tell him he is mentally retarded. He is indeed the mentally slowest of the team, which is no great achievement.

A woman comes up to Ron and admits she has a crush on him. The script gives us no indication why she would be attracted to Ron Burgundy.

Ron sees an attractive woman, Veronica Corningstone, who has no idea who he is. His introduction of himself is: "I don't know how to put this…but I'm kinda a big deal…People know me…I'm very important…I have many leather-bound books…and my apartment smells of rich mahogany." Not bad, but not great. Rewrite that speech and make it funny. Or simply watch Will Ferrell deliver the lines and figure out how he could have made them more interesting. Ferrell is the co-writer of the film, so he was writing this for his own performance. But as a performer he seems to think of those lines as merely jokes, and doesn't get the emotional subtext, which would have made them work better onscreen. Probably the flaws in Ferrell's writing and acting come from having done sketch comedy on *Saturday Night Live* (1975–forever). The writing on that show tends to be very sloppy, as does the acting, without the precision required for great comedy. At the end of the scene, Ron tells Veronica, "I want to be on you," and she very wisely leaves. We are 11 minutes into the film.

Ron goes home. Alone. Nice house. His dog Baxter is surely a reference to Ted Baxter. Ron complains about Baxter speaking Spanish, when all he is doing is barking. If Baxter had made some sound that could be interpreted as Spanish, the joke might have had a point, but it just lies there. The dog may be intended to show Ron's loneliness, but there is no evidence of it in the dialogue or in Ron's reactions to him.

At the station the next morning, Ed tells them that Ling Wong, the panda at the zoo (probably the only reason the film was set in San Diego), is pregnant, which everybody agrees will be the big story of the summer. The "Panda Watch" days on various newscasts give a minimal structural assist to the script. Compare this to how James L. Brooks uses the "domino" clip in *Broadcast News* (1987) to show the shallowness of television news. Ed also says the network is looking for a new anchor, which sets that plotline in motion. Ed tells the boys that the affiliated stations have been complaining about a lack of diversity. Big problem: why would the affiliated stations be complaining about another station's lack of diversity? Each station would more likely be reacting to local pressures. When Brooks wrote *Broadcast News*, he not only drew on his years in television, but spent a lot of time researching the news side of the business, as did Paddy Chayefsky on *Network*. Here's a dirty little secret: you have to be smart even when writing low-brow stuff. The audience *knows* when you are condescending to them. See how many laughs Chayefsky and Brooks get out of the *reality* of television news. Yes, they exaggerate a little, but always with a basis in truth.

There is a mediocre comic discussion of what diversity is, which leads Ed to introduce the station's newest reporter, Veronica. Ron is surprised, but that's about it. What other reactions could you give him? And what about her? If she was new in town, how did she get invited to that party last night? And if she knew anything about the station she was going to, she would have known who he was. And there is no indication in the party scene that she was shining him on. She says here that she hopes to add to the station's reputation. So did she know about Ron before or not? Later, in Ed's office, Champ and Brian are complaining to Ed that it is not right to have a woman doing the news. They are yelling, I suspect, to try to make up for the bad writing, a problem throughout the film, although later in the film one of Ferrell's best moments is one of his quietest. Brick complains about women in the newsroom, "I read somewhere their periods attract bears. Bears can smell the menstruation," a line more complex than Brick, the idiot, would be likely to come up with. Keep your jokes consistent with your characters. Champ starts pretending he is putting barbecue sauce on what he imagines to be Veronica's ass. She comes into the room, but it is not clear if she understands exactly what he is pretending to do, which diminishes a potentially interesting reaction shot. She leaves, and we get a voiceover from her that this is the same sort of thing that she ran into at other stations, and that she is determined to work her way up to the top. This is the only voiceover she, or any of the other characters, gets. Why do you suppose the writers put it in? They have already established a narrator who is more or less omniscient and could have told us this. One theme in the film is the battle of the sexes, which is why the film is set in the seventies, when women were getting more and more opportunities in television and elsewhere. The writers seem to deliberately avoid the possibilities of the theme. Brooks in *Broadcast News* got laughs—and more—by taking the issue of a woman in television journalism seriously. Ferrell and McKay aim lower and miss.

Our four guys are walking in the park (this may have been intended as a reference to the "team walk" in the news show's title sequence, but it is shot so awkwardly that the joke is lost) discussing what to do about Veronica. The team meets the news team from Channel 9, the competition. The first shot of the meeting is set up I think to parody the first meeting of the gangs in *West Side Story* (1961), but the wrong music kills that gag. If you need music for a specific gag, write it in and hope the producers can afford the rights. The two teams trade insults, mostly about their clothes, but since everybody's clothes look seventies-awful, the argument seems to emphasize how dumb *everybody* is.

Ed is on the phone dealing with his son, who seems to have brought German pornography into school, the first of a series of running gags about his son's troublemaking. This first one is mildly amusing (we only learn at the end of the conversation that Ed is talking to a nun), but the others are not. Veronica comes in to complain that she has been assigned to cover a cat fashion show. Now, we know that Veronica knows how sexist the workplace is, and surely it would be no surprise to her to get this assignment, so wouldn't it be smarter for her if she just does the assignment, but does it so well and so inventively she makes herself a star? In the great newspaper comedy *His Girl Friday* (1940), Hildy is already a star reporter at the opening of the film, and we see how smart a reporter she is throughout the film, which makes her a much more interesting character to watch. But then her leading man, her editor Walter Burns, is even smarter than that, which makes *him* interesting to watch, and makes their relationship *fabulous* to watch.

Champ, Brian, and Ron each try to hit on Veronica. She doesn't have any interesting reactions. Now imagine how Hildy in *His Girl Friday* would respond to these "advances." Christina Applegate (Veronica) can be a wonderful comic actress, but she is given very little to work with in this script. The writers are so focused on the male characters that they overlook both Veronica's character and the laughs they could get from her reactions to the guys.

As Veronica waits for Ron in the lobby, she has second thoughts about his offer to show her San Diego, but thinks he is cute. Well, maybe. We have all fallen for people who are wrong for us at some time in our lives, but the gap between Ron and Veronica is enormous, and the writers do not seem to realize the work they will have to do to convince us they should be together. Ron and Veronica go out to a restaurant and the manager asks Ron to play jazz flute. Who knew? Well, he does play, and play well. At last, something that Ron does well, and we are supposed to believe from Veronica's reaction that this is the deal-maker. Maybe, but she needs more lines and/or more of a visual reaction to make that work, especially in view of all the stupid things he has done. They go to bed, which cues a brief, partially animated sequence. The animation does not really tell us anything we don't already know. In the morning she says to him, "Well done, sir," which we have trouble believing, simply because we have seen nothing that would suggest it. How would you suggest he is good? And still keep the PG-13 rating? We are 37 minutes into the film.

She wants to keep their affair quiet. You know the film's writing well enough now that you can guess the next scene: he is shouting about their affair to the office. He and the guys discuss what it is like to be in love, and while the writing here is only so-so, it is acted not at top volume but at a normal conversational level, so it plays better. It also flows into the one charming scene in the movie, when the four guys break into the song "Afternoon Delight," again played at a normal volume level.

Ron's news team tells him about the pancake breakfast the next day, but he says he is going jogging with Veronica. The guys seem to be upset that he is more interested in her than them, but this is just stated, repeatedly, and not developed. The writers here are avoiding an interesting issue even more than Adam Herz did in the *American Pie* films.

Ron is driving and throws a burrito out of his car, which causes a motorcyclist to crash. In retaliation, the motorcyclist takes Baxter, who just happens to be in the car, and kicks him off the bridge they are on. Ron is so upset that he does not get to the station on time. Veronica's boss is reluctant to let her anchor the show by herself, but she says, "Mr. Harken, this city needs its news. And you are going to deprive them of that because I have breasts?… Exquisite breasts." We have not seen Veronica *use* her sexuality in that way, so it comes as a surprise. Applegate could also get more out of the line, especially the last two words. Listen to Julia Roberts's "They're called boobs, Ed" in *Erin Brockovich* (2000) to hear how it should be said. Veronica anchors the news, and the women in the studio—wait a minute, where did they come from? We have not seen them around the studio or the newsroom for the first fifty minutes of the film—are happy that she is a success. Ron, of course, is not.

Ed announces that the ratings are up (from one unscheduled appearance? Unlikely) and that Veronica will be Ron's co-anchor. At the end of their newscast, each tries to get in his/her signature line ("Stay classy, San Diego," "Thanks for stopping by, San Diego") last, after the other one. It is the one scene in the picture that works completely. Why? First, as my wife pointed out, "It's the one bit that wasn't shouted." Second, Ferrell and Applegate get a nice rhythm going, and they really *perform* the lines. Third, the director, Ferrell's co-writer Adam McKay, is smart enough to just set the camera down and watch Ferrell and Applegate do their thing. One of my former students, Tamra Davis, directed an Adam Sandler film, *Billy Madison* (1995). She told me what she learned from the experience was that in a comedy, the director has to put her talents at the service of the actors: if we do not see or hear what the actors are doing, we are not going to laugh.

We hear what the two anchors are really saying to each other as they smile under the credits. This should have been the equivalent of the mound scene in *Bull Durham*; instead it is a collection of mediocre insults by both of them. Maybe she is right for him, after all.

Now the guys try to play tricks on her. This should be an intensification from the previous scenes where they have complained about her, but it is just more of the same. Helen, one of the women who applauded Veronica's success, tells the guys they are children and need to grow up. She is right. I do realize that *Anchorman* is in the tradition of what the British call "laddish" comedy, in which twenty- and thirty- and sometimes forty-something guys behave like eleven-year-old boys, but do the films have to sound as though they were *written* by eleven-year-old boys? After all, in *Broadcast News*, James L. Brooks created a somewhat dense would-be anchor, Tom Grunick, but made him attractive enough so that the smart woman producer, Jane Craig, would be believably attracted to him. And how about the almost-adolescent-but-smart tricks Walter Burns plays on Hildy's fiancé in *His Girl Friday*? Okay, Burns was played by Cary Grant, but guys, there is nothing wrong with being an adult, even you are not Cary Grant.

The guys run into the news teams from Channel 9 and from the other stations. And they have a rumble. Huh? This is probably one of those ideas that sounded great in the room when they were thinking up ideas, and it does have a certain wacky appeal, but it seems to come out of virtually nowhere. It is, I suppose, sort of set up by the earlier confrontation with the Channel 9 team. But doing it as a rumble, with real weapons, at least one person killed, and one person having his arm cut off, is different from the tone of the rest of the film. Yes, we did have Baxter thrown off the bridge, but that's as black as the comedy has gotten.

After the rumble they are back in the office, and then (for about the twenty-seventh time) trying to figure out what to do about Veronica. Can you say "repetitive"? In an argument Veronica tells Ron he has bad hair. Now, that is a great insult to an anchorman, but the writers do nothing with it. There is very little reaction from Ron, or anybody else. We are 67 minutes into the film.

At a restaurant, Helen tells Veronica that Ron reads *anything* that is on the teleprompter. Veronica has "Fuck you, San Diego" put on the teleprompter, and Ron reads it, which upsets the bikers in the bar (remember them?) and by implication everybody else in San Diego. Ed has to fire Ron. For a livelier version of this scene, see Budd Schulberg's script for *A Face in the Crowd* (1957), and while you're at it, look at how Schulberg handles the relationship between a smart woman and a down-home country boy.

Veronica is now the sole anchor, and we are into Day 46 of the Panda Watch. Later Ed gets the call that Ling Wong is in labor, and the various news teams we saw at the rumble are all there. Ron is drunk, shabby, and bearded in a bar, telling the bartender that a "she-devil stole my heart," but he admits when he sees her on TV that she is better than him. The bartender tells him that the times are changing. The bartender is played by Danny Trejo, one of the toughest-looking men in the movies. The contrast between his appearance and his liberal sentiments makes the scene play better than it reads.

At the zoo, Veronica finds the perfect angle to film the birth, but the Public Television announcer pushes her into the bear pit, where she is surrounded by three sleeping bears. Remember the gross bear joke earlier? I don't think the writers did, since there is no reference to it in this scene. If you are going to have a joke that gross, you'd better give it a really good payoff.

Called back to work, Ron sees Veronica in the bear pit and must make a decision: cover the birth or rescue her. He jumps into the pit. She admits it was she who fixed the teleprompter and his howl of outrage wakes up the bears. The other three guys from the news team jump into the pit and wrestle with the bears. Baxter arrives. Surprise, surprise, he is not dead. We have seen him come out of a river and head for the zoo (uh, neat trick. The bridge he was thrown off of is over San Diego Bay, which is not connected to any river). Baxter jumps into the pit and has a conversation with the bears. Baxter says that in his travels he met a bear, Katow-jo, who happens to be this bear's cousin, so this bear will let the humans go. Baxter says, "I will tell tales of your compassion." The scene is off-the-wall, but works not only in plot terms, but as an out-of-nowhere-parody of similar scenes in wildlife films. It also works because both Baxter and the bear are not shouting, but woofing and growling in a normal conversational tone.

As our guys and Veronica are getting out of the bear pit via a ladder, the anchorman of Channel 9 threatens to push them back in, but then he says he respects Ron. This is a minor payoff for a minor character that simply slows down the end of the film. Veronica agrees to let Ron tell the story of the panda, but Ron brings her in as his "co-anchor." Veronica says, "There are literally thousands of men I should be with, but instead I am seventy-two percent sure I love you." I don't know about your reaction, but mine was: run, Veronica, run to *any* of the others.

The narrator tells us that he picked Ron and Veronica as his replacement, but we do not know what he was (a network anchor? An anchor in a larger-market city?). The narrator says they became the first "mixed-gender news team," and the next shot shows them as anchors, but it is not clear where they are anchoring. And the narrator tells us they are still at it, but if the makeup on Ferrell and Applegate is supposed to persuade us they are thirty years older than they were in the rest of the movie, it fails. At 89 minutes, the credits begin.

Anchorman: The Legend of Ron Burgundy cost approximately $26 million and brought in a domestic gross of $84 million, with an overseas gross of $5 million. In other words, by the time you subtract the percentage of the gross that stays at the theaters and the cost of prints and marketing, it made its cost back. It worked moderately well for American audiences, since the subject was local American television and there were enough people, unlike me, who found it at least partially amusing. Overseas audiences were just plain baffled, as often happens with gross-out American comedies.

Sources
The quotes from the script's dialogue are from my notes on the film and from the "memorable quotes" section on the film on IMDb, although it should be noted that there are quotes in that section from the trailer that are not in the film, and some from the outtakes that are also not in the film. The budget is from IMDb, and the grosses are from _Variety (w)_, January 17–23, 2005.

For discussion of writing for both the _Mary Tyler Moore_ show and _Saturday Night Live,_ see my _Storytellers to the Nation: A History of Writing for American Television_, 2nd Edition (Syracuse University Press, 1996). For a brief discussion of _Broadcast News,_ see a second or later edition of my _Framework_ (Syracuse University Press, 2000).

16
STAR WARS: EPISODE I, II, and *III*

STAR WARS: EPISODE I—THE PHANTOM MENACE
(1999. Screenplay by George Lucas. 133 minutes)

"**A** long time ago in a galaxy far, far away..."

Yes, I know that is the first line of the first film, but there is a reason Lucas has it at the beginning of the other films. In the first film, the line established quickly that this movie and its sequels would not take place in a realistic world. While much fun has been had over the years complaining about the "unrealistic" details in the scripts and films—and it has been fun, admit it—it is also fruitless to argue that: rocketships would not make noise in the vacuum of space; explosions in space would not be glorious fireballs because there is no air to sustain them; holes in the ships would suck the interior atmosphere and creatures into space; small rocketships would probably not have artificial gravity devices; strange planets would not have the same gravity and atmosphere as each other; temperature ranges on such planets would not allow people and creatures to walk around with minimal protective clothing; and, given my appreciation of the English language, my favorite is: the wisest being in the universe would probably have learned to speak the language grammatically correctly a little more than does Yoda.

Even if resistance to such things is futile, the scripts are deeply flawed as well, particularly in *Episode I, II*, and to a lesser extent *III*, both in the terms of their own universe and also in how they present it to the real universe we the audience live in. At least when we are not watching the films.

"A long time ago..." etc. is also a good opening for *Episode I*, since it came out sixteen years after the previous *Star Wars* film. The line pulls the audience back into the world of the films and sets up expectations of the kind of film *Episode I* will be: fast, light on its feet, with elaborate special effects, and possibly passable acting. The film starts dismantling those expectations immediately.

The first title crawl tells us that there is turmoil in the Galactic Republic. Good, turmoil is often fun to watch. But then we find out the turmoil is because "taxation of trade to outlying star systems is in dispute." Turmoil on screen fun, tax disputes dull. In *Star Wars*, the crawl was about the Rebellion against the Empire, which grabs the audience's attention in a more vivid way. The crawl in *Episode I* continues, telling us that the Supreme Chancellor has sent two Jedi Knights to the Trade Federation ships blockading the planet Naboo to settle the dispute. "Trade Federation"? "Naboo"? One name is dull, the other is silly. Lucas works more on a visual level than a literary one, to put it politely, but the use of language throughout all the *Star Wars* scripts is clumsy and sits badly on the dazzling visuals. If you are going to write a film that is primarily visual, make sure the language does not work against it. Three words: *Lawrence of Arabia*.

The crawl ends and the Jedi Knights land on the battleship. The two knights, Qui-Gon Jinn (the more mature) and Obi-Wan Kenobi (his apprentice), talk to representatives of the Trade Federation. This is not an action-packed opening sequence, unlike the opening of *Star Wars*, which establishes who the good guys are (the cute robots and the cute girl) and who the bad guys are (the stormtroopers, especially the one dressed in black). The Trade Federation leaders next talk to the hologram of their secret boss. Now, in a picture called *The Phantom Menace*, it is pretty clear to the audience that the person who a) orders the killing of the Jedi and b) cannot be clearly seen is the Phantom Menace. The difficulty is that the actor, Ian McDiarmid, has a very distinctive face and voice, which makes him recognizable when he shows up as Senator Palpatine. So how phantom can he be if he is so easily recognizable? The Knights discover a droid army onboard the ship and hide in ships to go down to Naboo to warn the planet. We are a little over 8 minutes into the film.

The Trade Federation leaders talk via hologram to Queen Amidala of Naboo. A political question here: how did a girl in what looks to be her late teens get to be Queen...of a democracy, as Naboo is later identified as? We will get sort of an explanation in *Episode II*, but for now we just have to accept it as part of the "galaxy far" etc. It will, however, come back to haunt us in the plotting of this and subsequent films, and particularly in the question of her character.

On Naboo, Qui-Gon stumbles over Jar Jar Binks, the most reviled of all *Star Wars* characters. The intent I suspect was to create a comic character not unlike Satipo, the cowardly assistant to Indiana Jones in the opening sequence of Lucas's *Raiders of the Lost Ark* (1981). These characters are comic relief and counterpoint to the brave actions of the heroes, Indy there, the Knights here. The problem with Jar Jar comes from George Lucas's tin ear for writing dialogue. In the haphazard English he has given Jar Jar, the phrase "I'm" becomes "meesa," a version I assume of "me is." "Meesa" unfortunately sounds awfully close to "massa," the traditional African-American slave dialect for "master." That, combined with his physical klutziness and his subservience, convinced many viewers, and not just African-Americans, that Lucas was making Jar Jar a racist stereotype. Lucas was probably just sloppy rather than racist. You see why you have to be careful about language in your script?

Jar Jar takes Qui-Gon and Obi-Wan to the underwater city of his people, the Gungans. The city is gorgeous, and we are given plenty of time to drink in the images, but the city is a minor element in the plot and is not particularly expressive in terms of the story, characters, or ideas. This is often true of visual elements of the films, and I suppose you can defend it on grounds that the films are in the grand tradition of American spectacles (Griffith, De Mille, etc.), but there can be too much of a good thing. How much do you need in your film?

The Gungans (the Gungan leader is another stereotype, of a tribal leader in films set in Africa or the South Seas) assign Jar Jar (why him?) as the navigator of the ship that takes them through the planet's core to the main city on Naboo. The ride is a show-off piece of CGI, a roller-coaster ride that so far has not replaced Star Tours at Disneyland. As I mention many times in this book, a screenplay is written for performance, and just as the city of the Gungans is written for the performance of the production designers, this ride is written for the performance of the CGI experts. It is done reasonably well, although we might wish that the big fish attacking them had eaten Jar Jar. We are about 18 minutes in.

After the spectacle of the establishing shots of the main city on Naboo, some action. The Jedi Knights rescue Queen Amidala from the Trade Federation. There are more lightsaber duels with droids, similar to those seen earlier on the battleship. Again, find ways to make your action scenes *seem* different. The Jedi need to get the ship repaired before taking the Queen to the Senate. The planet they land on is Tatooine, the home planet of Luke Skywalker in the first *Star Wars* film. So our attention picks up, half an hour into the film, longer than needed to get here.

Qui-Gon and Jar Jar go into the village, taking along with them a young woman introduced as Padmé. She is presented to them as a servant to the Queen, but since she is obviously played by Natalie Portman, who is playing the Queen, we might reasonably suspect that it is the teenage Queen finagling a day off from royal duties. But Qui-Gon accepts her as the servant. A word here about Qui-Gon and Obi-Wan. Go back and look at how many times so far I have just referred to them as "the Jedi Knights." That is because they have virtually no characters of their own. One of the dramatic limitations of the whole concept of the Jedi Knights is that, while looking good in action, they are dramatically inert. Liam Neeson, brilliant in the well-written role of Kinsey, is unable to do anything with Qui-Gon other than look noble. Ewan McGregor has at least found an acting exercise to amuse himself with, and I wonder if Lucas as the director was even aware of it. McGregor has adopted the accent of the young Alec Guinness, who played the older Obi-Wan in the first three films. Listen to Guinness in *Great Expectations* (1946) if you don't believe me.

Our threesome goes to a spare parts shop. There they meet the young Anakin Skywalker, who is about ten. Now, people who are aware of the first three films are going to know immediately that he grows up to be Darth Vader, so it is a bit of a surprise to see him as a ten-year-old boy. Since the audience also probably knows he is going to father Luke and Leia with the Queen/Padmé, their meeting is rather creepy. She is much older than he is, and apparently much more mature. So why is this young woman interested in a ten-year-old boy whose main interest seems to be pod racing? She may have a thing for little boys. She may be enjoying her holiday from royal duties. She may have a natural curiosity about everything. She may feel maternal toward the boy. She may have a bit of a rebel streak in her (after all, where did *that* come from in Princess Leia?). It could be all of the above. But the script gives us no idea.

Poor Natalie Portman is a wonderful actress (see *Garden State* [2004]), but here she is given nothing to play. A word here on the acting. People in the Lucasfilm empire were concerned before the release of the film about the performance of Jake Lloyd (Anakin). He is flat, but all the other actors are as well, so his performance doesn't stand out as any worse than the others. Lucas has defended the flat acting in *Episode I* and *II* on the grounds that in the old serials the *Star Wars* films are inspired by, the acting tends to be flat. By the same logic, Lucas's special effects should have been cheesy. But they are not, and the acting should not be. Part of the problem is that the dialogue is so thuddingly flat that it would be difficult for actors to do anything with it. Also, when Lucas directed *Episode I*, he had not directed a film since 1977. Lucas has never been a particularly good director of actors, although if given a good cast, as in *American Graffiti* (1973), he does not get in their way.

Anakin takes them all home to meet his mother, Shmi. Anakin has built what is clearly C-3PO, who gets introduced to R2-D2. The writing of the first meeting of the two liveliest characters in all six films is not distinctive. What would you do with that scene?

Back on the ship, Obi-Wan tells Queen Amidala that her call for... wait a minute. Queen Amidala? Isn't she off talking pod races with young Anakin? Well, no, officially that is her servant. But if she is the one with Anakin, then *this* one is her servant and double, so why is she talking policy? It will get worse.

At Anakin's house, Padmé is surprised to discover that there is slavery on Tatooine, but her reaction comes out of nowhere and goes nowhere. If she's the Queen, wouldn't she have a bigger reaction? And if she is just the servant, wouldn't she be filing this away to tell the Queen? And when Anakin says he feels that the Jedi Knights have come to end slavery, Qui-Gon has hardly any reaction at all, although he later tells Obi-Wan he has a feeling about the boy. Reactions, especially immediate ones, show us character.

Qui-Gon realizes the only way to get the parts they need is to bet money on the pod races, since betting is the only way to make money with the Hutts. We find out that the other kids have laughed at Anakin's attempts and that he has never even finished a race, all of which sets us up for the pod race. As he tries out his pod, Padmé looks on, smiling. Why is this woman smiling?

Qui-Gon talks with Shmi and says he thinks the Force is strong in Anakin. Qui-Gon tests a blood sample from Anakin. The midichlorian count is higher than Yoda's. Qui-Gon, the most mature person in the film, says he does not know what it means, but he has already talked to Shmi about Anakin and the Force. Okay, we don't literally know what the midichlorian count means, but really, we do. We are way ahead of the film. You never want to let the audience get this far ahead of you. Ideally you want the film to be a little ahead of them, so they have to work to catch up. It involves them more.

At 55 minutes into the film, we get the pod race, the best sequence in the film. You may think that is because it is Pure Cinema, like Hitchcock. Yeah, right. This is the best sequence in the film because it is the best-*written* sequence in the film. The meaning of the action has been established in the discussions of pod racing. As much as we are rooting for anyone in this film, we are rooting for Anakin to win. And in spite of director Lucas's flattening the acting, the sequence demands reactions.

The details around the race add a texture to it that no other scenes in the film have. The cute CGI figures of the other racers are given specific things to do and, lo and behold, reactions to have. There are two announcers, all right, as we discover, one announcer with two heads, and Lucas has given them good parodies of our friends the sports clichés. There is even a creature walking around in the crowd selling really weird-looking food. Or really weird-looking souvenirs. It's hard to tell.

The race itself, patterned most distinctly on the chariot race in the 1959 version of *Ben-Hur*, has, unlike its model, a variety of scenery for the racers to go through. Instead of the interlocking wheels of the chariots, it is the machinery of two of the racers that get caught. On the other hand, the outcome does not carry the emotional weight of Messala's death in *Ben-Hur*. If the sequence is writing for the performance of the CGI filmmakers, it is also writing for the performance of Ben Burtt, who handled the sound design on all of the *Star Wars* films. Just *listen* to this sequence once to learn what sound can do for a sequence.

Needless to say, at the end of the fifteen-minute sequence, Anakin wins and Qui-Gon gets the parts. Qui-Gon has made a side bet with the shop owner, and Anakin is now free. His mother is not, and being a noble mom, she is willing to let Anakin go. Lucas, in the first *Star Wars* film, borrowed from films as diverse as *The Wizard of Oz* (1939), *Triumph of the Will* (1935), and, of course, *Lawrence of Arabia*. In the goodbye scenes here, he has passed up the opportunity to borrow from two of the best. Because Qui-Gon is so noble, it never occurs to Lucas to suggest any sort of romantic interest on his part in Shmi. I am not suggesting *Y Tu Mamá También*, but perhaps the unspoken attraction between Shane and the farmer's wife in *Shane* (1953). It could add texture. And if you want to see a great good-bye scene between a mother and a son she is sending off to what she hopes is a better life, look at *Citizen Kane*. Mankiewicz and Welles focus on the mother and her reactions. Purnilla August, the Swedish actress playing Shmi, is perfectly capable of matching Agnes Moorehead in *Kane*, but the writing and direction are not.

Darth Maul arrives on Tatooine and we have yet another lightsaber duel. Qui-Gon escapes, and the ship goes to the planet where the Senate meets, 80 minutes into the film. Queen Amidala meets Senator Palpatine and High Chancellor Valorum. This is the first time we have seen Palpatine as himself, and we recognize him as the not-so-Phantom Menace.

Anakin stops to visit Padmé, but only the Queen is there. Now wait a minute. If the woman he's been hanging out with is the real Queen, shouldn't she give some sign that she recognizes him? Nothing big, but maybe a wink. Or is she just blowing him off because she got what she wanted from him: spare parts for the ship? We have no idea. In the Senate, the Trade Federation wants to send a group to investigate the situation, but Queen Amidala is upset, calls for a vote of no confidence, and decides to return to Naboo. As suggested by Qui-Gon, Anakin is tested by the Jedi Council, who thinks he is too old to start training. Qui-Gon wants him as his apprentice. Have you gone out to get popcorn yet? In practical terms, that is what these dreary dialogue scenes are for.

The Council sends Qui-Gon, Obi-Wan, and Anakin to Naboo, although it senses Anakin has an "uncertain future." See what I mean about the flatness of Lucas's dialogue? In *Star Wars* Lucas has the sole screenplay credit, but he brought in his co-writers of *American Graffiti*, Willard Huyck and Gloria Katz, to help with the dialogue and add a little humor, especially in the repartee between Leia and Han Solo. On *The Empire Strikes Back* (1980), Lucas did the story, but Lawrence Kasdan (*Body Heat* [1981]) and Leigh Brackett (*The Big Sleep* [1946]) wrote the script, and Kasdan and Lucas shared the screenplay credit of *Return of the Jedi* (1983). On *Episode I* and *III*, Lucas is the sole screenwriter, and the second screenwriter on *Episode II* does not help much. Sometimes writers should not be allowed to direct their own scripts, and sometimes directors should not be allowed to write their own scripts. To be fair, Lucas has come to realize his screenwriting limitations. While accepting the American Film Institute Life Achievement Award in 2005, he referred to himself as the "king of wooden dialogue."

Jar Jar takes Queen Amidala to the Gungans. Okay, now it is obvious to us that Padmé is standing behind the Queen as they approach. So maybe Padmé really is a servant. But then she steps forward and says she is the real Queen, and the one made up like the Queen is her double. Lucas has had the Queen dressed up in outlandish outfits, with even more outlandish hairdos, probably to help with the idea of the doubles. It doesn't really, and it makes it impossible for poor Natalie Portman to act under the weight of all the accessories. If she tried using her body language, the hair would collapse. We will see in *Episode III* that Lucas has finally let Portman let her hair down, literally, and her performance is better. You could claim that this hair and costuming is writing for the performance of the stylists and costume designers, but do not write costume and hair requirements for your characters that will keep the actors from acting.

Amidala will use the Gungans as a decoy so she can get into the city and capture the Trade Federation Viceroy. The final action scenes have been set up, and we are now 105 minutes into the film. The Gungan army fights the droid army while Qui-Gon, Obi-Wan, Anakin, and

Amidala sneak into the palace to try to kidnap the Viceroy. Anakin finds a rocketship to fly. Lucas cuts between the four action scenes: the battle, the rocketship, the duel between Darth Maul and the Jedi Knights, and Amidala finding the Viceroy. Jar Jar, fighting with the Gungans, mistakenly lets loose a collection of blue balls that chase after him and help destroy the Gungan tanks. Some Lucas fans will see this as a variation of the rolling boulder in *Raiders of the Lost Ark*, while film historians will reference the landslide in Buster Keaton's *Seven Chances* (1925). Keaton's and the *Raiders* scenes work better because you want Keaton and Indy to escape the rolling boulders. With Jar Jar…

At the end of the duel, Darth Maul mortally wounds Qui-Gon. We should be as moved as we were in *Star Wars* when Obi-Wan was killed, but we are not. We have not connected to Qui-Gon as we had to Obi-Wan. And we may also know that Qui-Gon, in the world of *Star Wars*, is very likely to show up again in future pictures in cameo appearances. This is an example of where knowing the rules diminishes the impact of the scene.

Anakin gets his rocket going again and destroys the Trade Federation battleship, which destroys the protective shield of the droid army, letting the Gungans win. Obi-Wan kills Darth Maul. Qui-Gon, who has been waiting to die, tells Obi-Wan that Anakin is the "chosen one." Palpatine, now the Chancellor, arrives on Naboo and tells Anakin he will watch his career with interest, not a terrible bit of foreshadowing.

Obi-Wan tells Yoda that he wants Anakin as his apprentice and Yoda says the Jedi Council will agree. Yoda and Mace Windu agree that Darth Maul was a Sith, but since Siths come in pairs, there is another one out there, and it is not clear to them who it is, and which one was the Master and which the Apprentice. All of this is setting up the next two episodes in the most obvious ways. Lucas ends with a victory parade on Naboo, but the marching band seems like something out of an American high school. You can take Lucas out of Modesto, but you cannot take Modesto out of Lucas.

If the script is as bad as I claim, and if audiences despised Jar Jar Binks, why did the film end up the third highest grossing film until that time? The easy but not entirely correct answer is that there was such a buildup of anticipation in the sixteen years since the first trilogy that *Star Wars* fans felt they *had* to see it. We wanted to see how the story we had grown to love over many viewings had started. The first three films brought us into not just one world, but several, that we wanted to go back to.

That only explains why it opened big, not why it continued to pull in the audiences. I think part of the appeal was that, for all the flaws in the script, the film delivered at least some of what it promised. We see some of the old characters again and some new ones, even if the new ones are not as compelling. We are dazzled by the spectacle we know Lucas can provide. While you can anticipate characters and story, the kind of spectacle that the *Star Wars* movies have has to be experienced firsthand, preferably on the big screen. While not completely satisfying, the film was satisfying enough. The question was whether the unsatisfactory elements would diminish the appeal of *Episode II*.

> **STAR WARS: EPISODE II—ATTACK OF THE CLONES**
> (2002. Story by George Lucas. Screenplay by George Lucas and Jonathan Hales. 142 minutes)

"A long time ago..." Of course.

The introductory titles tell of unrest in the Galactic Senate, and that several thousand solar systems (nothing like thinking big, although we never see *that* many) are thinking about leaving the Republic. The separatist movement under Count Dooku (try saying that name out loud and not laughing) has made it difficult for the Jedi Knights to keep the peace. A better opening title than on *Episode I*, since it promises active conflict. The titles continue, telling us that Amidala, formerly known as Padmé and "the former Queen of Naboo" (She was overthrown? She quit? It will be a while before we get an explanation), is on her way to the Galactic Senate. Her rocket lands (listen to Ben Burtt having fun here: the sounds are those of World War II-era airplanes) and she is blown up in an explosion. Nope, it's one of her doubles, the most dangerous job in the universe. The first question in the movie is why somebody would want to kill Amidala. We never really get an answer, although there is a hint of one later on. She is now a Senator, so why is she still allowed to use all those doubles?

Chancellor Palpatine talks to Yoda and Mace Windu about his efforts to try to stop the war. Apparently no one has *yet* realized he is the Phantom Menace. Obi-Wan (McGregor is now up to the middle-period Guinness of *Bridge on the River Kwai* [1957]) and Anakin are coming to see Amidala. Anakin is now a young man (although Amidala has apparently not aged a bit) and has not seen Amidala in ten years. He is nervous because he had a crush on her. Amidala recognizes Ani. How? He was Jake Lloyd then and is Hayden Christensen now, and they do not look that much alike. She notes that he has grown up. Ani says that she is beautiful, and she says, "You'll always be that little boy I knew on Tatooine." Okay folks, here is where this begins to turn into the worst *Star Wars* film ever. The major dramatic movement of this episode is going to be Ani and Amidala falling in love. Unfortunately, this is not the sort of thing Lucas is good at, either as a writer or director. His co-script-writer here is the English writer Jonathan Hales, whose credits include the television series *Dallas* (1978–1991) and another called *Dempsey and Makepeace* (1985–1986), about a New York City male cop paired up with a British woman cop in London. Whatever skills he brought to those when writing about men and women are not on view here. We simply cannot tell from Amidala's reactions how she feels about Ani. After noticing he has grown up, she says he will always be a little boy to her, which makes her later behavior weird. This scene should set up that there is an attraction, however unwanted, by either or both of them.

There is some tension between Obi-Wan and Ani. Ani wants to investigate the attempt on Amidala's life, but Obi-Wan wants to follow their instructions. Jar Jar tells Ani that Amidala is glad to see him, but how does Jar Jar know? Ani thinks that Amidala has forgotten him, but was he not listening when she said she recognized him?

A woman (yes, really) soldier sneaks a vial of something poisonous via a flying device into Amidala's bedroom. Ani destroys the vial and, at 14 minutes into the film, the first big action scene begins. In a pod flyer, Ani and Obi Wan chase the soldier. This is a modestly exciting sequence, but goes on way too long as the CGI effects take over, a recurring flaw in the film. The soldier's flyer crashes and Ani chases her into a nightclub. This is one of the few times in *Episode I, II,* and *III* that we actually get a sense of the culture of Lucas's various planets. The pod races in *Episode I* are, I suppose, the galactic equivalent of NASCAR. The nightclub here, written for the performance of the art directors and set decorators, is a combination of Las Vegas and Tokyo, but you have to pick up the texture on your own in the corners of the screen, which is not necessarily a bad thing. Obi-Wan catches the soldier, who is about to tell him the name of the bounty hunter who hired her when she is killed by a dart.

The Jedi Council suggests that Ani take Amidala to her home planet of Naboo to protect her. In terms of strategy this makes no sense, since the idea was to keep her hidden. But she is a Senator, so why did the Council think her absence would not be noticed? We do get a brief scene between Ani and Palpatine in which Ani refers to him as his "guide," which will help us in *Episode III.* Yoda, Mace, and Obi-Wan discuss how arrogant Ani is becoming. But if that is true, why are they entrusting Amidala to him? Lucas needs a way to get Ani and Amidala together, but this doesn't make a lot of sense.

Amidala asks Jar Jar to speak for her in the Senate, telling him, "I know I can count on you." Did she not see *Episode I*? And there is no evidence that Jar Jar has gotten any smarter. She also tells Ani that he has grown up, but he is behaving like a spoiled adolescent brat. Her judgment appears seriously warped in this scene, and there is no indication that she has fallen in love with Ani yet. When he stares at her, she asks him not to look at her "like that." He asks why, and she says, "It makes me feel uncomfortable." But there is nothing in her reaction to tell us why or how she feels uncomfortable. Does she just think he is a creep? Is she bothered that she finds herself attracted to him? Not a clue.

Obi-Wan goes into a very fifties-looking diner, complete with waitresses on roller skates, so we get a little texture as he talks to an old friend, Dex, a much more successful CGI character than Jar Jar. Dex recognizes the dart from a distant planet. Obi-Wan tries unsuccessfully to look it up in the archives (another slight nod to culture, although did they have to make the librarian an older woman, her hair in a bun with two pencils stuck in it?). Ani and Amidala are eating at the café on the transport and she asks him if a Jedi can love, and he says that the Jedi must show compassion, which is an unconditional love. Just what a girl wants to hear.

Obi-Wan shows Yoda a hologram of the universe (if he had this, why go to the archives?), which does not show the missing planet. Yoda says the gravity is there, suggesting the planet is still there. Thirty-eight minutes into this episode, we finally get an explanation of the political setup on Naboo. Amidala says that she was the youngest Queen ever elected and she was not sure she was ready for the job. Ani notes that they tried to change the constitution so she could serve more than two terms. But she says she was relieved when her two terms were up. The next Queen asked her to be a Senator and she felt she could not refuse. This scene has very much the air of having been jammed into the script because fans had the same problems with the Queen business in *Episode I* that I had. They talk to the new Queen, who looks even younger than Amidala did in *her* Queen days, and Amidala decides she will be safer in the Lake District.

Obi-Wan finds the missing planet, Camino, and on it two hundred thousand units of a clone army for the Republic ready, and one million on the way. Obi-Wan is a bit surprised, since the Jedi who ordered this ten years ago has since died. He learns that the army was cloned from the bounty hunter Jango Fett.

On Naboo, Ani and Amidala go to a castle on the lake. He says his planet was sand, not smooth like Naboo. He touches her bare back and they kiss. She pulls away, saying, "I shouldn't have done that." He apologizes. End of scene. We get no sense of whatever passion there may be between these two. The dialogue does not get it across, and the actors, under Lucas's direction, do not go for any subtext.

At a lake with gorgeous waterfalls, Ani and Amidala are having a picnic. Now, is that not a great location for a love scene? It starts promisingly, with Amidala talking about her first boyfriend, but then evolves into a political discussion. Yes, they do roll around in the field, but it is still a waste of a great location. The central problem of this script is that Lucas and Hales have no idea how to tell this love story. Here are a couple of possible ways. One is to think of Ani as a fifties teenage hood and Amidala as the good girl who is attracted to the bad boy. If that is the *The Wild One* (1953) version, the *Roman Holiday* (1953) version is: princess gets tired of her royal duties, runs away, falls in love with a commoner, and then decides that she has to return to duty. We got a hint of that version in *Episode I*, but it was undeveloped then and now. Look at either or both of those fifties films to see how compelling the story can be.

Ani and Amidala are in a room with a roaring fire in a fireplace. Almost as good a location as the waterfall for a romantic scene, but the writers geek it here as well. She says flatly, "I will not give in to this." Compare that with the scene in the car between the princess and the reporter in *Roman Holiday*, or better yet, her line back in the embassy when she is reminded of her responsibilities: "If I were not completely aware of my duty, I would not have returned tonight. Or, indeed, ever again." *That's* how you break an audience's heart. We are close to an hour into the film.

Obi-Wan has a lightsaber duel (the first one in this film, a bit of a relief from the other films) with Jango Fett. (By the way, Fett has a son, who seems out of place in all these goings on. You have to be one of the real *Star Wars* fanatics, and/or have seen a cast list, to realize that the boy is Boba Fett, who will grow up to be a bounty hunter in *Episode V* and *VI*.) Fett escapes, but Obi-Wan follows him to yet another planet. On Tatooine, Ani discovers from his old boss that his mother, who he dreamed was in pain, was sold to Cliegg Lars. Obi-Wan follows Fett through an asteroid field, a scene reminiscent of *The Empire Strikes Back*. It is more visually complex, but not as compelling, because that complexity gets in the way of telling the story.

Ani and Amidala meet his stepbrother Owen (who will later become Luke's uncle), his fiancée Beru, and Owen's father Cliegg, who tells them that raiders have stolen Shmi. Obi-Wan hears Count Dooku saying he intends to have the largest army in the galaxy. We are about 1 hour and 15 minutes into the film. Ani finds his mom and she dies in his arms. Since we have not seen her since early in *Episode I*, her death here does not have the impact on us that it should. Yoda feels that Ani is in pain and Obi-Wan tries to send a message to Ani, since Tatooine is closer to the planet he is on than the one where Yoda is. This is one of the few times in the entire series where such a practical point about time and space is brought up. It will soon be overshadowed by other time and space problems, which are particularly bad in this film.

Ani is upset that he could not save Shmi and says that when he becomes a full Jedi Knight he will keep people from dying. This sets up part of his motivation for being seduced into the dark side in *Episode III*, but here it just makes him seem deranged with grief. This is not helped when he goes into a monologue about the number of people he has killed as a Jedi, of which we have seen no evidence. This is one of the more confusing and unsatisfying scenes in the whole film. They have a funeral for Shmi, but it has none of the simple emotional grandeur that John Ford gets out of similar scenes in his westerns. Ani then hears the message from Obi-Wan, which ends abruptly, so Ani and the Jedi Council assume Obi-Wan is under attack. Amidala, finally showing some of the spunk her daughter Leia will become noted for in the years to come, tells Ani she will go to help Obi-Wan, since they are closer than the Jedi Council. Since he must protect her, he goes too.

Palpatine says he needs an amendment to raise an army, but no Senator would propose it. Another person says Amidala would if she were here. Now the attempt on her life makes no sense. If she is the only one brave enough to propose it, why would Palpatine, the not-so-Phantom Menace, a) try to have her killed and b) assist in sending her away? And it makes even less sense when they very easily appear to get Jar Jar to make the proposal. Okay, maybe Palpatine knew that she would *not* make such a proposal. But nobody else would, either. He may also have known that she would oppose such a proposal, but that is not clear in the film.

Count Dooku tries to convince Obi-Wan that he, the Count, is behaving with the best interests of the Republic at heart, and that the Senate is controlled by a Dark Lord of the Sith. And Obi-Wan still has not figured out it is Palpatine! Ani and Amidala arrive to help Obi-Wan, but find themselves trapped on and around a conveyer belt that looks like something out of a classic Warner Brothers cartoon. They are captured, and Amidala says she is not afraid to die. She tells Ani, "I've been dying a little bit each day since you came back into my life." Not a terrible line, except for that fact we have seen nothing in her behavior, nor heard anything from her lips, that would lead us to believe that is true.

At 105 minutes, Obi-Wan, Ani, and Amidala are brought out into an arena, which is very similar to the Coliseum in *Gladiator*. The reference may be to the arena scenes in *Quo Vadis* (1951), but since this film came out just two years after *Gladiator*, that is the film fresh in the audience's minds, so the next sequence seems a little too dated, as opposed to the variation on the chariot race in *Episode I*, which was so old it was new again. Steal not only from the best, but from the oldest, so a lot of your audience will not remember it very clearly. Our three are tied up to three large poles (see *Quo Vadis*) and three large beasts are let out of the cages to go after them. Amidala does the old "use the hairpin to unlock the handcuffs" trick to get free, and the others make a fight of it with the other beasts. One of the crowd thinks this is not fair, but that is as close to texture as the writers get, as opposed to the pod race in *Episode I*.

Our trio is fighting off the clones under Count Dooku's command (that's what the manufacturing on this planet is about, I assume, unless he has stolen the other clone planet's clones. Or had *them* cloned. Is your head beginning to hurt as much as mine trying to keep the clones sorted out?). And now the Jedi Knights arrive, backed up a bit later by the Republic's white uniformed troopers. There is no indication that our three were held for more than another few hours before the arena scene, so how did the Jedi Knights and the Republic get all those clones, transport them across the great distances of space, and still make it there in time? Yes, we suspend our disbelief, but sometimes it just gets to be too much, and the ending of this film is one of those times.

The troopers land their ships in the arena and save our trio, as well as Mace Windu, who finally, after standing around saying bad dialogue for nearly two whole movies, gets an action scene. Count Dooku wonders how the Republic got its army up and running so quickly—a very good question. But then when somebody suggests he use *his* clones, he says it would take too long to get them. Weren't they being made on this planet? If the Republic can get there that quickly, why can't his clones?

A brief pause in the action here to consider the glory that is Christopher Lee, who plays Count Dooku. Lee, having spent a lot of time in the Hammer horror movies of the fifties and beyond, knows how to deal with really bad dialogue. Listen to him in the latter part of this film, especially how he gives enormous variations on lines that have no variation in them. He is also able to keep a straight face while saying lines such as these. No small accomplishment for an actor.

A little after the two-hour mark, Obi-Wan duels Count Dooku, is beaten, and is followed by Ani, who ends up with his right arm sliced off. Who arrives to save the day? Yoda. And here is a great conundrum of screenwriting. We know Yoda. We have seen him in three films before this one. We know he hardly moves, and when he does, he uses a cane. Everything we know about Yoda suggests that he is not a duelist of the first order. Yet here he bounces all over the place and is stopped from killing Count Dooku only to save Obi-Wan and Ani. Turning him into a whiz with a lightsaber is wrong. Wrong, wrong, wrong, and WRONG!!! Did you hear the audience reaction when he started? They *loved* it. I, who as you may have noticed like at least a little consistency, loved it. Why does it work when it goes against everything we know about screenwriting? We can only guess. Some of it may be that the movie is so bad that we were ready for a surprise, which the writers have not given us at any point in the film. Some of it I think is that since *The Empire Strikes Back* we have loved Yoda as a character, mangled syntax and all, and we love to see this new side of him. Maybe we just want somebody to save the day. Maybe he is just Vivien Leigh in *Gone with the Wind* (1939). Why do you think it works? Or, if you are even more pinch-faced about logic than I am, why do you think it did not?

The Jedi Council talks over whether a Sith has taken over the Senate. Geez guys, how slow are you? And on Naboo, Ani and Amidala get married. At least we think that's what happens, since there is no dialogue. Now guys, how hard a scene could that be to write?

At 136 minutes, the end credits begin.

As with *Episode I*, the question is, if it is so bad, why was it so successful? I think the answers are similar to the ones I gave for *Episode I*. It certainly does deliver the spectacle, even if the story slows down for a lot of what Lucas would later refer to as "jazz riffs" (see below), at least some of which were mildly entertaining. I discussed earlier the importance of context for a line of dialogue. I think context is also important for a film, and here the context is part of a series of films that already has great emotional meaning for many millions of people. Would it extend to *Episode III*, or were *I* and *II* together bad enough to kill the franchise?

STAR WARS: EPISODE III—REVENGE OF THE SITH
(2005. Screenplay by George Lucas. 140 minutes)

"A long…" Yeah, we know, but it still works.

The opening crawl tells us that the Republic is in trouble, since General Grievous has kidnapped Supreme Chancellor Palpatine. Okay, we know from paying attention in *Episode I* and *II* that Palpatine is the not-so-Phantom Menace. So why are his associates kidnapping him? Maybe they are the good guys? We never find out.

What we get instead is an attempt to rescue Palpatine by two Jedi Knights, Obi-Wan and Anakin. This begins with a spectacular set of shots of Grievous's battleships with assorted rocket fighters in dogfights around it. This is one of the most dazzling openings of the *Star Wars* films and gives us a feeling that after *Episode I* and *II*, Lucas may be back on track. The shots are not only visually stunning, but set up the Jedi's rescue attempt. They come on board not to talk, as at the beginning of *Episode I*, but to fight. Anakin kills Count Dooku. This tells us that nobody is safe in this movie if you kill off the sixth-billed star in the first fourteen minutes of the film. Always a nice way to keep the audience on their toes. The Jedi try to land the disintegrating battleship on a nearby planet. They do, of course, 22 minutes into the film. Now *that's* the way to start the movie: play to your strengths as a screenwriter, in this case, action, narrative speed, and writing for the performance of the CGI crew.

Ah yes, but then we have dialogue. Anakin and Amidala talk. She's in the family way. Anakin is still the sullen teenager and she's the occasional royal, and the dialogue is just as flat as before, but Christensen and Portman are actually allowed to show a little emotion. And her hair is not in any of the elaborate dos of the earlier films, so she can move both her face and her body. It makes a difference.

Lucas is also smart enough to break up the dialogue scenes into short scenes intercut with other short dialogue scenes so it diminishes the dreariness of listening to the bad dialogue of *these* characters by having now to focus on the bad dialogue of *those* characters. So we now get a scene of the holographic Phantom Menace (and still nobody knows… oh, never mind) assuring Grievous that there will soon be another apprentice to replace Dooku. And back to Amidala and Anakin. She wants to have the baby on Naboo. She makes a reference to the Queen. Yep, another one.

Anakin has a dream of Amidala dying in childbirth, setting up one of the motivations that will drive him in this film. Yes, an actual motivation in a *Star Wars* film. Anakin talks to Yoda about the dream, and all Yoda can tell him is, "Train yourself to let go of everything you fear to lose." Huh? Is Yoda turning into a bit of a nihilist here?

Palpatine appoints Anakin as his personal representative to the Jedi Council, beginning his seduction of Anakin. The dialogue is still "on the nose," but Ian McDiarmid, like the other actors in the film, is actually allowed to *act*. He manages to find ways to get a variety of implied emotions in his scenes. (It has been rumored that British playwright Tom Stoppard helped with some of the dialogue, but being a fan of Stoppard, I will require a notarized statement that the playwright of *Arcadia* was anywhere near this script.)

The Jedi Council is upset by Palpatine's appointment of Anakin, and they do not give Anakin the rank of Master, which provides another motivation for him. We have in these scenes, if not outright conflict, certainly dynamic tensions between Anakin and everybody else.

About 42 minutes into the film, Lucas gives us something we have not seen before in a *Star Wars* film: a suggestion of high culture. The culture we have seen in the films has been mostly pop culture. Here Anakin appears in an ornate theater lobby. Who knew they had high-class theater in a galaxy far, far, etc.? The show seems to be a galactic *Cirque du Soleil*, except with elongated goldfish in a large bowl rather than acrobats. Palpatine suggests to Anakin that the Jedi are conspiring against him. He has figured out that the Council wants Anakin to spy on him. He also suggests the power of the Dark Side of the Force. Lucas is laying out the seduction of Anakin in a series of scenes that will bring him to turn to the Dark Side. The dialogue is no better than before, but the structure of the scenes provides a dynamic that helps them stand up against the special effects scenes.

The Jedi Council sends Obi-Wan to deal with Grievous while Yoda goes off to develop an alliance with the Wookies, one of whom turns out to be Chewbacca. His introduction is no more impressive than the meeting of R2-D2 and C-3PO in *Episode I*. It is not clear to me from one viewing of the film if the Wookies are training for combat or are engaged in some sort of battle. If it's training, why are things being destroyed? If it's a battle, why don't we see the outcome? An article in *Entertainment Weekly* mentions that this sequence was reduced in the editing process; that I will not require a notarized statement to believe.

Palpatine's seductions are beginning to work on Anakin. Ani tells Amidala that he wants more. Okay, as more or less satisfactory as these dialogue scenes have been, we are coming up on an hour into it, so it is time for an action scene. So we get a lightsaber duel between Obi-Wan and Grievous. Palpatine offers to teach Anakin the ways of the Force, including the Dark Side, and he suggests that this can help save Amidala from the death Anakin has seen in his dream. Anakin begins to think (about time) that Palpatine is a Sith Lord. Go back and read the description of the theater scene above. See how this scene is a progression from it?

Anakin tells Mace that Palpatine is a Sith Lord. Mace goes to arrest Palpatine. Now, here is a problem. Except for some involvement in the battle scene at the end of *Episode II*, Mace Windu has been underemployed. So if Mace is going after Palpatine, I really want to see him "go medieval on his ass." After all, this is Samuel L. Jackson, Jules his own self from *Pulp Fiction* (1994). No such luck, though, just a regular lightsaber duel. Palpatine kills Mace. Anakin agrees to help Palpatine if Palpatine can save Amidala. Palpatine gives Anakin the name, but just the name, Darth Vader. We are 76 minutes into the film.

Yoda outwits the troops sent to kill him, and Senator Organa escapes as well. Anakin is sent to the lava planet Mustafar to protect the Viceroy. Mustafar is one of the most expressive sets/locations/CGI constructs in all of the *Star Wars* films. It may not be as visually dazzling as some of the others, but it has more suggestive power, as Lucas seems to understand. Mustafar will be useful in the scarring of Anakin that will lead him to visually become Darth Vader. The roiling lava suggests Anakin's inner turmoil, much more so than Christensen's acting. Christensen has subtlety as an actor, but he does not necessarily have the power he needs to be convincing as someone who becomes what we know Darth Vader to be.

Palpatine attacks the Jedi plot against him in the Senate and Amidala has an actual reaction to him *in a reaction shot*. There's something you do not see a lot of, at least in *Episode I, II, and III*. Obi-Wan learns Anakin is a Sith and tells Amidala, then asks if Anakin is the father of her baby. Well, duh. Haven't any of these wise people even thought to ask her about this? After all, she has been showing her pregnancy since the beginning of the film, and isn't Anakin the obvious choice? She is at least a Senator, as well as a former Queen. Wasn't anybody interested enough to ask before this? And then (at 103 minutes in) she goes to Mustafar to talk to Anakin. Excuse me, but wouldn't the atmosphere there be a little tough for a woman about to deliver? And should she be flying at her stage of the pregnancy? Okay, if they have solved all those medical problems, why haven't they invented an ultra-sound machine that will tell her she is carrying twins?

Anakin tells her that the Dark Side will save her but she wants him to run away. Obi-Wan and Anakin duel with lightsabers. The duel is intercut with Yoda confronting Palpatine and their fight, which takes place in the Senate, another use of a set/CGI construct in an inventive way. The physical destruction of the Senate parallels its political destruction. Obi-Wan defeats Anakin and leaves him burning (at 121 minutes). Palpatine rescues Anakin, while Obi-Wan takes Amidala to Organa, who says, "We'll take her to the medical center quickly." Jimmy Smits (Organa) is an excellent actor, but there is nothing he can do with that line.

Lucas then intercuts the medical "repair" of Anakin and the birth of Luke and Leia. Anakin gets fitted with the famous mask and begins to talk like James Earl Jones, which is a real jump from Christensen's voice, but there is something satisfying about that moment. The context makes the moment, as it does the birth of the twins. The droid doctor says that Amidala has lost the will to live, which we would buy a whole lot better if her love had been shown more convincingly in

Episode II. She dies. The funeral of Amidala is held on Naboo, with, I guess, this month's Queen.

Organa takes Leia to his wife, and we end with Obi-Wan delivering Luke to Uncle Owen and Aunt Beru, who stand in the final shot that recalls one of the more poetic images of the first *Star Wars* film: the desert planet with the two moons. Everything has fallen into place, which is satisfying for long-term fans of the series. But couldn't there be at least one surprise? Probably not. At 133 minutes in, the credits begin.

Okay, I will grant you that *Episode III* is better than *Episode I* and *II*, and you could make a case for it fitting more accurately into my Not-Quite-So-Good category. If you want to cut up your copy of this book and paste it into that section, be my guest. The story does move quicker, as Lucas himself recognized. He told *Entertainment Weekly* that sixty percent of the "prequel" story he dreamed up is in *Episode III*, with only forty percent in the first two films. That gave him time to do what he called "jazz riffs…things I enjoy" in the first two films, but that works against Lucas's strength as a maker of fast-moving films. And some of the riffs, notoriously Jar Jar Binks, simply do not work. He got back to narrative drive, although much of that came in the editing process, which is where he found the focus the story has to have. The limitations of the writing, both in characterization and especially dialogue, keep the film from achieving what it could have been. It still made a *big* pile of money because of what it did deliver.

As Elaine Lennon, who read the first-draft manuscript of this book, said, referring to sense of family that the *Star Wars* films created in their audiences, "That Lucas guy was on to something, I tell ya…"

Sources

The story on *Episode III* that includes the quotes from Lucas is by Jeff Jensen, "What a Long Strange Trip It Has Been," *Entertainment Weekly*, May 20, 2005. The quote from Lucas at the AFI Awards is from Susan King, "Lucas Earns His Own Star," *Los Angeles Times*, June 11, 2005. I have not quoted him directly, but Jeff Goldsmith's two reviews of *Episode III* on *CS Weekly* (May 20, 2005), one without spoilers, one with, are very perceptive about the script flaws of that film.

17
SHORT TAKES ON BAD SCREENPLAYS

THE films are in chronological order of release.

> **DUNE** (1984. Based on the book by Frank Herbert. Screenplay by David Lynch, but he took his name off the credits as writer of the 137-minute theatrical release. He put his name back on the 190-minute television version, although critical reaction was that it was marginally worse than the theatrical version.)

I have to admit that I have never seen this film all the way through, either in its theatrical or television version, but you can learn from movies you do not see. You can look at the reviews of the films and what is written about them elsewhere. There is an enormously helpful web site, www.rottentomatos.com, which provides links to reviews in newspapers and magazines all over the country. Since you do not want to spend all your time and money watching bad movies, checking out the reviews is also a helpful way to see what is so bad in the scripts that even, ahem, reviewers notice them. You can save money and learn about screenplays at the same time. Win–win.

In the case of *Dune*, I had a friend who saw the film and told me a very interesting thing. She was a huge fan of the Herbert novel, and while watching the film, she kept saying to herself, "They are only on page twenty," "They are only on page forty," "Only on page fifty," etc. Two points.

Point one: if you are adapting a novel, particularly a long novel, you have to be ruthless. Remember David Benioff and *Troy*? Novelists can spend pages and pages writing about stuff you do not need to have in a two-hour film. What parts of the novel do you *need* in the film?

Point two: one of the difficulties in writing a science fiction script is establishing the world of the film. If you first show us a man with a gun on a horse in the desert, we know, until you tell us otherwise, that we are in a western, and we pretty much know what the rules are. In a science fiction film, you have to establish the rules of the universe the film is taking place in. In a novel you can spend many pages describing those rules, but you cannot in a film. Go back and look at what I wrote about the openings of the various *Star Wars* films.

> **HOWARD THE DUCK** (1986. Based on the comic books by Steve Gerber. Screenplay by Willard Huyck and Gloria Katz. 110 minutes)

I am sorry to say I did see this one. And the rest of the ones in this chapter as well.

I had not read the *Howard the Duck* comic books, but I knew enough about them to know that, in the comics, Howard was a foul-mouthed, obnoxious character, which was his charm. In other words, Donald Duck taken to his logical conclusion. He was so softened by the movie that fans of the comic book felt cheated, as did those who had only heard about him. If you are going to make a movie about Howard the Duck, make a movie about Howard the Duck.

In fairness to Huyck and Katz, their original take was smaller and darker, but the studio, Universal, wanted it bigger and brighter. Sometimes you just have to walk away from a project.

Source

There is not a lot about *Howard the Duck* in the official and unofficial writing about its executive producer, but Charles Champlin's *George Lucas: The Creative Impulse* (Harry N. Abrams, 1992) does have a brief page on it and Huyck and Katz's original approach.

> **WILLOW** (1988. Story by George Lucas. Screenplay by Bob Dolman. 126 minutes)

This film is exhibit A for the prosecution in the case against Joseph Campbell and the use of his Hero's Journey paradigm as the basis for structuring a film. Yes, it follows Campbell's line, and borrows from many classic mythologies. Willow, the Nelwyn, must return the chosen one, the infant Elora Danan, to restore...zzz, zzz. Wake up, there is also a Darth Vader-like General Kael (hey, one laugh, naming the villain after film critic Pauline Kael), but then there is a goat who becomes a sorceress, and...zzz.

Unless the story and characters are compelling, it will do you no good to follow anybody's Hidden Secrets of the Great Mythologies of the West. Or the East, for that matter.

And elaborate special effects, as we should all know by now, do not make up for a lack of story and characters.

Source
See Champlin's book for some details of the production.

> **THE BACHELOR** (1999. Based on the 1925 screenplay *Seven Chances* by Jean C. Havez, Clyde Bruckman, and Joseph A. Mitchell, which was based on the 1916 stage play *Seven Chances* by Roi Cooper Megrue. Screenplay by Steve Cohen. 101 minutes)

Buster Keaton's *Seven Chances* is flawlessly structured, elegant, and brilliantly paced. And don't forget funny. And it is the quintessential *silent* film.

The story is simple: Jimmy Shannon discovers he will inherit seven million dollars on his twenty-seventh birthday if he is married by seven o'clock on that day. He learns this on, of course, his twenty-seventh birthday. Okay, no problem. He can propose to the girl he's in love with, Mary. But he bungles the proposal. So now he has to propose to every girl he comes across, all of whom turn him down. Until his associate puts an ad in the paper that mentions he will inherit the money. Now he has hundreds of would-be brides chasing him: along city streets, through the rockslide Lucas borrowed for *Episode I*, etc. Needless to say, he ends up with Mary.

I have no idea what the original stage play was like, but you can see why it makes a perfect silent film. We know he is proposing to each woman; we do not need to *hear* it each time. This means Keaton and his writers can focus on the women's reactions to his proposal, which is where the humor lies. Look at the different reactions they have. And the chase by the brides provides great slapstick comedy in the last third.

The makers of *The Bachelor* get everything wrong. Keaton's Jimmy is a shy, awkward, sympathetic character. We cringe when he gets the first proposal to Mary wrong. *The Bachelor*'s Jimmy is an obnoxious jerk from the word go, and we cringe when this Jimmy proposes to Mary because we feel sorry for her.

Then we have scene after scene of him proposing, but we *hear* them all. Cohen tries to make each of the women at least part of a character, which ends up taking away from the thrust and speed of the story. Well! Here I have been not so subtly promoting better writing of women characters all throughout this book. This is the exception that sort of proves the rule: you do not need characters of depth for these scenes. Shallow, funny characters would be enough *here*. But *good* shallow, etc.

Cohen then unfortunately does not rethink the horde of would-be brides at the end. In 1925 film audiences would simply assume that the women would want to get married, especially for the money. Cohen assumes the same thing, rather than rethinking why contemporary women might want to marry this guy and his money. Cohen is missing a lot of potential satire.

Finally, *Seven Chances* is 56 minutes. *The Bachelor* is 101 minutes. Longer is not better. Watch both if you do not *yet* believe me.

Source
Background on *Seven Chances* is from Tom Dardis's *Keaton: The Man Who Wouldn't Lie Down* (Charles Scribner's Sons, 1979).

> **GODS AND GENERALS** (2003. Based on the book by Jeffrey M. Shaara. Screenplay by Ronald F. Maxwell. 231 minutes)

In 1993 Ronald F. Maxwell wrote and directed *Gettysburg*, based on the novel *The Killer Angels* by Michael Shaara. Originally intended to go straight to television, the film received a theatrical release to better reviews than box office. It cost approximately $25 million, and brought in only $10 million. That should have been a warning to Maxwell and his partners.

Gettysburg worked as well as it did because it provided an epic look at the most important battle of the Civil War. There was not only action but a sense of the strategy of both sides. The film was marred by a lot of incessant announcements from the Southern officers about how they were fighting for "duty, honor, and country." The spectacle was enough to overcome the talkier patches.

Unfortunately, it looks as though Maxwell thought the film did as well as it did *because of* the "duty, honor, country" speeches rather than *in spite of* them. So for *Gods and Generals*, based on a book by Shaara's son Jeffrey, the warfare is shortened, while we get speech after speech after speech about, you guessed it. After a couple of hours of this, or probably less if your people, like mine, fought for the North, you just want to slap Stonewall Jackson upside the head and tell him to stop trying to pretend that protecting slavery is a noble cause. As a Southern relation of mine would say, that dog won't hunt.

And you know the film is pro-Southern when the only battles shown are the ones the South won. The budget for the film was $56 million, and it grossed only $12 million.

Source
The budgets and box office results of both films are from IMDb.

SINBAD: LEGEND OF THE SEVEN SEAS (2003. Screenplay by John Logan. 86 minutes)

There have been many films about Sinbad the Sailor. Ray Harryhausen, the master of stop-motion animation, worked on at least three over the years. A particularly tacky Sinbad film was *Son of Sinbad* (1955), a film made by RKO primarily, from the look of it, so studio owner Howard Hughes could have his pick of the many women extras.

The story of the 2003 film concerns Sinbad being falsely accused of stealing the *Book of Peace*. He has one chance to find it and return it, or his friend Proteus will be killed. Sinbad decides to sail to Fiji, a new twist for a Sinbad movie and something Howard Hughes might have approved of, but Proteus's fiancée Marina stows away, and then tries to convince Sinbad to rescue Proteus. So far so good. Sinbad is the lovely Brad Pitt, who would be okay if his character actor rather than movie star self showed up. Marina is the equally lovely Catherine Zeta Jones. And the evil goddess Eris who puts this all in motion is Michelle Pfeiffer, whom nobody hit with an ugly stick when she was born, either. So what's the problem?

It's an animated film.

Did you see anything I told you in the paragraph before last that demanded the film be animated? No. The characters are not particularly well written, and with the exception of Eris do not really demand good vocal acting. Virtually every situation could be done live-action. Harryhausen was smart enough to use live actors in his Sinbad films and save the stop-motion for the skeletons, monsters, et al. If you are writing an animated film, then you had better take that into consideration and write for the performance of the animators.

The only thing in the picture that requires brilliant animation, and gets it, is Eris's hair. But will an audience pay ten dollars just to see great animated hair?

Mind the GAPs.

THE STEPFORD WIVES (2004. Based on the book by Ira Levin. Screenplay by Paul Rudnick. 93 minutes)

Ira Levin's 1972 novel was an inventive gloss on male fears about the women's movement: in a suburb, men have gotten together to have their wives "fixed" so they are beautiful but docile. The 1975 film played the story more or less as written, as a horror story in which one of the wives discovers what is really going on.

By 2004 things had changed. First of all, the term "Stepford Wives" had entered the culture, via both the book and the film. Everybody knew the story and what the term meant, which meant that the audience was way ahead of the story. Also, as with *The Bachelor*, the culture had changed. Much had improved for women, much had not, but the culture was simply not the same, so there was no way the original story would have the resonances it had in the seventies.

One way the filmmakers tried to "update" the story was to make one of the couples two gay males. I would love to have been at the pitch meeting where this idea was suggested. Paul Rudnick is a funny writer, and I'm sure he was great in the room discussing the possibilities. Unfortunately, the gay couple stops the film dead in its tracks, and not in a good way. Levin's story is only about married couples on the surface. At its heart it is about men's attitudes toward women.

If you are going to remake a classic, remember that today's audience is not the same as the audience of the classic's day. Which brings us to...

THE MANCHURIAN CANDIDATE (2004. Based on the novel by Richard Condon and the 1962 screenplay by George Axelrod. Screenplay by Daniel Pyne and Dean Georgaris. 129 minutes)

Condon's book and Axelrod's screenplay take a darkly comic, highly skeptical look at what was in the public eye at the time both were written: brainwashing by both the North Koreans and the anti-Communists in our government. The 1962 film was the first to parody McCarthyism on film, and at a time while the Cold War was still on.

Of the credited writers on the new version, Dean Georgaris worked on the material first. In the original book and film, Raymond Shaw is the would-be assassin. Ben Marco, his commanding officer in Korea, figures out what has happened and chases down Shaw at the end. Georgaris made Marco the would-be assassin. Which means, for those who remember the original, that when Shaw answers the phone and gives it to Marco saying, "It's for you," it should be a heart-stopping moment. It is not, because now it seems artificial and contrived. And it kills the last half-hour of the picture, since Marco has been our stand-in, and now we do not get to see Rosie, whose role has been upgraded in this version to a federal investigator, chase him down. Bad for the star playing the character the audience most identifies with to go missing for such a long time at the end of the film.

Daniel Pyne's work was to update the material from its Cold War setting. His idea was that the brainwashing would now be done not by the North Koreans, but by a large corporation. Okay, if obvious (and Pyne found the news stories about Iraq, Enron, et al. ahead of him), but he has not developed the idea well. Go back to the original to see how Condon and Axelrod have created *characters* for the North Koreans, notably Dr. Yen Lo. The people at the conglomerate in the new version are simply generic businessmen. In updating a classic, either officially or unofficially, think about how the story and situation will work for today's culture.

Pyne and Georgaris's updating of Shaw's mother makes her a more contemporary figure, but not nearly as compelling as the original. Rosie is the only character whose change seems to help the film, since she is now more involved in the plot, but the old Rosie was a relief, both for Marco and for us, from the tension of the story. How do your characters function in your script, and how can you protect both that function and the characters?

Sources
Jeff Goldsmith's article "Coming Soon: *The Manchurian Candidate*," in *Creative Screenwriting*, July/August 2004, deals with the changes in characters. Daniel Pyne's "Suicide Mission: Writing *The Manchurian Candidate*," in *Scr(i)pt*, July/August 2004, deals with updating the brainwashing plot.

> **BROKEN FLOWERS** (2005. Written by Jim Jarmusch. 106 minutes)

The idea is not bad: a Don Juan type gets a letter saying he is the father of a nineteen-year-old son he didn't know he had. So he sets out to track down the women he was dating twenty years ago who might be the mother. And finds the son.

Oops. In Jarmusch's script he does *not* find the son. That would be okay, if he would give us something in its place. I *think* that what Jarmusch is trying to do at the end is make us think that Don Johnston will think *every* nineteen-year-old boy he sees might be his son. Sorry, but it's not enough. What ending could you come up with that would be satisfying? Can you come up with one where he does not find his son? How?

Part of the problem is that, as written and played (by Bill Murray), Don is simply not convincing as a Don Juan. He doesn't look as though he has the energy to get out of the house, let alone seduce anybody. I know Jarmusch's style and Murray's recent style, as in *Lost in Translation* (2003), is minimalist, but at least in *Lost in Translation* Murray's Bob Harris had a reason to be listless: jet lag.

The scenes with the women he reacquaints himself with are a mixed bag. The first woman, Laura, and her daughter Lolita have some life to them, and Don's bafflement with them seems earned. The second sequence, with Dora and her husband Ron, makes its point very early and then goes on longer than it should. The third, with Carmen, the animal shrink, simply seems flat. The fourth, with the biker chick Penny, just never gets going. What sort of women would you write for Don to meet?

I know Jarmusch is a minimalist filmmaker, but in his best films, such as *Stranger Than Paradise* (1984) and *Mystery Train* (1989), there are real characters. Weird, sure, but that's half the fun.

QUESTIONS

I have raised a lot of questions, some specific, some general, about the screenplays and films I have discussed in this book. Here, in a convenient list for everyday use, are some of the general questions that kept coming up, questions you may want to ask as you read a screenplay and/or watch a film. Of course, these are general, and there will be, as there have been in this book, many specific questions that may and should come to mind as you read and watch.

Where is the film starting?
    The present?
    The present, jumping to the past?
    The past, jumping to the present?
How is it establishing the characters?
    By showing?
        What they do.
        What we see.
    By telling?
        What they say.
        What we hear about them.
        What other people say *to* them.
Are these the right characters for the film?
Is this the right story for these characters?
What is the screenwriter telling us or showing us?
    Or not telling us?
    Why?
How is the film moving?
Is the story developing?
Are the characters developing?
Are the characters behaving stupidly?
    Why?
Do we need to know this?
Is the screenwriter following the Syd Field or the Joseph Campbell pattern too closely?

Is the film getting away from what the movie is about?
Is it stealing from the best?
Endings:
    Does this finish off the story it started out to tell?
    Does it satisfy the viewer?
    Does it go on too long?
Does the film deliver what it promised?
What is this movie about?

And then, of course, you should ask yourself the same questions when you write your screenplay.

Several readers of the first draft of this book suggested writers should post this list next to their computers, typewriters, quill pens, etc. Let me add to that suggestion. If you are working on a computer, make a separate file of these questions. Then you can update it easily when you think of a new one. And by all means you should send it to me via the publisher when you think of it.

After all, as novelist and occasional screenwriter Rita Mae Brown said, "Computers don't help you write, but they sure help you rewrite."